Vyacheslav Likhachev

Political Anti-Semitism
in Post-Soviet Russia

Actors and Ideas in 1991-2003

Edited and translated from Russian by Eugene Veklerov

SOVIET AND POST-SOVIET POLITICS AND SOCIETY

ISSN 1614-3515

Recent volumes

29   *Florian Strasser*
Zivilgesellschaftliche Einflüsse auf die Orange Revolution
Die gewaltlose Massenbewegung und die ukrainische Wahlkrise 2004
Mit einem Vorwort von Egbert Jahn
ISBN 3-89821-648-9

30   *Rebecca S. Katz*
The Georgian Regime Crisis of 2003-2004
A Case Study in Post-Soviet Media Representation of Politics, Crime and Corruption
ISBN 3-89821-413-3

31   *Vladimir Kantor*
Willkür oder Freiheit
Beiträge zur russischen Geschichtsphilosophie
Ediert von Dagmar Herrmann sowie mit einem Vorwort versehen von Leonid Luks
ISBN 3-89821-589-X

32   *Laura A. Victoir*
The Russian Land Estate Today
A Case Study of Cultural Politics in Post-Soviet Russia
With a foreword by Priscilla Roosevelt
ISBN 3-89821-426-5

33   *Ivan Katchanovski*
Cleft Countries
Regional Political Divisions and Cultures in Post-Soviet Ukraine and Moldova
With a foreword by Francis Fukuyama
ISBN 3-89821-558-X

34   *Florian Mühlfried*
Postsowjetische Feiern
Das Georgische Bankett im Wandel
Mit einem Vorwort von Kevin Tuite
ISBN 3-89821-601-2

35   *Roger Griffin, Werner Loh, Andreas Umland (Eds.)*
Fascism Past and Present, West and East
An International Debate on Concepts and Cases in the Comparative Study of the Extreme Right
With an afterword by Walter Laqueur
ISBN 3-89821-674-8

36   *Sebastian Schlegel*
Der „Weiße Archipel"
Sowjetische Atomstädte 1945-1991
Mit einem Geleitwort von Thomas Bohn
ISBN 3-89821-679-9

Vyacheslav Likhachev

POLITICAL ANTI-SEMITISM
IN POST-SOVIET RUSSIA

Actors and Ideas in 1991-2003

Edited and translated from Russian by Eugene Veklerov

ibidem-Verlag
Stuttgart

Bibliografische Information Der Deutschen Bibliothek

Die Deutsche Bibliothek verzeichnet diese Publikation in der Deutschen Nationalbibliografie; detaillierte bibliografische Daten sind im Internet über <http://dnb.ddb.de> abrufbar.

Cover picture: A rally of the anti-Semitic *Natsional'no-derzhavnaya partiya Rossii* (NDPR, National Great Power Party of Russia) in Moscow on November 19, 2002. The two men in the middle (not holding posters) are the Party's leaders and well-known Russian nationalist activists: Stanislav Terekhov (left), and Aleksandr Sevastyanov (right, with a beard). The poster contains thinly veiled anti-Semitic slogans in the form of a rhyming pun.
The left poster reads: "'Eti' – '*anti*fashisty', poznyary i ZhvIDkYe khuzhe Gebbel'sa, no NDPR im ne po zubam, a po *zubam*!" In English: "'These' [so-called] '*Anti*-Fascists', Pozners [Pozner – a liberal TV commentator] and Zhvidkoys [misspelled Shvydkoy – a liberal former Minister of Culture] are worse than [Joseph] Goebbels, yet the NDPR is a hard nut for them to crack; but [let's] crack their teeth!" The four capitalized letters in the former Culture Minister's name form the word "zhidy" – a derogatory term for Jews comparable to the English "kikes".
The right poster adapts a famous line from Russian poet Mikhail Lermontov and makes it sound like an anti-Semitic slogan: "Skazhy, Luzhkov, naskol'ko darom Moskva toboy zdana khazaram?" In English: "Say, [Moscow Mayor Yury] Luzhkov, did you really surrender Moscow to the Khazars for free?" (The Khazars were a Turkic people who founded an independent medieval kingdom in what is now southern Russia and adopted Judaism. In contemporary Russian "patriotic" lexicon, Khazars are a code word for Jews.)
The photograph can be found on the web at: http://ndpr.ru/data/photo/02s.jpg.
© 2002 <u>Национально – Державная партия России</u>. Printed with permission from the webmaster of http://ndpr.ru.

<u>First Russian-language publication:</u>
Vyacheslav Andreevich Likhachev, *Politicheskii antisemizm v sovremennoi Rossii* (Moskva: "Academia", Moskovskoe byuro po pravam cheloveka, 2003). 240 pp. ISBN 5-87532-052-4.

∞

Gedruckt auf alterungsbeständigem, säurefreien Papier
Printed on acid-free paper

ISSN: 1614-3515
ISBN-10: 3-89821-529-6
ISBN-13: 978-3-89821-529-9

© *ibidem*-Verlag
Stuttgart 2006
Alle Rechte vorbehalten

Printed in Germany

Contents

Book Editor's Preface by Eugene Veklerov   9
Abbreviations   15
Glossary of Organizations' Russian Names   17
Foreword   19

Introduction: Anti-Semitism in Mass Consciousness   23

I   Politics

1   Russian Political Parties and Anti-Semitism   31
       1.1   Leftist-Nationalist (Communo-Patriotic) Parties   33
       1.2   National-Patriots   42
       1.3   Eurasians   49

2   Radical Rightist Movements in Contemporary Russia   62
       2.1   Radical Rightists in Contemporary Russia:
              Who Is Who   64
              Classification Problems   64
              Russian National Unity   66
              National Bolshevik Party   72
              Other Radical Right Wing Groups   77
              Uniting Right-Wing Radicals   80
              "Old Right-Wingers": Black Hundred
              and Orthodox Fundamentalists   85
       2.2   Activity of Right-Wing Radicals:
              Defeats in Elections and Successes in Crime   90
              Right-Wing Radicals in Elections   90

	Illegal Activities of Right-Wing Radicals	93
2.3	State Policy on Nationalist Radicals	98
	Registration Denial	98
	Banning Existing Organizations	103
	Current Situation and Future of the Right-Wing Radical Movement	108

II Propaganda

1	The Anti-Semitic Press: What Is It?	113
1.1	General Overview of the Nationalist and Communist Press	113
1.2	"Nazi Gold"	124
2	Ideological Anti-Semitism and its Aspects	132
2.1	The Social Aspect of Anti-Semitic Propaganda	137
2.2	The Conspiratorial Aspect of Anti-Semitic Propaganda (the "Plot Theory")	141
2.3	The Religious Aspect of Anti-Semitic Propaganda	145
2.4	The Racial Aspect of Anti-Semitic Propaganda	149

III Religion

1	Anti-Semitism, the Russian Orthodox Church (ROC) and the State in Contemporary Russia	153
1.1	Religious consciousness and intolerance	154
1.2	Orthodox Christianity and Anti-Semitism	157
1.3	"Church Liberals": Post-Holocaust Theology on Orthodox Soil	161
1.4	"Zealots of the Orthodox Devotion": Fighters against "Jesus-Haters"	164
1.5	The ROC Episcopate: Moderate Conservatism	172
1.6	State and Church: Present and Future	175

2   Russian Muslims and Anti-Semitism   179
    2.1   Muslims in Contemporary Russia   179
    2.2   Dogmatic Anti-Judaism: Ideology
          of Muslim Fundamentalists   185
    2.3   Anti-Zionism: Ideology Amenable to Masses   192

3   Right-Wing Radicals between God and Nation   197

Conclusion   215

Selected Bibliography   217

Book Editor's Preface

When Dr. Andreas Umland, the editor of the series *Soviet and Post-Soviet Politics and Society*, told me about his idea to publish an English version of this book and asked me if I would like to be its translator and editor, I immediately agreed and here is why. As a Jewish child who grew up in the Soviet Union, I was not interested in anti-Semitism, but anti-Semitism was interested in me, so that eventually I had to reciprocate. This Introduction is not an appropriate platform for personal reminiscences, but suffice it to say that in the schizophrenic reality of the Soviet Union, anti-Semitism was everywhere and nowhere at the same time. You could encounter it everywhere from Nazi-style cartoons in *Pravda* to derogatory slurs on buses, but had you had enough guts to complain, you would have been officially told that anti-Semitism did not exist there, and had you persisted, you could have been jailed for slander. To be exact, official propaganda did not really use the word 'Jew'. Instead, it used code phrases, like 'Zionist circles' or 'rootless cosmopolitans'. But however complex the code phrases were, the rank-and-file anti-Semites always managed to decipher them.

Among other things, we were barraged by propaganda ranting that Jewish, oops, Zionist money controls everything in America, and America, of course, was our enemy number one, since its main goal was to conquer the Soviet Union. To prove the tenet that the Jews control everything in Washington, the propaganda often mentioned the two most prominent and wealthiest Jews who had America in their pockets: Ford and Rockefeller.

It took me a long time to discover that the above proof was slightly flawed: neither man was Jewish. In fact, Henry Ford donated his money to support anti-Semitic causes. Many other prominent Americans were perceived to be Jewish, such as Mark Twain, perhaps because the name Mark was popular among Russian Jews. Which reminds me of Sholom Aleichem's characters who believed that Abraham Lincoln was Jewish, because his first name was such a quintessentially Jewish name in Russia that it was used as a derogatory name for all Jews. But since Lincoln was a 'good' president according to the official propaganda, the Russian media was careful to spell his first name differently from the equivalent Russian Jewish name, lest the Jews get an undeserved credit. Namely, Abraham Lincoln's first name was spelled as 'Avraam', whereas the Russian Jewish version of that name was spelled as 'Abram'. (It is common in the Russian language to spell proper foreign names like Michael or John phonetically. In other words, the media made an exception for Honest Abe by using the Russian Biblical version of his name).

The same Mark Twain I mentioned above (who, of course, was not Jewish) has more in common with our subject than his "Jewish" name. Specifically, the evolution of Twain's own position on the Jewish question mirrors, to some extent, similar processes occurring in Russia. As a young writer, Twain embraced the negative stereotypes of the Jews that prevailed in Missouri in the 1850s and used those stereotypes in his early newspaper articles. As he personally got to know more Jews and their contributions to the contemporary society, Twain gradually changed his position and in the later part of his life he became a staunch and ardent defender of the Jews against anti-Semitism.

Many, if not most, Russian citizens have followed a somewhat similar path. So far as anti-Semitism is concerned, Russia is largely a success story. To be precise, there are many anti-Semitic groups, including those that espouse violence. But such groups are relatively small and marginalized. Some 15 years ago, there were grim predictions – some of which were made by reputable academics – that Russia would follow the path of the Weimar Republic, i.e. e. it would slide into a Nazi-style dictatorship or chaos. Yet, the Russian people turned out to be mature enough to choose another path. There are still many local pockets harboring anti-Jewish feelings, notably in areas populated by Muslims, and there is plenty of social anti-Semitism. But as far as the government policies and mainstream public opinion are concerned, the trend is definitely positive.

The anti-Semitism among the Muslim minorities in Russia is a sad new development. The author of this book, Vyacheslav Likhachev, seems to attribute this intolerance to the influence of foreigners and especially the Wahhabi sect. Interestingly enough, the Jews and the Muslims lived amicably in the past. Back in the 1960s and 1970s, the Crimean Tatars, who had been deported from the Crimea by Stalin, started to demand their right to return home. At that time, the foreign Muslims ignored their plight, and the only champions of their cause were the Soviet human rights activists, notably A. Sakharov, P. Grigorenko, D. Kaminskaya, N. Scharansky. In particular, human rights activists, disproportionately many of whom were Jews, were active in the defense of Mustafa Dzhemilev who had been imprisoned by the Soviet government and who is presently Chairman of the Crimean Tatar *Mejlis* (Parliament).

In the middle of June of 2006, when the work on this translation was largely over, leaders of the Muslim and Jewish communities in Russia held a successful forum titled "Islam and Judaism: Prospects for Dialogue and Cooperation". Its active participants included Ravil Gainutdin, Head of the Council of the Mufties of Russia, and Adolf Shaevich, Russia's Chief Rabbi. Both sides appealed for friendlier relations between the two communities. However, since both communities are considerably fractured, it remains to be seen how persuasive their appeals will be.

We live in a topsy-turvy world. As anti-Semitism lessens in Russia and other historically anti-Semitic countries, it is increasing in other parts of the world. Newspapers accuse the Mayor of London of making anti-Semitic remarks and show photographs of the Mayor of Moscow lighting the first candle of the Jewish menorah on Chanukah. Here are two more pieces of recent news. "The majority of Russians do not harbor negative feelings toward Jews and the percentage of Russians who disapprove of anti-Semitism has increased since last year, according to a new nationwide poll. <...> Seven percent of the respondents distrust or dislike Jews, 84 percent do not have these feelings and 9 percent found it difficult to answer this question"[*]. Poland, which is another "country so many Jews love to hate has consistently pursued a pro-

---

[*]   Krichevsky L. Poll: Russians don't dislike Jews, www.jta.org/page_view_story.asp?intarticleid=16282&intcategoryid=2.

American and pro-Israel policy. <...> Israel events at this country's major universities draw large and positive audiences, while the rare anti-Israeli demonstrations are so small they do not even make it to the local media"**. Compare that with growing anti-Semitism in England, France and on many US college campuses. Hopefully, the positive trend in Russia and Eastern Europe will continue, while the negative trend in the West will reverse.

This book deals mainly with anti-Semitism in political life, in media and in religion in contemporary Russia. In other words, its author is interested in anti-Semitism as it appears in political and religious ideology, rather than in the more common sense as persecution of, or discrimination against, Jews or Judaism. The author is a young man, born in 1979, who pursues the study of anti-Semitism in his homeland as an academic subject. Appropriately, the book is written in a dispassionate style that largely conceals the author's views and makes the book more credible. To his credit, he manages to be consistent and to refrain from editorializing even when he describes really bizarre anti-Semitic stories, such as those based in astrology or quoted from an alleged document from an unidentified "World Zionist Congress" which contains insidious plans to increase the acidity of the goyim's blood.

As the translator and editor, I added footnotes explaining certain terms or concepts that may be less familiar to a Western reader. My footnotes are easily distinguishable from the author's footnotes, as they are labeled E1, E2, etc. With all due respect to the author, I disagreed with him on a few occasions and took the liberty of using a couple of my footnotes to express my opinions on those occasions. To make reading of the book easier, I also added a Glossary that lists the Russian names of political and religious groups, parties and organizations and their English translations. The Glossary also contains a list of commonly used abbreviations in the text.

The Russian version of the book was completed by the summer of 2003. Hence, the author could only make guesses about the 2003 Duma election, in which case I used Editor's footnotes to provide the actual results. Finally, the

---

**   Taube T. Who's one of Israel's best friends? www.jta.org/page_view_story.asp? intarticleid=16289&intcategoryid=2.

English version corrected a few minor errors in the original, such as misspelled English words and names in the References, and removed textual duplications.

A few terminological explanations are also necessary for the English reader. Russia is a multi-ethnic state. In addition to the ethnic Russians, the country is populated by other Slavic and non-Slavic ethnic groups, which often maintain their languages and other attributes of their culture. Hence, the English word 'Russians' is ambiguous and, in fact, it corresponds to two distinct Russian words – *Russkie* (the members of the Russian ethnic group) and *Rossiyane* (the people permanently living in Russia). When the meaning of the term was not clear from the context, I tried to clarify it.

Since the Soviet Union was an atheistic state, the word 'Jews' was not used in the religious sense for 70 plus years, and it has largely lost that sense. Rather, it usually denotes belonging to the pertinent ethnic group the way the words Ukrainians, Armenians or Tatars do. Thus, an ethnic Russian who chose to convert to Judaism would still be referred to as a Russian. Conversely, a person who was born to Jewish parents, but later got baptized and even became a Russian Orthodox priest may still be referred to as a Jew, and in fact, this book includes such examples.

Having a specific ethnicity was obligatory in the Soviet Union and it was inscribed in one's internal passport. To make things more confusing, it was inscribed under the item *natsionalnost*, a Russian word that sounds similar to the English word nationality. For the English speaker, however, the word nationality appearing in a passport would automatically refer to citizenship, whereas the Russian word *natsionalnost* does not have the same denotation for the Russian speaker.

Also, the reader should be careful about the usage of the words 'left' and 'right' in this book. For example, the author classifies Eduard Limonov's National Bolshevik Party as a radical right-wing party. In fact, its ideology is so eclectic that it might as well be classified as a left-wing party. Perhaps, that is just an example of a worldwide phenomenon, whereby the extreme left and the extreme right actually merge, instead of being opposite as geometry suggests. A good example would be the meeting of David Duke and Albert Makashov in 1999 covered by the press. The former is an ex-leader of the American Ku Klux Klan, a racist and a rabid anti-Communist. His notion of "Jewish crimes" is exemplified by the case of the Rosenbergs who stole American nuclear secrets and sent them to the Soviet Union for ideological reasons. Makashov is a prominent leader of the Russian Communist Party and a big fan of Stalin. One could not think of more implacable enemies, yet common anti-Semitism turned a Communist and an anti-Communist into allies. They had a cordial meeting covered by *Zavtra* under a characteristic title: "Duke to Makashov – 'We are Brothers in Arms'"[***].

A final word of caution applies to anti-Semitic expressions attributed to prominent figures of the past. Such expressions may not necessarily be judged as anti-Semitic; it all depends on the historical context and on the norms prevailing at that time. Applying our standards of political correctness to people who lived centuries ago would be misleading, as would taking those quotations out of historical context.

Several friends and colleagues have provided useful comments to me as I was working on this translation. Dr. Basya Gale read the English version twice. Her numerous suggestions substantially improved the style of the book and I am deeply indebted to her. Bett Martinez, Dr. Lawrence A. Shepp and Doreen Stock also read fragments of my translation. I am grateful to them for their comments.

Eugene Veklerov
University of California

[***]   "My s vami brat'ya po bor'be!", www.zavtra.ru/cgi/veil/data/zavtra/99/306/82.html.

Abbreviations

CCRNP -	Coordinating Council of Radical Nationalist Parties
CIS -	Commonwealth of Independent States
CMR -	Council of the Mufties of Russia
CMSB -	Central Muslim Spiritual Board
CPRF -	Communist Party of the Russian Federation
CRU -	Christian Revival Union
EP-URP -	Eurasian Party - Union of Russian Patriots
FP -	Freedom Party
FSU -	Former Soviet Union; a group of independent states formed after the disintegration of the Soviet Union
LDPR -	Liberal Democratic Party of Russia
MP -	Moscow Patriarchy
MSA -	Movement in Support of the Army
MSB -	Muslim Spiritual Boards
MSBES -	MSB of the European part of the USSR and Siberia
NBP -	National Bolshevik Party
NPGR -	National Party of Great Russia
NRPR -	National Republican Party of Russia
NSF -	National Salvation Front
NSRM -	New Social Russian Movement
PNP -	People's National Party
PPPR -	People's Patriotic Party of Russia
PPRU -	Popular Patriotic Russian Union
RA -	Movement "Russian Action"
RAU -	Russian All-People Union
RCWP -	Russian Communist Workers' Party
RF -	Russian Federation
RMC -	Russian Muslim Community
RNC -	Russian National Council
RNU -	Russian National Unity

RNU-KK -   Russian National Union (headed by K. Kasimovsky)
RO -   Russian Orthodox
ROC -   Russian Orthodox Church
ROCA -   Russian Orthodox Church Abroad
RPPM -   Russian Patriotic People's Movement
SU -   Slavonic Union
TOC -   Russian True Orthodox (Catacomb) Church
UOB -   Union of Orthodox Brethren
UOC -   Union of Orthodox Citizens
UOG -   Union of Orthodox Gonfaloniers
UPP -   United People's Party
URF -   Union of Right Forces

Glossary of Organizations' Russian Names

Christian Revival Union - Soyuz Khristianskoe vozrozhdenie

Communist Party of the Russian Federation - Kommunisticheskaya Partiya Rossiyskoy Federatsii

Eurasian Party - Union of Russian Patriots - Evraziyskaya partiya - Soyuz patriotov Rossii

For Holy Russia - Za Rus' Svyatuyu

Freedom Party - Partia Svobody

Interregional Movement Unity - Mezhregionalnoe dvizhenie Edinstvo

Joined People's Party - Obyedinennaya Narodnaya Partiya

Joint Detachment of RNU - Svodny otryad RNE

Liberal Democratic Party of Russia - Liberalno-demokraticheskaya partiya Rossii

Memory – Pamyat'

Movement in Support of the Army - Dvizhenie v podderzhku armii

Movement "Russian Action" - Dvizhenie "Russkoe Deystvie"

National Bolshevik Party - Natsional-bolshevistskaya partiya

National Party of Great Russia - Natsionalno-derzhavnaya partiya Rissii

National Republican Party of Russia - Natsionalno-respublikanskaya partiya Rossii

National Salvation Front - Front natsionalnogo spasenia

New Social Russian Movement - Novoe obshchestvennoe russkoe dvizhenie

People's Nationalist Party - Narodno-natsionalnaya Partiya

People's Patriotic Party of Russia - Narodno-Patrioticheskaya partiya Rossii

Popular Patriotic Russian Union - Narodno-patriotichesky soyuz Rossii

Russian All-People Union - Rossiysky obshchenarodny soyuz

Russian Communist Workers' Party - Rossiyskaya kommunisticheskaya rabochaya partiya

Russian National Council - Russky Natsionalny Sobor

Russian National Union - Russky Natsionalny Soyuz

Russian National Unity - Russkoe Natsional'noe Edinstvo

Russian Nationalist-Socialist Party - Russkaya natsional-sotsialisticheskaya partiya

Russian Party - Russkaya Partiya

Russian Party of Russia - Russkaya partiya Rossii

Russian Patriotic People's Movement - Russkoe patrioticheskoe narodnoe dvizhenie

Russian Phalanx - Russkaya Falanga

Russia's Revival - Russkoe vozrozhdenie

Salvation - Spas

Slavonic Union - Slavyansky Soyuz

Slavonic Unity Party - Partiya slavyanskogo edinstva

Union of Officers - Soyuz ofitserov

Union of Orthodox Brethren - Soyuz pravoslavnykh bratstv

Union of Orthodox Citizens - Soyuz pravoslavnykh grazhdan

Union of Orthodox Gonfaloniers - Soyuz pravoslavnykh khorugvenostsev

Union of Realists - Soyuz realistov

Union of Right Forces - Soyuz pravykh sil

United People's Party - Ob"edinennaya narodnaya partiya

White World - Bely mir

Working Russia - Trudovaya Rossia

Foreword

This book is based on the research conducted by the author in 2000 – 2002 in collaboration with several organizations. Most of the material was commissioned by the Moscow Bureau for Human Rights. Certain parts were prepared within the project "Anti-Semitism and Xenophobia in the Russian Federation" carried out by the author through the sponsorship of the Moscow Office of the Anti-Defamation League, the Russian Jewish Congress and the Tolerance Foundation; part was presented as talks at various conferences and published in scholarly journals and collections of papers. Most of the talks that formed the basis for further research (and took advantage of valuable comments made during the discussions) were presented at multidisciplinary conferences on Judaica organized by the Center for Researchers and Teachers of Judaica at Sefer[E1] colleges. The main part of the text consists of information that the author gathered and processed for many years as part of his work in the Information and Research Center Panorama. I am sincerely grateful to all organizations mentioned above for their support of my research projects. These materials in a recast form comprise the skeleton of this book.

I would like to express my gratitude to my colleagues who have helped me in my work in the last several years. It is impossible to mention every colleague I had while I carried out my research; I will list only those without whom this book would not have seen the light of day. I am deeply grateful to Viktor Aleksandrovich Shnirelman, my first teacher and advisor. His suggestions and demanding style of work were extremely helpful to me at the first steps of my research activities in the field of ideological anti-Semitism. I am thankful to Vladimir Valerianovich Pribylovsky, possibly the greatest specialist in political history of post-Soviet Russia, who taught me research methodology in the area of the most recent Russian political history. It is impossible to overesti-

---

[E1]   Sefer is an organization that coordinates the teaching of Jewish studies at universities and colleges.

mate his contribution to shaping my research skills. I am proud of my acquaintance with him.

I am grateful to my relatives and close friends whose support and understanding made this work possible. I would like to express my special appreciation to my spouse, Anna Nekrasova. Her love and friendship help me live.

I am grateful to everyone who has read this manuscript. Their comments and friendly criticism certainly improved the book substantially. Particularly valuable comments were made by Aleksandr Verkhovsky, Valentin Oskotsky, Vladimir Pribylovsky, Anatoly Podolsky, Artur Fredekind and Viktor Shnirelman. Naturally, all errors and inaccuracies remain the author's responsibility.

Within my specialization, I am mainly interested in anti-Semitism in the political life of contemporary Russia. Actually, anti-Semitism in the strict sense of the word is primarily a political ideology, whereas widely spread prejudices are secondary. Religious issues are covered only insofar as they are part of the political context. However, it is impossible to talk about political anti-Semitism without examining the issue of how common this bigotry in mass consciousness is. Not being an expert in sociology, I have summarized results of specialized studies and have referred the reader to the specialized literature that I used.

The main part of this book is divided into three parts. The first part is devoted to an analysis of anti-Semitism in the context of the political parties in the contemporary Russian Federation (RF). Two elements of this issue are discussed: moderate anti-Semitism in the ideology of 'serious' parties belonging to the political mainstream, and the situation in marginal groups on the extreme right (ultra-nationalist and religious fundamentalist groups). In addition, we discuss the attitude of the state towards such movements.

The second part of this book is concerned with anti-Semitic propaganda. We describe in detail the anti-Semitic press and its financial resources. Then, in a very general way, we discuss and analyze the structure and content of anti-Semitic propaganda in periodicals and newspapers.

Finally, the subject of the third part of this book lies on the boundary between the study of politics and religion. This part is devoted to the analysis of the function of anti-Semitism in the Russian Orthodox Church (ROC) and in Islam in contemporary Russia. The last chapter of the third part offers an analysis of the Russian extreme right-wing movement as a 'religious' movement.

Each part and each chapter can be viewed as independent articles devoted to specific issues.

The work on this book was largely completed in the beginning of the summer of 2003. Undoubtedly, by the time it reaches the readers, the rapidly changing political life in post-Soviet Russia – accelerated by the upcoming elections – will bring further corrections. The reader should not forget this.

Introduction: Anti-Semitism in Mass Consciousness

In order to evaluate the extent to which anti-Semitic prejudices are common in Russian society, we have to turn to the results of public opinion polls. The most prominent sociologist working on this problem is Lev Gudkov. His studies are used as the basis for the following[1].

According to Gudkov[2], the core of the most convinced anti-Semites (i.e. the people providing consistently negative answers to most of the questions) is a cluster of respondents whose percentage may be approximately estimated as 6% – 9%. Their relative numbers practically do not change from year to year. They are the people paying extraordinary attention to the 'Jewish question'. Anti-Semitism is a substantial element of their view of the world. About 1% - 1.5% of the polled people (the margin of error in such sociological studies is plus or minus 2% - 2.5%) are ready to support, or already participate in, radical nationalist organizations such as *Russkoe natsional'noe edinstvo* (Russian National Unity, RNU) or *Pamyat* (Memory). They regularly read anti-Semitic and xenophobic periodicals and books.

The percentage of those who gave manifestly negative answers only to certain diagnostic questions about the Jews is much larger: 15% - 18%. For these people, anti-Semitism is not the main, or even an important, part of

---

[1]   Analyzed results of several public opinion polls sponsored by *Vserossiyskiy tsentr izucheniya obshchestvennogo mneniya* (All-Russian Center for Public Opinion Study) and conducted by L. Gudkov were published in the following publications: Gudkov L., Levinson A. Otnoshenie naseleniya SSSR k evreyam i problema antisemitizma. *Vestnik Evreyskogo Universiteta v Moskve*, No.1, 1992; Gudkov L., Levinson A. Izmenenie v otnoshenii k evreyam naseleniya respublik na territorii byvshego SSSR. *Vestnik Evreyskogo Universiteta v Moskve*, No.4, 1993; Gudkov L. *Antisemitizm v postsovetskoy Rossii – Neterpimost' v Rossii. Starye i novye fobii.* Moscow Carnegie Center, 1999 (further referred to as *Neterpimost' v Rossii*).

[2]   Gudkov L. *Antisemitizm v postsovetskoy Rossii*, pp. 74 and on.

their ideology. Rather, their attitude is caused by their generally intolerant xenophobic position.

About half of the respondents (from 35% to 52%) form the outer, disparate layer of the distribution of the anti-Semitic feelings. Their anti-Semitism is passive and defensive, meant to set limits. The most negative reaction was in response to the question about whether a Jew could be a Russian president (64% of the respondents answered in the negative). A general characteristic of this group of people is their negative attitude on issues such as letting the Jews have their active political parties, letting them have loud and in-your-face celebrations of their religious holidays, etc. Many respondents from this group doubt the Jews' loyalty.

Therefore, according to Gudkov, the most common negative anti-Semitic reactions have a defensive or compensatory character. They are directed towards restricting the Jews' access to positions that are symbolic of the Russian national consciousness.
Apparently, the last group making up 35% - 52% of the population should be defined as sharing anti-Semitic opinions.

According to the results of the same public opinion polls, consistently pro-Jewish (philo-Semitic) groups in the society are as small as overtly anti-Semitic ones: their size does not exceed 10% - 12% of the polled. Combined with liberal respondents who are deliberately tolerant towards various ethnic groups, the size of this layer reaches 18% - 20%. Such a small size of the consistently tolerant population should not cause a panic. This social layer has a high prestige in the society, because it includes more highly educated, professional people holding influential positions in the media, in politics and the economy, and therefore, significantly influencing the society at large.

According to the results of another public opinion poll commissioned by the Anti-Defamation League (ADL) in 1999 (the results were published in September)[3], strong anti-Semitic views are held by 44% of the polled. The ab-

---

[3]   Highlights from the September 1999 Anti-Defamation League *Survey on Anti-*

sence of anti-Semitism was demonstrated by 19%, and 37% belong to the gray area. The respondents were asked to say if they agree or disagree with eleven statements, such as "Too many Russian banks are controlled by Jews", "The Jewish businessmen tend to be dishonest" or "The Jews are more concerned about the interests of Israel than those of Russia". Those who agreed with 6 – 11 statements were categorized as 'consistent anti-Semites'; those who agreed with 2 – 5 statements were put into the gray area.

Of course, from the sociological point of view, the public opinion poll was implemented incorrectly for various reasons that we are not going to discuss here, as we are not experts in this field. But a strong side of the ADL methodology is the fact that a similar system has been used in the USA for dozens of years and we can compare the results. In the United States in 1998, 12% of those polled supported anti-Semitic views consistently, 53% demonstrated essential tolerance. In 1964, the results were 29% and 31%, respectively. Hence, the situation with anti-Semitism in Russia in 1999 was worse than that in the USA in 1964.

According to a very common point of view, the strong position of anti-Semitism in the mass consciousness is caused by traditional stereotypes of 'populist', 'rural', 'patriarchal' consciousness. These stereotypes, in turn, are rooted in the rudiments of the religious view, on the one hand. On the other hand, they are rooted in narrow-mindedness, lack of education, provincial aggressiveness towards strangers, etc. However, recent sociological studies (their results have not been verified yet) carried out by a Siberian group showed that anti-Semitism in contemporary Russia does not conform to traditional stereotypes. Rather, it is part of the urban culture. The modern Russian society does not have much in common with a traditional society. The intense and partly forced modernization intentionally destroyed the rudiments of the patriarchal culture and radically changed the people's mentality. Although sociologically, the arguments of the proponents of the idea above are not flaw-

Semitism and Societal Attitudes in Russia. Published by the Anti-Defamation League.

less, the suggested theory seems reasonable. In any case, it deserves further verification.

To understand anti-Semitism adequately in the context of the social life of modern Russia, it is necessary to point out this important fact: the Jews, obviously, are not the main target of the ethnic phobias. The prejudices against natives of the Caucasus, Gypsies, etc. are much more widely spread, more radical and more overtly stated. The primary role in shaping the phobias towards the natives of the Caucasus and the Muslims is played by the recent events (military actions in Chechnya and Dagestan, ethnically flavored terrorism, migrations, a difficult economic and ethno-demographic situation, etc) and, to a greater degree, their distorted coverage by the media[4].

According to public opinion polls, the respondents feel the most negative emotions towards the Chechens and other groups from the Northern Caucasus, Armenians, Azeris, Gypsies, Blacks, the Balts, and only then towards the Jews followed by the Tatars and Americans[5]. According to Zinaida Sikevich[6], on the average, 40.9% of the polled in Russia openly expressed some hostility towards another ethnic group. In other polls detecting 'latent' rather than declared xenophobia, that number reached 85% of the respondents, out of which almost three quarters (from 69% to 76% depending on the region) targeted only the natives of the Caucasus. According to the same data, hostility towards the Jews was declared by 5.6% of the polled.

---

[4]   We are not talking about nationalist and radical publications that are xenophobic by definition – they have a small circulation and a very small effect on mass consciousness. However, the contemporary Russian press is widely contaminated with subconscious xenophobia – on the level of terminology, the choice of topics, subtle accents, etc. It is hard to say which comes first: does the media form mass xenophobia or does mass xenophobia determine the demand, and therefore, shape the media in its own image and likeness? The book written by a group of authors – Verkhovskiy A. (editor) *Yazyk moy... Problema etnicheskoi i religioznoy neterpimosti v rossiyskikh SMI*, Moscow: Panorama, 2002, deals with the role of the media in shaping negative ethnic stereotypes.

[5]   See, for example, the table "The attitude of the Russians towards other nationalities". *Neterpimost' v Rossii*. p. 48.

[6]   Sikevich Z., *Etnicheskaya nepriyazn' v massovom soznanii rossiyan – neterpimost' v Rossii*. pp. 107-108.

The figures above are supported by other public opinion polls[7], including more recent ones, and they seem reliable.

We should add that the polls sense a nearly constant level of the anti-Semitic feelings in the society starting in 1990 (a small growth in anti-Semitic feelings was noticed in 1993 – 1995). In the meantime, the layer of tolerant and essentially tolerant people slightly increased, mainly owing to the attitudes of young people. This increasing attitude of tolerance among young people provides grounds to predict a further growth of such feelings in society.

Besides, while there was a relatively common anxiety (or a hope, for those on the 'other side') in the early '90s that extremes, like anti-Jewish pogroms, were possible within a year, lately such expectations almost do not exist[8]. Public opinion is, of course, not the best indicator in this case, but one may draw certain conclusions based on it.

In the study referred to above, L. Gudkov claims that "the attitude towards the Jews in Russia is about the same as it is in Western or Eastern Europe, more tolerant than it is in Austria, Germany or Poland, but worse than it is in the Czech Republic, Hungary or Ukraine". That gives reason for optimism. However, as Gudkov states later, the most important structure of the value system in the Russian society is deeply sick, since its consolidation occurs "not because of positive values and achievements. Rather, it occurs because of a general oversimplification of collective life, including keeping a hostile attitude towards those who are ethnically 'other', who are often imagined or fantasized, and indifference towards the problems of people who are the object of

---

[7]   See, for example, the results of public opinion polls in: Gessen M. Iz chego tol'ko sdelany natsi. *Itogi*, May 12, 1998.

[8]   In 1990, in response to the question "Are anti-Jewish pogroms probable in Russia this year or next year?", 12% of the respondents said "very probable" or "sufficiently probable" and 43% - "less probable" or "not probable at all" (the rest could not answer). In 1997, the results were 5% and 77%, respectively. See the table "Opinions regarding anti-Jewish pogroms and anti-Semitic feelings". *Neterpimost' v Rossii*, p. 79.

antipathy and hostility"[9]. This analysis was given before the beginning of the second Chechen campaign. Unfortunately, the analysis was confirmed by the following course of events.

The modern Russian mass consciousness is characterized by a negative model of collective self-identification. While the positive model of national self-identification ("we are good, nice, cultured, etc.") stabilizes the society and provides a high level of tolerance, the negative one ("they are bad, evil, aggressive, etc.") leads to a high degree of xenophobia and bitterness. Clearly, elements of both the positive and the negative models of self-identification always co-exist in reality and form a complicated value complex of mass consciousness. However, the problem of the collective self-identification for contemporary Russians lies in the fact that the negative elements prevail both qualitatively and quantitatively. Indeed, the trend to consolidate by demarcating the boundary between 'us' and 'them' is extremely strong both at the top and at the bottom of the society. This demarcation assumes an enemy (often fantasized) who possesses clearly expressed ethnic characteristics. The xenophobic emotions are shamelessly exploited by the high-level leaders in order to consolidate the population (the sociological term is 'ethnic mobilization'), which makes the problem very serious. The fact that they presently use anti-Chechen rather than anti-Semitic feelings should not confuse anyone[10]. The very existence of such feelings is what is dangerous.

Western studies similar to ours are often accompanied by recommendations to State bodies. Such bodies in the West tend to pay attention to the opinions of independent experts and public organizations. That is part of the mechanism still lacking in our civic society. The ethno-political situation in the RF is so complex that it is very difficult to give definite and, more importantly, realistic and workable recommendations. Nevertheless, let us try to formulate our

---

[9]   Gudkov L. *Antisemitizm v postsovetskoy Rossii*, pp. 95-96.

[10]   For the sake of fairness, let us note that the concept of xenophobia under the conditions of suppression of a military center of ethnic separatism has a connotation different from that in a multi-ethnic state without hot spots. However, discussion of this issue may lead us too far away from out main subject.

opinion on desirable changes in the most problematic spheres in the area of inter-ethnic relations and human rights.

First, state bodies should rein in chauvinistic and xenophobic propaganda and activities promptly and vigorously, especially when they originate from the state bureaucrats themselves. Naturally, the actions countering extremism should be carried out in a deliberately polite and lawful manner, without the illegal arbitrariness common in Russia (this obvious principle is not presently observed). To lower xenophobic feelings in the society, high-level statesmen should promptly denounce specific instances of intolerance and chauvinism, especially aggressive ones. Any discrimination against ethnic minorities (Turk-Meskhetians, Gypsies, Chechens and ethnic migrants) by law-enforcement or other state bodies should definitely cease. There should be no inequality of various religious groups from the point of view of the state. In general, the state's interference in religious affairs should be minimal.

Second, it is necessary to develop and implement a number of steps (primarily, in the sphere of education and mass culture) aimed at forming a tolerant consciousness. It seems to us that it is especially important to implement educational programs devoted to the danger of racism, chauvinism and xenophobia, and fostering a respectful attitude towards cultural diversity among state employees, especially the police, judges and other law enforcement officials.

We may state that, for the most part, however, the situation may be radically changed with only systemic changes solely in the area of implementing the laws that already exist 'on paper'. So far, the formation of a civic society and law-abiding state is a dream for Russia. However, as the world's experience has shown, this dream is achievable.

I   Politics

1   Russian Political Parties and Anti-Semitism

This part of our book is devoted to the analysis of the role played by anti-Semitism in the ideology and propaganda of the wide spectrum of 'mainstream' parties in contemporary Russia. Of course, it would be useless to look for evidence of anti-Semitism among the liberal or centrist politicians. For a number of reasons, however, anti-Semitism is a visible phenomenon among organizations following a nationalistic ideology even when the nationalism is in its very mild form.

This chapter deals with the major political forces in the country. Of course, anti-Semitism in major parties represented in parliament and enjoying wide popularity is not as overt as it is in marginal neo-nazi groups. However, the very fact that parties with significant anti-Semitic elements in their ideology belong to the 'mainstream' is a cause for concern. Obviously, we are not talking about crude slogans calling for killing of the Jews. Anti-Semitism of large parties is more concealed, disguised. That is exactly why it is seriously dangerous: camouflaged anti-Semitism thus acquires 'respectability', legitimacy within the political area.

Today, more than ten years since the post-Soviet Russian democracy has been in existence, it is obvious that the country has avoided sliding into a nationalist-radical ('fascist') state. The thesis about a "Weimar Russia"[11] proposed in the early 1990s by analogy with Weimar Germany did not materialize. Looking back from 2003, one may confidently state that very powerful authoritarian and xenophobic sentiments among a large segment of the people did not ensure the victory for the chauvinist forces, but rather they chose

---

[11]   This term was introduced by an American political scientist of Russian extraction, Alexander Yanov, see Yanov A. *Posle Yeltsina. "Veymarskaya" Rossiya*. Moscow, 1995.

other directions in their evolution. The power of the state happened to be tougher than that in Germany of the 1920s and the society more stable. Lately, the extreme nationalist organizations have been rapidly losing even the shaky positions that they managed to hold in the mid 1990s.

Organizationally, the radical nationalists present a rather pitiful sight now. However, National-Patriotic ideas not overtly suggesting violence or massive violations of human rights of people based on their ethnic, religious and political affiliations are still very common in the society. In the political spectrum, nationalist ideas are used by both nationalistic-populist movements and communo-patriotic ones.

In dealing with such a complex issue as the influence of the radical nationalist ('fascist') concepts and approaches on the ideology of Russian major political parties, one should be very careful and avoid falling into extremes. On the one hand, clearly there is no objective reason to claim (as is done by some respected but excessively emotional journalists and researchers) that Gennady Zyuganov and Vladimir Zhirinovsky are 'fuehrers' of the Russian 'Nazis' who are struggling to grab power (and are very close to it) in order to set up a huge concentration camp in Russia. One the other hand, one should not dismiss numerous and very serious nationalist-radical and xenophobic elements in the ideology and propagandist rhetoric of a number of influential Russian political leaders.

Many elements of the nationalist-radical ideology have been 'smuggled' into the area of 'big politics'. Of all these elements, we are interested in manifestations of the intentional hostility towards Jewry. In principle, a nationalist, or even a radical, position does not necessarily imply anti-Semitism. Theoretically, there may exist an ultra-nationalist organization free from anti-Semitism. However, for a number of reasons (not the least of which is the pressure of the political tradition in our country), in actuality, most of the Russian nationalist patriots are anti-Semites to some extent anyway. A variant anti-Semitic mythology is a prerogative of the radical right wing playing the role of the 'brains' generating and propagating the Jewish conspiracy theory. Like circles in water, the anti-Semitic mythology spreads farther away from the original center covering a wide ideological and political space. As these circles reach the periphery, they lose their intrinsic logic and, oftentimes, their radicalism too, keeping only the separate non-cohesive accusations, as well as a negative emotional charge. Anti-Semitism is present in the ideology and propaganda of a large group of Russian political parties exactly in the form of such disjointed elements.

The purpose of this Chapter is to shed some light on the entire spectrum of those major political organizations in contemporary Russia in whose ideology anti-Semitism plays a significant role or whose propaganda uses anti-Semitic motifs. Here is the last preliminary comment of a methodological type. It would be futile to look for anti-Semitic statements in the official programs of the political parties, with the exception of the groups not laying real claims to political participation, such as *Russkaya partiya Rossii* (Russian Party of Russia) of Viktor Korchagin. But that is not the main point: in contemporary Russia, generally, the programs themselves do not tell much about the real positions taken by a political group. More often, a program presents a party ideology in a superficial way – they are written for the Ministry of Justice, not for the people. The voter (we are talking about motivated voters supporting a certain ideology) votes not for the 'program' (even party members, as a rule, do not read it), but rather for the position expressed by the leader or published in the party press. Therefore, we will concentrate on the statements made by political leaders and on the analysis of publications. That will help us sort out the positions of various parties on the "Jewish question".

1.1   Leftist-Nationalist (Communo-Patriotic) Parties

The largest communist organizations traditionally took an internationalist position. However, in the situation created in post-Soviet Russia, they have shifted to the 'right' and taken a place in the quite conservative part of the political spectrum[12]. In case of the *Kommunisticheskaya Partiya Rossiyskoy*

---

[12]   We tend to link the increasing role of anti-Semitism in the Russian communist movement with exactly this ideological evolution from internationalism to Soviet patriotism. A detailed description of this evolution (as well as a detailed description of

Federatsii – the Communist Party of the Russian Federation (CPRF) – such a shift to the right was also accompanied by a de facto refusal to support its leftist ideals in economics, at least in their radical form. A similar evolution of opinions on economic issues did not take place in radical neo-Stalinist groups and they do not enjoy as much popularity in the society despite their exploitation of Imperial-Soviet patriotism [13].

Obviously, the positions of classical Communists-Internationalists are extremely weak in Russia. Most of the groups and publishers calling themselves 'Communist' tend to exploit National-Patriotic rhetoric in one degree or another. By doing so, they invoke either the traditions of Stalinist imperial nationalist-bolshevism, or the 'Soviet patriotism' of the 70s – 80s of the past century. Putting the stress on the patriotic themes draws most of the contemporary Russian Communists (or communo-patriots, to be exact) close to the Nationalists. It is clear that they have less in common with respect to the positive parts of their platforms (quite a few Nationalists tend to assess the Soviet period in Russian history and the rule of the Communist Party of the USSR negatively) than with respect to the exploiting of the negative images. Anti-Semitism occupies a solid position among various forms of xenophobia that

---

the gradually increasing role of anti-Semitism) may be found in the following: Agurskiy M. *Ideologiya natsional-bol'shevizma.* Paris: YMCA, 1980; Mitrokhin N. *Russkaya partiya. Dvizhenie russkikh natsionalistov v SSSR. 1952 – 1985.* Moscow: Novoe literaturnoe obozrenie, 2003. It is possible to argue that the Russian communists did not abandon the ideology of their mentors but, on the contrary, came back to it. Indeed, Karl Marx himself and others, if not the majority of the radical social democrats of the third quarter of the XIX century, professed rabid social anti-Semitism. In their propagandist rhetoric, it was related to anti-capitalism (V. Shnirelman brought that problem to my attention). However, that point of view is refuted by the obvious fact: our home-grown Communists lack the desire to 're-invent' Marx, not to mention other authors who are simply unfamiliar to the rank-and-file members of the Communist party. If CPRF members read Marx less and less and have negative feelings towards the Jews more and more, then the anti-Semitism of CPRF is not related, at least not immediately, to the position of the founder of scientific communism.

[13]   For the most detailed analysis of the entire spectrum of the leftist political parties and groups in post-Soviet Russia, see Tarasov A., Cherkasov G., Shavshukova T. *Levye v Rossii: ot umerennykh do ekstremistov.* Moscow: Institut eksperimental'noy sotsiologii, 1997.

have long become a staple of communist propaganda, such as anti-Westernism and Americanophobia.

The anti-Semitic position is consistent with the modern communist ideology. Moderate anti-Semitism in domestic politics and loudly declared anti-Zionism in foreign politics are usually associated by both the average man in the street and by politicians with the late Soviet period, and rightfully so. That's why pro-communist public figures with a positive attitude towards the Soviet period of Russian history frequently exploit anti-Semitic rhetoric.

Aside from the strong traditions of Soviet anti-Zionism, there is another important factor. The Communists in contemporary Russia occupy a conservative-protective niche and position themselves primarily as an avant-garde of the 'popular-patriotic' groups. Since the liberals may be very cautiously called pro-Westerners in the contemporary political spectrum, then the communists, on the contrary, became Slavophiles, squeezing classical National-Patriots from that field. The Russian Orthodox (RO) nationalists (except for the populists like Zhirinovsky) have achieved significant successes during the entire post-Soviet decade only when they formed a broad coalition with communists and Soviet patriots. In the 1990s, such coalitions were *Russky Natsionalny Sobor,* (Russian National Council, RNC) (G. Zyuganov was a co-chairman of *Duma* – the ruling body of RNC, other leaders of RNC included open neo-nazis, such as Aleksandr Barkashov) and *Front natsionalnogo spasenia,* (National Salvation Front, NSF). Stalinist Communists played the key role in NSF; we may mention Nikolay Lysenko among other prominent nationalist-radicals who participated in NSF activities. Another coalition in the second half of the 1990s was *Narodno-patriotichesky soyuz Rossii,* (Popular Patriotic Russian Union, PPRU) created under the auspices of CPRF; a substantial role in PPRU was played by radical anti-Semites Nikolay Kondratenko and Vladimir Miloserdov, the leader of *Russkaya Partiya* (Russian Party).

The communists turned out to be strong organizers. They very skillfully played on the nostalgia of a large part of the Russian population about the 'great empire' that was also a 'socially equitable state with universal prosperity' and, thus, managed to seize the popularity among the nationalistically inclined Russians. This characteristic of the modern Russian communist movement caused, to a large extent, the marginality of the National-Patriots proper. It also caused a wide spread of nationalist and xenophobic (including anti-Semitic) feelings in a large group of people.

CPRF is the most numerous Russian political party. Its membership officially reaches 500,000 people. Strictly speaking, CPRF was the only real political party in the country during the 1990s. Its leader is Gennady Zyuganov. It publishes the following large-circulation papers: *Sovetskaya Rossiya* (Soviet Russia), its editor-in-chief is Valentin Chikin, circulation – 300,000 copies, published 4 or 5 times a week, *Pravda* (Truth), its editor-in-chief is Aleksandr Ilyin, circulation – 65,700 copies, published 3 times a week, *Pravda Rossii* (Truth of Russia) its editor-in-chief is Vladimir Ryndin, circulation – 74,000 copies, published once a week

The contemporary CPRF is much more National-Patriotic than communist. The fact that Gennady Zyuganov, rather than Valentin Kuptsov, became its leader at the Founding Convention in 1993 under the pressure of the radical wing (primarily General Albert Makashov), caused the nationalist bent in the party ideology. For a long time, the party ideology was de facto shaped by Aleksey Podberezkin. Even though he was not a party member officially, his ideological influence on Zyuganov was so great that he was called the "Gray Cardinal" of the CPRF leader. His Social-Democratic rhetoric notwithstanding, Podberezkin holds National-Patriotic views on the most important issues.

Despite a common opinion that the communists are losing popularity in the country, CPRF has improved its results from election to election. It got 12.4% of the vote in the election for the State Duma[E2] in 1993, 22.3% in 1995, and 24.29 in 1999 even taking the lead over the pro-government bloc *Mezhregionalnoe dvizhenie Edinstvo* (Interregional Movement Unity). A detailed analysis of the electoral statistics refutes another common stereotype related to CPRF – that its electorate consists of less educated country and small town dwellers and is aging. On the contrary, the percentage of city dwellers,

---

[E2]   The State Duma is one of the two chambers of Russia's Parliament.

young people and college educated people voting for the communists increases from election to election.

The Communist Party was a highly diverse organization during the entire 1990s. It consisted of several distinct groups. Frank xenophobes such as A. Makashov[14] and Viktor Ilyukhin were on its nationalistic wing. These politicians occupying the top of the party hierarchy systematically made and condoned anti-Semitic statements. Anti-Semitism plays an important part in their world outlook. Furthermore, the image of the 'Jew' is interpreted by them in social terms. Thus, General Makashov claimed (although perhaps not quite sincerely) that the word *zhid*[E3] means a dishonest man, a banker, a pawnbroker, an exploiter.

Anti-Semitic innuendos are sometimes detectable in the writings of the CPRF leader G. Zyuganov. For example, he gingerly discusses the role of the Jewish factor in forming the capitalist market and the mechanism for exploiting the workers in his book 'Beyond the Horizon'. However, we should add that the main part of the text concerning the role of the Jews in the capitalist system was contained only in the first printing of the book, published in Orel with a limited circulation but it was not included in the later, 'canonical' version published in Moscow. In his other writings and speeches, the secrecy-minded CPRF leader carefully avoids any identification of the fantasized enemy. His writings use the depersonalized 'subversive forces', 'world power behind the scene', etc., rather than Jews or Zionists.

This gap in the communist ideology is filled by the second-rank party leaders. In their speeches, the enemy is 'Zionists' (although significantly less often than 'Imperialists', 'Americans', the 'West' or 'traitors'). According to the genre laws, the web of intrigue requires personification. And since xenophobia is generally pretty strong in Russian consciousness, the opposition leaders are

---

[14] A. Makashov stated with all candidness: "We are anti-Semites and we should win", Khitarov D. General-kommunist sobiraet svoyu "chernuyu sotnyu". *Itogi*, March 2, 1999.

[E3] The word zhid is used in the modern Russian language as a derogatory term for a Jew.

ready, naturally, to see 'enemies' not only, and not so much, in political opponents or in the country leaders, but rather in ethnic, religious or cultural images of 'them'. That is why it is quite logical that, when one specifies a social or political enemy, it pays to attach characteristics of 'them' to him, such as his belonging to the Church of Scientology or to a different ethnic origin.

The terms 'Zionist' or even 'zhid' for communists functions as a marker of social alienation. When communist Vasily Shandybin stigmatized the head of NTV 'Zionist Jordan'[E4], he probably meant exactly such a peculiar expression of social anti-Semitism. The same thesis was illustrated even more lucidly by the statement made by Duma member and communist Yury Nikiforenko that the "Zionist circles in China" were interested in the resignation of the Governor of the Maritime Territory Evgeny Nazdratenko. The former Governor of the Krasnodar Territory Nikolay Kondratenko is known for equally absurd statements. Even though he was not a CPRF member, he collaborated with the communists both within PPRU and on a regional level. In the elder's speeches, the Zionists were ascribed such demonized and abstract characteristics that they seem to have nothing at all to do with the real Jews. When Kondratenko really meant the Jews proper, he seemed to use the term 'zhido-mason'[15] which was less common in his lexicon. The communo-patriotic code language definitely confuses different concepts: the word 'Zionist' may refer to an Israeli, or to a Jew by birth, or generally to any 'enemy of Russia'.

General Makashov's infamous anti-Semitic statements made in 1998 brought to a head the issue of Judeophobia in the leadership of the Communist Party. CPRF officials could not break party solidarity and censure the General / anti-Semite. However, their silence cast a shadow of anti-Semitism over the entire Party. That ambivalence was fully utilized by anti-Communist journalists and political spinners who made many efforts to split the Left Camp into the 'moderate' and 'radical' parts. Thus, Makashov's speech was a pretext for

---

[E4]   Boris Jordan is a non-Jew.

[15]   Mikhaylovskaya E. Kondratenko – natsionalist v Senate. In Verkhovskiy A., Mikhaylovskaya E., Pribylovskiy V. *Natsionalizm i ksenofobiya v rossiyskom obshchestve*, pp. 106-119. Moscow: Panorama, 1998.

Stanislav Govorukhin to leave the PPRU leadership. Although a real party split did not occur, as a result, the radical anti-Semitic communists took part in the 1999 elections not as part of CPRF. Rather, they joined the electoral group *Dvizhenie v podderzhku armii* (Movement in Support of the Army, MSA). A. Makashov even suggested to rename it the Movement Against the Zhids. Their attempt to gain Duma seats as an independent group ended up lamentably: the radicals did not manage to divert any sizable number of votes from the communists, which was an obvious aim of pro-Kremlin politicians. The electoral group MSA led by Albert Makashov, Viktor Ilyukhin and Yury Savelyev got 0.58% of the vote in the 1999 Duma elections. Makashov did not get a Duma seat through a single-mandate district in the Samara region either − his registration was rescinded on a technicality. The General's attempt to participate in additional elections in a majority district in the Sverdlovsk region (Verkh-Isetsky District Number162) was not crowned with success either.

V. Ilyukhin who became a formal MSA leader after the death of its founder Lev Rokhlin made and condoned harsh anti-Semitic statements against 'Zionists' who 'looted the country'. Ilyukhin turned out to be luckier than Makashov and he was elected in a majority district. At present, he prefers to project the image of a solid politician who courageously fights corruption, defends the country's strategic interests, and does not bring up the Jewish issue any more.

MSA is an obscure group now but its niche has been taken by *Narodno-Patrioticheskaya partiya Rossii* (People's Patriotic Party of Russia, PPPR). Well-known nationalists and anti-Semites of a pro-Communist orientation, such as Vladimir Miloserdov and Nikolay Kondratenko, have joined PPPR.

Anti-Semitism is a distinctive mark of not just the radical wing of the communists, who have complicated relations with the party leadership, but of the party propaganda as a whole. It is clear from the results of the analysis of publications on the Jewish theme in the newspaper "Soviet Russia" that communist propaganda shapes a negative image of a Jew in two spheres: anti-Israeli rhetoric and the idea about a very negative role of the Jews in

Russian history, especially in the post-Soviet period. As far as the anti-Zionist theme is concerned, it was clearly inherited from Soviet propaganda of the late period, and logically, it is exploited in a communist publication. Perhaps, articles castigating 'Zionist occupiers[16]' and exposing their brutality are not, strictly speaking, anti-Semitic. However, it is obvious that their exorbitant and inappropriate rhetoric creates negative emotions towards the Jews in general among the readers. Besides, a thorough study of Soviet anti-Zionist propaganda clearly showed how easy it is to move from criticizing 'Zionist brutality' to cruelty and viciousness of the Jews in general, that is, to anti-Semitism in its most precise sense.

Outright anti-Semitic material shows up in "Soviet Russia" too, but less often. Typically, this theme may be brought up not by editorial materials, but by letters, poems and cartoons sent in abundance to the newspaper by readers. Oftentimes, the 'Jewish Question' is broached casually. For example, a letter to the editor may claim that the 'Zionists' want to rob the Russian people of their identity and that's why the item 'ethnicity' was dropped from the internal passport, etc. Rarely, major editorial material may be devoted to the Jewish subject. Thus, the newspaper has published a discussion by critics of the book "Two Hundred Years Together" by Aleksandr Solzhenitsin. The participants of the discussion constantly reminded each other that prejudices, superstitions and excessive emotionalism are inappropriate. Yet, the entire discussion was reduced to a replay of standard anti-Semitic accusations: "Jews pushed Russians into drinking in taverns", "bribed landowners", even organized "anti-Russian pogroms" ("seizing Russians, the Jews beat them ruthlessly, beat old men, beat women and even children") which "shows a certain archetype, a model of behavior rising at the dawn of the Jewish people"[17].

Therefore, although CPRF officially dissociates itself from anti-Semitism, the latter plays a significant role not only for the party radicals, including those in its leadership, but for the party propaganda in general too.

---

[16]   See, for example: Tetekin B. Izranen khram Rozhdestva Khristova. *Sovetskaya Rossiya*, November 24, 2001.

[17]   Kazintsev A., Kozhemyako V. Evrei, russkie i Solzhenitsyn. *Sovetskaya Rossiya*, October 20, 2001.

The second most influential and second largest Russian Communist organization is the movement *Trudovaya Rossia* (Working Russia). It is more radically inclined both in the social and in the national spheres.

Working Russia is a Communist organization of a neo-Stalinist orientation. Its leader is Viktor Anpilov. Its central publication is the newspaper *Molniya* (Lightning) (Editor - Viktor Anpilov, circulation – 21,000 copies, periodicity – biweekly). The "Stalinist Bloc" founded at the initiative of Working Russia got 0.61% of the vote in the 1999 election to the Duma. But in the previous Duma election, the electoral coalition "Communists – Working Russia – For the Soviet Union" led by V. Anpilov and Viktor Tyulkin almost achieved the 5% threshold. However, the split between the two leaders of the radical communists (partly caused by Tyulkin's disapproval of the nationalist bent among a large part of the leadership of Working Russia, including Anpilov) not only divided their electorate – but it also disappointed a large number of communist voters who quite reasonably decided that it is better to vote for the 'opportunist' CPRF than squander their votes in support of clearly hopeless electoral coalitions.

Strictly speaking, the anti-Semitism of Aniplov's comrades is not much different from the position of CPRF. However, the "Working Russia" leaders do not care about a respectable image and allow themselves to make nastier statements in print or, more commonly, in speeches. Few of Anpilov's speeches are without the word 'zhid' (usually as an adjective) or without accusing Zionists of anti-Soviet and anti-Russian activities. Obviously, from the standpoint of his personal psychology, Antipov is a Judeophobe, like Makashov and Yury Khudyakov, the second-ranking official in Working Russia, and unlike Zyuganov.

Publications of Working Russia eagerly make the most of the Jewish background of Russian 'oligarches', 'Zionist TEL-AVIsion', and earlier they even called the then President 'Baruch Eltsin'[E5].

A similar position is taken by *Soyuz ofitserov* (Union of Officers). Even though its leader Stanislav Terekhov has not been heard making public anti-Semitic statements (which was noticed more than once by the Union's regional leaders), he demonstrates a high level of Judeophobia in private conversations. In 2001 – 2003, Terekhov was a member of the leadership of *Natsionalno-derzhavnaya partiya Rissii* (National Party of Great Russia, NPGR) and anti-Semitism takes the most prominent part in their ideology.

Some publications ostensibly independent of the communist parties, such as the newspaper "Duel", also generally adhere to the communo-nationalist positions, including anti-Semitism.

One may summarize the situation in the communist organizations as follows. The communists in contemporary Russia are mostly communo-patriots (CPRF, PPPR, MSA, Working Russia, Union of Officers). Anti-Semitism in a veiled form is part of their ideology and propaganda. However, the reality has shown that emphasizing anti-Semitism does not pay. Whenever leftist patriots have openly tried to take advantage of that theme as the main or substantial component of their propaganda, they have been disappointed. The electoral support of the overt radical anti-Semitism is minimal, while the risk of being subjected to public ostracism is substantial. The example of MSA is typical in that respect. CPRF has possibly found an ideal strategy from the point of view of public support. It is a skillful utilization of moderately anti-Semitic ideas in a veiled form, a tolerant attitude towards 'its own anti-Semites' and a respectable image based, in particular, on an official denial of Judeophobia in its ideology.

[E5] Boris Yeltsin's name corrupted in such a way that it sounds like a Jewish name (he is not Jewish).

1.2   National-Patriots

Originally, the combination of the words "National-Patriots" was the way a number of political groups identified themselves. By now, that term has entered the political and scholarly vocabulary and it refers to the groups adhering to various versions of the ideology of Russian nationalism. "National-Patriots" are 'primarily' nationalists, the nationalist issue is the most important one for them. How they treat that issue is a totally different matter.

Nationalist organizations acting in the political arena of contemporary Russia adhere to various ideologies. They may be classified on the basis of different criteria. As we are mainly interested in the national question, it will be useful for us to divide the wide the National-Patriot field according to different concepts of a nation. Thus, we may tentatively identify 'imperial' and 'ethnic' nationalists. The former are 'authoritarians'. First and foremost, they care for the interests of the state, they support its military power, and often, its territorial expansion, suppression of separatist movements within its borders, etc. Following common sense, they realize that Russia is a multi-ethnic entity. Hence, they believe in the supremacy of the state over the nation and they view the latter as a civic rather than ethnic community. The latter, on the other hand, believe in the supremacy of the nation over the state and they primarily champion the interests of the nation as an ethnic rather than civic community.

The largest member of the 'imperial' movement is the Liberalno-demokraticheskaya partiya Rossii (Liberal Democratic Party of Russia, LDPR). LDPR is the largest nationalist party. Its leader is Vladimir Zhirinovsky, its official membership is 300,000, its central publication is the newspaper 'LDPR' (the editor-in-chief is Viktor Kulybin, circulation – 200,000, periodicity – from weekly during elections to monthly). The "Zhirinovsky bloc" got 5.98% of the vote in the election for the State Duma in 1999. LDPR demonstrated even more impressive electoral successes earlier: 22.92% in the federal elections in 1993, 11.18% in 1995. According to some sociological studies, LDPR may not make it into the 2003 Duma. However, V. Zhirinovsky has time and again demonstrated his outstanding PR skills. Hence, it is impossi-

ble to exclude a chance of the LDPR presence in the next Duma if they conduct a successful campaign[E6].

It is hard to call LDPR a nationalist organization in a strict sense of the term.
Although V. Zhirinovsky and his followers made many blatantly extremist and
xenophobic statements, it is impossible to talk about a comprehensive, radical rightist party ideology (or any 'ideology' of LDPR for that matter). The real
activity of the Liberal Democrats, such as their voting record in Duma, has as
little to do with their propaganda rhetoric as the party's name with its political
substance. By the way, Zhirinovsky once offered a humorous 'translation' of
the party name into Russian as a "National Liberation Party". In terms of contemporary Western political science, LDPR accurately fits the term of a 'populist' party, as that term implies a nationalist bent and taking advantage of
xenophobia. The LDPR leader has an amazing talent for telling his audience
exactly what it wants to hear, he being, figuratively speaking, some sort of
projection of an unconscious crowd.

Zhirinovsky repeatedly makes statements against "excessive influence" of
non-Russians in business and government, against international Zionism, and
for the supremacy of the Russian people in business and government ("And
look who hold the key positions in the central government and in the republics
where the majority of the people are Russians. Jews, Caucasian natives,
Tatars, Bashkirs, Yakuts, etc! No other country but Russia has such excessive influence of ethnic minorities in government, business and economy, in
scientific and cultural organizations!"[18]). Statements like "The main principle
of the state politics should be: Whatever is good for the Russians is good for
Russia"[19] are typical for V. Zhirinovsky. Although we should stress the super-
ethnic interpretation of the Russian community once more, that interpretation
is not followed consistently[E7]. Zhirinovsky was the first among prominent poli-

---

[E6]   The author refers to the possibility of failing to pass the 5% of the vote threshold for
        parliamentary representation. In fact, LDPR got 11% of the vote in the 2003 Duma
        election
[18]   Zhirinovskiy V. O patriotizme. *LDPR,* No. 2 (104), 2000.
[19]   Zhirinovskiy V. Russkiy vopros i LDPR. *LDPR*. No. 2 (107), May, 2000.
[E7]   The Russian language has two distinct words corresponding to the word 'Russian'
        in the English language. The first word, Russky, has a narrow, ethnic connotation.

ticians who suggested the elimination of the line specifying 'nationality' in the Russian internal passport.

On the record, the LDPR leader has repeatedly denied anti-Semitism as part of his party ideology. For a long time, Zhirinovsky concealed his own Jewish roots, but when they became known, he began talking about them with deliberate pride. Nevertheless, the LDPR chairman does not really avoid making anti-Semitic statements. For example, here is the way he exploits the Jewish conspiracy myth in one of his books: "I am just trying to explain the situation. Most of the Bolshevik leaders were Jews. Most of the contemporary 'Democrats' are Jews too. Most of the party leaders (about 60%) who form ideology are Jews too... I am just stating the fact. The country is in a deep crisis. What conclusion can we draw?"

One may hear a claim that Zhirnovsky has stopped exploiting the Jewish issue after his own roots became public, but that is not so. His recently published novel "Ivan, Close Your Soul" contains a host of anti-Semitic statements. For example, "Communism was invented by Jews. My universities, my studies were marked and hugely influenced by that Jewish germ... The Jews are the source of that super-germ, a plague of the 20th century called communism"[20].

If one is interested, one can find anti-Semitic statements in publications serving as ideological party documents rather than its leader's verbosity. Thus, an article titled "USA and Russia in the New Century" published in the newspaper LDPR and signed by "Analytic Center of LDPR" claims that "Jews created the USA and control it. Naturally, they do not want to lose their control... Under that model, Americans and their allies need an enemy – real or mythical"[21]. Further, it claims: "Our main enemy is the political elite of the United

---

The second word, Rossiysky, refers to all inhabitants of Russia. When the meaning is not clear from the context, we try to convey the difference by using the words ethnic and super-ethnic.

[20]   Quoted from *Ya – Russkiy*, No. 9-10 (91-92), May, 2002.

[21]   Analytic Center of LDPR. USA and Russia in the new century. *LDPR*, No. 2, January, 2001.

States. This elite dreams of the destruction of the Russian people"[22]. Another example is a leaflet notifying members of the next party meeting; its back side is a photomontage of pictures of Berezovsky, Gusinsky, Lebed, Dudaev, Maskhadov, Basaev and others with a six point star on the background[23].

By and large, however, one may assert that anti-Semitism in LDPR does not play a significant role. The party ideology is very xenophobic in general and the Jewish issue is by far not the most frequent one in the party periodicals and in its leader's writings. Although Zhirinovsky allows himself to make much more furious xenophobic attacks than, for example, Zyuganov does, generally anti-Semitism is not as intrinsic to the party ideology of LDPR as it is to CPRF. Generally, because of political traditions, anti-Semitism is a very 'ideological' phobia requiring complex arguments and an organic intertwining with general conceptual constructs. Yet LDPR is the least 'ideological' organization. Of course, LDPR includes anti-Semites in the strict sense of the word. The party positions itself as a nationalist one. In the Russian political context, it implies anti-Semitism as well. Yet anti-Semitism is not essential for Zhirinovsky-ists, unlike anti-American and anti-Chechen motives, and it has no clear ideological foundation.

The largest organization among 'ideological' imperial nationalists is *Rossiysky obshchenarodny soyuz* (Russian All-People Union, RAU). RAU is the largest classical National-Patriotic organization. It has 50,000 members, its central publication is the newspaper *'Vremya'* (Time), (the editor-in-chief is Pavel Bychkov, circulation – 20,000, periodicity – weekly). RAU got 0.37% of the vote in the election for the State Duma in 1999. In 1995, it formed a bloc called "Power to People" based on RAU and got 1.61%.

RAU was reorganized to the National Revival Party *"Narodnaya Volya"* (People's Will). A few nationalist politicians who did not belong to RAU earlier joined People's Will. They included the former Moscow regional leader of "Russian National Unity" and later the deputy chairman of the group "Russian

---

22   Zhirinovskiy V. Pravda ostaetsya za LDPR. *LDPR,* No. 2, January, 2001.
23   LDPR leaflet in the author's archive.

Revival" Yury Vasin, the former leader of the group *"Spas"* (Salvation) Vladimir Davidenko, as well as non-nationalists - the former chair of *"Soyuz realistov"* (Union of Realists) Nina Zhukova.

RAU leaders always claimed that, first and foremost, they care about the interests of the Russian people. According to the party ideology, the "Russians are 'not only' a nationality in the Russian Federation, they are the state-building nationality"[24] (newspaper "Time"). Speeches of the party leaders include similar statements put in a more categorical form. As is the case with LDPR, it is not always clear what is meant by the "Russian people". Insofar as we can judge, the imperial meaning prevails. They are talking about the Russians 'in spirit' rather than blood: those who belong to the ROC or even wider – those who view Russia as their motherland and Russian culture and history as theirs. Ethnically non-Russian minorities, such as Tatars, Bashkirs and Balts, are widely represented in the party.

RAU / People's Will surely includes ethnic nationalists as well. Thus, the RAU coordinator in the South of Russia for a long time was Nikolay Lysenko, one of the best known nationalist radicals. Interestingly, N. Lysenko refused to work with traditional Russian patriots in early 2003 and now he advocates Islam as the last stand against the West. In the middle of 2002, there appeared some information that members of the regional branches of the overtly racist *Narodno-natsionalnaya Partiya* (People's Nationalist Party) joined People's Will at the request of V. Davidenko in order to strengthen its radical wing.

RAU's central publication "Time" sometimes allows itself to publish anti-Semitic articles, although not too often and in a mild form. Non-ideological anti-Semitism (a suspicious, contemptuous and generally negative attitude towards the Jews that is not justified by either conspiratorial, or by social constructs) is typical for RAU. For example, the author of an article about a conflict within the Jewish community in Russia used a cynical and disparaging tone: "Everything began with a provocation of the now ex-Rabbi of Russia Shaevich who, as a member of the Jewish Russian Congress, could not dis-

---

[24]   *Vremya* (Omsk), No. 11, May, 2000.

obey the President. Not the Russian President Putin, but that Congress' President Gusinsky. Berezovsky took advantage of Shaevich's bleat in the "Washington Post" and sicced Berl Lazar, who speaks Russian worse than the late Golda Meir, on gusiguenots"[25].

Sparse materials in "Time" that exploit ideological anti-Semitism are of religious nature. For instance, a large article, in the spirit of RO fundamentalism, published in the newspaper claimed that the conflict between Christianity and Judaism is the main driving force of history: "From a Christian point of view, Judaism has no positive meaning. Since the crucifixion of the Messiah, Jesus Christ, by the Jews, militant anti-Christianity has become the main part of Judaism"[26]. "The Jewish conspiracy" is viewed solely through a religious prism. Subsequently, the article attributes this statement to some Rabbi speaking at "one of the secret meetings": "Every war, every revolution, every political or religious crisis in the Christian world brings us closer to the moment when we reach our supreme goal". According to the author's understanding of the Jewish religion, that goal for Jews is "domination over other people"[27].

Both RAU and LDPR are rather moderate parties even though they include radical elements. It should be noted here that neither ethnic, nor imperial approach to nationalism does not inherently mean moderation of the latter. For example, the *Natsional-bolshevistskaya partiya* (National Bolshevik Party, NBP), that is one of the most radical among the sizable political groups in the country, also holds a position of super-ethnic nationalism. If we recall historical examples, Italian Fascism took on an etatist (state) rather than ethnic character too. Summarizing, we may still state that the super-ethnic nationalist patriots are less radical in general. In particular, they are less inclined to exploit anti-Semitism than the ethnic nationalists are. Yet, practically no nationalist patriotic party has been able to completely avoid anti-Semitic emotions among part of their cadre and anti-Semitic materials in the party press.

---

[25]   Perminov Yu. Vserossiyskiy sabantuy. *Vremya* (Omsk), No. 23, August, 2000.

[26]   Ioan (Snychev), Metropolitan. Tvortsy kataklizmov, *Vremya* (Omsk), No. 36-37, 2000.

[27]   *Ibid.*

Naturally, the imperial nationalists are not known for being involved in direct calls for anti-Jewish violence or other anti-Semitic actions.

The ethnic nationalists foster a more radical ideology than the imperial nationalists do, but they substantially fall behind the latter in numbers and in popularity. The central part in their world outlook is occupied by the purely ethnic concept of the "Russian Nationality". Therefore, they relate to non-Russians, especially those who are not members of any indigenous peoples of Russia, with intolerance and hostility to one degree or another. The notions of the "international Jewish conspiracy" and religious anti-Semitism are most popular among ethnic nationalists. There are open Hitlerites dreaming of the "final solution of the Jewish question".

However, all these organizations practically have no major part in the political process and they do not affect the public opinion. As this chapter covers the parties that are, or hope to become, a substantial political force, we will cover the activities of radical ethno-nationalist parties and groups in a separate chapter. Unlike moderate National-Patriots, ethnic nationalists do not hide the anti-Semitism in their ideology and propaganda, so it does not have to be 'uncovered'.

1.3   Eurasians

During the 1990s, the communists and national-patriots were the only noticeable force among ideological movements that exploited anti-Semitic ideas. Fundamentally, a chapter devoted to 'reputable' parties could have been limited to these two movements. However, another political force crystallized in the last two years and it is of interest to us. We are talking about neo-eurasians.

In the multiplicity of the ideological heritage of the past rediscovered in the late 1980s – early 1990s, Eurasianism happened to be one of the most attractive and acceptable concepts. Its popularity among the Russian intelligentsia is outstanding. Partly, it was due to the talent of the founders of the

Eurasian movement as well as the brilliance of the person who bridged the Eurasian classics with modernity – Lev Gumilev[28]. But a more likely explanation of the popularity of the Eurasian ideas in modern Russia lies in their phenomenal flexibility. In fact, one should talk about a methodology rather than a strict political ideology. Eurasianism has turned out an acceptable alternative both to radical Westernism and to discredited versions of Slavophilism. The idea of a global Eurasian civilization, distinct from both European democracy and Asian despotism, explained the historical path of the Russian Empire – the Soviet Union – the Russian Federation, it flattered the Russian middle class and it was a source of its pride. Fuzzy constructs allowed everyone to interpret the ideology of Eurasianism any way they wanted to. For the patriots, Eurasianism was a unique chance to declare the "objective impossibility" of building a Western political and economic model. It also gave them a chance to provide the Russians with self-identification based on positive associations and images. Never mind that the Eurasians' prescriptions are strictly theoretical and not applicable to reality. They happen ideally to fit the post-Soviet mentality that could not accept the collapse of a great power and could not understand why. Basically, Eurasianism in the contemporary conditions may be reduced to a simplistic thesis. Yes, all attempts to build a Russo-Soviet empire have not been quite successful. However, an empire for Russia is an objective necessity due to a number of historical, cultural, political and economic factors.

Eurasianism gave a second wind to super-ethnic nationalists and it was mostly they who jumped on the bandwagon. Works by classic Eurasianists and their followers were published by laarge literary journals known for their National-Patriotic orientation. In 1991-1992, the "organ of the spiritual opposition" - newspaper *"Den"* (Day) - was the main tribune for the neo-Eurasianists. However, Eurasianism quickly spilled over the boundaries of the "patriotic ghetto" and onto the wider political space.

---

[28]   For the "Jewish problem" in the Eurasian ideology, beginning with the founding fathers of the movement and ending with its post-Soviet representatives, see Evraziytsy i evrei. *Vestnik Evreyskogo Universiteta v Moskve*, pp. 4-45, No. 12 (11), 1966. For Gumilev's anti-Semitism, see Rogachevsky A., Lev Gumilev i evereyskiy vopros. *Evereyskoe slovo*, No. 36 (110), September 11-17, 2002. See also ref. 85.

During the first post-Soviet years, the Eurasianists acted as theoreticians and journalists but not as public politicians. They championed Eurasianist ideas in the pages of books and magazines, by contrast to some political party leaders who enunciated certain Eurasianist slogans from high platforms. Many concepts belonging to politicians of very different orientations, such as Gennady Zyuganov (communist), Sergey Baburin (nationalist), Yury Luzhkov (centrist) and Sergey Shakhray (democrat), were expressed in Eurasianist terminology. Leaders of other post-Soviet states seeking a union with Russia (Nursultan Nazarbaev, for example) began to appeal to Eurasianism too. Eurasianist argumentation turned out to be attractive to the Russian authorities: it allowed them to consistently formulate the necessity of keeping Russia united. Both bureaucrats and ordinary people felt strongly that Russia should not disintegrate into small states. But that feeling was purely emotional, it could not be reasonably justified within the ideological choice made by the country towards a Western liberal political model. The apogee of the impact of that ideology on the government was demonstrated in statements made by Vladimir Putin in 2000 that may be quite reasonably treated as Eurasianist.

Since then, Eurasianism has begun to form as an independent political force. At present, it is represented by two political parties already registered on the Federal level according to a new and pretty strict law: "Eurasia" (its leader is journalist Aleksandr Dugin) and *Evraziyskaya partiya – Soyuz patriotov Rossii* (Eurasian Party – Union of Russian Patriots, EP-URP) (Chairman of its political council is a member of the State Duma Abdul-Vahed Niyazov).

The leader of "Eurasia", Dugin is a very colorful person. This ideologue of the Eurasianist movement began his political career in the late 1980s in the National-Patriot Front *"Pamyat"* (Memory) and was a member of its Central Committee. In the early 1990s, he participated in shaping the ideology of the united opposition and actively propagandized a mixture of some elements of Eurasianism, geopolitics, traditionalism and conspiracy theories and some concepts of the new European right. Dugin stated his views on the pages of the newspaper "Day" and his own magazine "Elements". By the middle of the

1990s, he was an ideologue of the National Bolshevik Party and he remained there until 1998 when he dropped out of the party. In the late 1990s, he was involved in propaganda activities and worked with various political leaders. Thus, he was involved in writing the program and ideological documents for Gennady Seleznev's movement "Russia". Besides, the former ideologue of National Bolshevism managed to become an Old Believer (or more exact, "Uni-Believer"[29]), a semi-official Russian geopolitical expert and in that guise he put forward the idea of moving the nation's capital to Kazan.

After the election of Vladimir Putin as Russian President, Dugin announced the creation of his own movement whose mission was to 'totally' support the head of the country and supply the government with ideological material. The Founding Convention of "Eurasia" was held on April 21, 2001. The composition of the movement that was soon transformed into a party was rather mixed. It included Dugin's young 'disciples', representatives of various religious denominations (for example, the head of the Central Spiritual Board for Muslim Russians, Talgat Tadzhuddin), former intelligence workers (Petr Suslov) and even representatives of the radical religious Zionists. (Avrom Shmulevich, an Israeli, was listed in the polit-council of "Eurasia" while it was still a movement, although he denied his formal membership in the movement). An active participant in the party activities is a Chechen businessman and public figure named Khozh-Akhmed Nukhaev ("Khozha"). "Khozha" has been accused of many robberies and thefts and he has been called a 'godfather' of the Chechen mafia. Nukhaev attended public party activities despite the fact that the police looked for him as a suspect in the case of "Lazovsky's gang" (about bus explosions in Moscow).

The party promulgates active propaganda and Dugin and his allies are readily invited to TV. Even though taken by itself, the party "Eurasia" is little known (yet, perhaps), its ideological writings could very well be attractive both to the authorities and to the people. This pretty strange, if not absurd, gathering of extremists, secret agents and clergy got a friendly coverage in the govern-

---

[29]   The Uni-Belief (Edinovercheskaya) Church is an extremely small movement in the Old Belief Church. It keeps the pre-Nikon rite but recognizes the jurisdiction of the Moscow Patriarchate of ROC.

ment controlled press, which clearly shows the empathy towards it that at least some Kremlin-oriented spin doctors feel.

As for our main subject, we should state that anti-Semitism is present in Eurasia's ideology, but in a peculiar form. Warm contacts with ultra-Zionist circles, including Israelis, should not confuse us: many anti-Semites relate favorably to Zionism as a political movement aiming at the repatriation of the Jews to the Holy Land.

In his propaganda, Dugin widely uses elements of the traditionalist school founded by the French philosopher René Guénon[30]. In the last few years, however, the name Guénon has appeared more rarely in Dugin's speeches and publications. Yet he has never publicly reconsidered his fervent attitude towards that French esotericist, or towards his own works in the field of traditionalism. However, Dugin has re-examined Guénon's and his followers' numerous theses, including their view of Judaism.

According to the classic traditionalist scheme by Guénon and his student Julius Evola, there is a single, primary, sacral Tradition, a "set of God-given

---

[30]   A. Dugin is a member of the second generation in our country of the traditionalists belonging to René Guénon's school. The first people who began to read, translate and spread the works of that French metaphysicist were the late Yury Stefanov and Evgeny Golovin. One may get an idea of Yu. Stefanov's views from his posthumous collection of papers (Stefanov Yu. *Skvazhiny mezhdu mirami*. *Kontekst*, No. 9, 2002). A collection of lectures and papers by E. Golovin was published recently too (Golovin E. *Priblizhenie k snezhnoy koroleve*. Moscow: Arktogeya-Tsentr, 2003). Students of the latter (by seniority) are writer Yury Mamleev, Geydar Dzhemal and Aleksndr Dugin. Dugin has made more efforts for spreading Guénon's ideas and, in turn, brought up the third generation of Russian traditionalists. They are Vadim Shtepa (the author of the book "*INversiya*" (Moscow, 1998, special issue of the magazine "*INache*") containing perhaps the most accessible description of Guénon's ideas in Russian), Aleksy Karagodin, Arkady Maler (the author of the book *Strategy of the Sacral Meaning*, Moscow 2003). However, Dugin has broken relations with the above-mentioned people and he does not consider them as his students. At the same time, several traditionalist groups, independent of Yu. Stefanov and E. Golovin, appeared in the early 1990s. The history of the development, as well as misunderstanding and distortion, of Guénon's ideas (who undoubtedly was one of the greatest thinkers of the 20th century) has not been written in Russia yet. I am planning to address this most interesting subject (in my opinion) in the near future.

revelations" that is a foundation of esoteric schools of all traditional religions, including Judaism. The negative traits of the contemporary society result from a departure from Tradition's "Light of Truth", from secularization. The forces affecting the world negatively are called "counter-initiating". That is a profane and paradoxically satanic metaphysical pole opposite to the pole of God's original tradition. The development of the world is involution, degradation, departure from the Tradition, sinking into matter, profanation, disregard of God-given truths contained in esoteric religious doctrines (including Judaism in no less degree than any other religion)[31]. Even Evola (who, unlike Guénon, was an outright anti-Semite and who collaborated with the nazi and Fascist regimes), did not deny esoteric Judaic concepts (mainly in Kabbalah) the right to a full and equal part of the Tradition. He believed that the cause of the "depravity" of the Jews was their departure from the religion[32].

Dugin's scheme is more complex. From his point of view, absolute counter-initiating does not exist, just as there is no single universal esoterism that might be traced in every religion. That means that "every sacral form, having its own metaphysical specifics, forms its own theory of what constitutes counter-initiating for it, and only for it"[33].

Certain religions are intrinsically antagonistic. For example, "Hinduism bases its tradition on a formula opposite to the Persian Tradition even though they

---

[31]   René Guénon's concepts are described following Genon R. *Krizis sovremennogo mira*. Moscow: Arktogeya, 1991; *idem, Tsivilizatsiya kolichestva i znameniya vremeni*. Moscow: Belovod'e, 1994; *idem, Traditsiya i metafizika*. St. Petersburg: Azbuka, 2001; *idem, Izbrannye proizvedeniya*. Moscow: Belovod'e, 2003 (in two volumes).

[32]   See for example, Evola Yu. *Yazycheskiy imperializm*. Moscow: Arktogeya, 1994; Evola Yu. Evrei i matematika. *Era Rossii*, pp. 6-7, No. 8, March, 1995. Evola Yu. Lyudi i ruiny. Moscow: *Nasledie predkov*, 2002. The position of the Austrian writer Gustav Meyrink whose novels Evola translated into Italian was close to that of Evola. In his novel *The Golem*, Meyrink drew the esoteric sacred side of Judaism with empathy. However, he showed the image of a Jew as a social figure with a pathological antipathy, see a Russian translation, for example, in Maynrink G. *Golem. Val'purgieva noch'*. Moscow: Prometey, 1990. Evola's position supports Hanna Arendt's reasonable idea that anti-Semitism per se was caused by the assimilation of the Jews and by the beginning of their mass participation in the social life of the surrounding peoples. (See: Arendt Kh. *Istoki totalitarizma*, pp. 37. Moscow: TsentrKom, 1996).

[33]   Dugin A. *Messianstvo Kabbaly. Konets sveta*, p. 347. Moscow: Arktogeya.

developed from the same source. It is known that even Gods' and demons' names in Zoroastrianism and Hinduism are inversely analogous[34]. According to that logic, "from the point of view of the RO esoterism, the religion in direct opposition is undoubtedly Judaism"[35].

However, the matter is not limited to the "relative" anti-traditionalism (that is, according to the traditionalist logic, to demonism, Satanism) of Judaism. Declaring the lack of unity in the traditional doctrines, Dugin, nevertheless, does not reject the notion of Tradition. Despite irreconcilable internal contradictions, the esoteric concepts still could be united on the basis of some common meta-ideology. That is possible, for example, "in reverse" – making a start from the contemporary "anti-traditionalist society based on the principles exactly contrary to the whole complex of what forms the basis of any tradition"[36]. Yet, "even in that context where most of the traditions are completely consistent, Judaism is an exception"[37]. Unlike other traditions, Judaism is in complete accord with the ideas dominating in the modern 'profane' world. Furthermore, according to Dugin, that world is viewed by the Jews as a prelude to their Messianic triumph.

"Orthodox Judaism, taken together with its underlying esoteric reasons, is the metaphysical pole opposite to the entire complex of all other traditions"[38], claims Dugin elsewhere. And one can imagine nothing more dreadful within the framework of traditionalist logic.

Besides, staying within the framework of the stereotypic RO anti-Judaism, Dugin asserts that it is a religious duty for the Jews to kill 'goyim': "At its

---

[34]   *Ibid.*, p. 348.
[35]   *Ibid.*, p. 348.
[36]   *Ibid.*, p. 349.
[37]   *Ibid.*, p. 349.
[38]   *Metafizika natsii v "Zokhare". Konservativnaya revolutsiya.* Moscow: Arktogeya, 1994. Zohar is one of the main works of Jewish mysticism. We should note that Dugin indeed knows Hebrew (but it is hard to say how well) and reads original texts. It is also true that, given an a priori opinion, one can easily find whatever one wants to find in a book (especially in such a complex book). Or, instead of presenting the original text to the less educated reader, one can boldly present one's opinion of it.

deepest level, not only does the Jewish eschatology[E8] permits ritual genocide, but it also insists on it, justifying its necessity by a series of consistent and somewhat logical identities... It is quite natural that such a vision leads the Orthodox Jew to nothing but an infinitely ferocious and 'sacred' hatred towards all other peoples. That hatred is even promoted, as a 'sacral virtue'. Indeed, the destruction of peoples who tried to build the Tower of Babel and ended up with a variety of languages is a prerequisite for the coming of the Messiah, for the beginning of the Great Shabbat"[39]. (The peculiarity of the source' punctuation is preserved).

We could have finished the chapter Eurasia at this point after having demonstrated a high degree of anti-Semitism in its ideology. But contradicting himself, Dugin takes a somewhat different view of the problem in his paper "Jews and Eurasia"[40]. (The paper's title refers to Yakov Bromberg, one of the Eurasianists who tried to look at the 'Jewish question' within the framework of the Eurasian ideology).

According to the idea of the paper, two opposite tendencies have always existed in Jewry. They may be called "Jewish Eurasianism" and "Jewish Westernism". Accordingly, the activity of the former is beneficial for Russia, and that of the latter is disadvantageous. The demarcation line within Jewry may be traced on both the religious and social levels.

Dugin categorizes the Hasidim, Kabbalists and mystics as "Jewish Eurasianists" representing the exalted movement in Judaism. During secularization, that movement turned into a socialist revolutionary movement, religious in essence. (Dugin finds religious overtones even in Marx). The activity of Jewish Bolsheviks, whose messianic charge resonated with that of Russia, happened to be beneficial for the country. The Jewish Westernism on a religious level was part of the 'rational' Maimonidean Judaism. During secularization, it

---

[E8]   Eschatology is an area of theology concerned with the events related to the end of the world.

[39]   *Ibid.*, p. 279.

[40]   The paper was published several times. See, for example, *Russkiy evrey*, No. 1 (3), 1998.

turned into usurious capitalism, enlightened materialism and a bourgeois-democratic mentality. That part of Jewry is the focus of destructive Capitalism.

The scheme above is the foundation of the official attitude of the Eurasia party towards the Jews. The Orthodox Jews, the radical Zionists and the Hasidim deserve nothing but respect and approval from the Duginists, which does not prevent them from castigating the Jewish bankers, politicians and journalists in the spirit of classical anti-Semitism[41].

In a nutshell, this duality in the attitude towards the Jews is expressed by captions of two pictures (collective pictures of archetypical "Jews") in the magazine Elements edited by A. Dugin[42]. The first caption reads: "... the image of a 'Jew' is equated with pawn-brokering, capitalism, cynical and corrupt journalists, with clannishness, with the contempt for the goyim, with unjust wealth, with readiness to betray and sell out, or in short, with the System". The next one reads: "Indigent, harassed people faithful to their traditions and to their unique piety, focused on a strange spirit of the people, with a sign of pain for mankind, thirsting for justice, filled with the drama of fathomless destiny, the Kabbalists, Hasidim, mystics, socialists... Their fervent anguishing spirit is a truthful and full-fledged element of any genuine revolution, be it a national or a conservative one, regardless of what anti-Semites say".

Such dualism in perceiving various phenomena is characteristic of Dugin in general. He divides Russia into two components along the same lines. He believes that there are two parallel Russias. The first one is official, pro-Western, appearing on a religious level as 'warm' Nikonian Christianity[E9] and

---

[41] The penchant of the Russian radical rightists to find two opposite forces within "Jewry" is a separate and interesting theme. For an attempt to analyze this issue see Likhachev V. Mifologema o "dvukh evreystvakh" v ramkakh pravoradikal'nykh politicheskikh ideologiy sovremennoy Rossii. Tirosh. Trudy po iudaike. Vol. 4, pp. 279-287. Moscow: 2000.

[42] Elementy, No. 8, 1998, p. 71.

[E9] Nikon was a Russian Patriarch of the 17th century who undertook reforms of the ROC.

on a secular level as a mechanistic state bureaucracy. The second one is rooted in soil, the Absolute Motherland of the mystics, schismatics, sectarians, revolutionaries and nonconformists.

The second organization with a similar ideological platform, but with a different leadership mentality is EP-URP. Eurasianism in their interpretation is primarily an anti-European choice for Russia, its openness to Asia and Islam. Anti-Westernism according to Niyazov is even more significant for neo-Eurasianism than it is for Dugin.

It is unclear yet what kind of popularity EP-URP may claim. In its present form, the party lays claim to being a party just for the Russian Muslims, its contacts with non-Muslim political movements are sporadic. Niyazov has joined the Unity faction in the State Duma, but has been expelled for making extremist statements. Perhaps, EP-URP may hope to get the electoral niche of the All-Russian Muslim movement "Nur" headed by Vafa Yarullin that got 0.57% in the party list vote in the election for the State Duma in 1995. Yet another electoral bloc that tried to exploit Islam in 1995 was Soyuz Musulman Rossii (Union of Muslims in Russia, UMR). UMR did not manage to collect enough signatures to register, but its leader Nadirshakh Khachilaev was elected in a single-mandate district. EP-URP's immediate predecessor was the movement Refah, while Refah, in turn, succeeded UMR, on the one hand. On the other hand, it imitated a Turkish Islamist party under the same name headed by Nidzhmetdin Erbakan. (Now it is the Turkish government party but its present name is Fazilet). Both the movement UMR and EP-URP are strongly influenced by an ideologue of homegrown Muslim radicalism named Geydar Dzhemal.

Even though Dzhemal has made very negative (sarcastic rather than angry) comments on Eurasianism[43], he is active in the area of Islamic politics and his

---

[43]   For example, in his speech at a meeting called "Eurasianism is the Future of Russia" Dzhemal said: "The specific phenomenon of the Eurasian spiritual pot has yet to go through a full cycle of decay before the appearance of a new human material capable of realizing a fundamentally new and universally meaningful project on the territory of the ex-USSR". (http://www.kontrudar.ru/speech_1.html)

close connections with Niyazov are no secret. Geydar's son, Orkhan Dzhe-
mal worked as the party press-secretary for a while. Probably, as far as both
Dzhemal and Niyazov are concerned, EP-URP is the party of Muslims in
Russia rather than a group following Trubetskoy and Savitsky.

Dzhemal's anti-Semitic position is well known. He ran for the State Duma on
the list of the above-mentioned Movement in Support of the Army led by
Makashov – Ilyukhin in 1999. Dzhemal bitterly attacked Israel and "the Zionists' criminal policies". Moreover, he believes that the Jews fight Islam everywhere and use the 'post-Christian' West[44] for that. Besides, in his religious
and metaphysical articles, Dzhamal views Jewry as an expression of forces
of the ontological negative[45].

---

[44]   For example: "Indeed, it is Judaism that fights Islam trying to put exhausted, worn
       out, duped Christians on the front line of this drama. These Christians have been
       long controlled from other Messianic centers". See: Ognennyy islam (interview with
       G. Dzhemal). *Zavtra*, No. 43 (412), October, 2001. Besides, world Jewry controlling
       the West threatens Russia too. (Dzhemal views that idea as the foundation for col-
       laboration between radical political Islam and the Russian nationalist movement).
       "The system of international Zionism establishing a liberal-cosmopolitan dictatorship
       on this planet is a mortal enemy of Islam. All these forces are hostile towards Rus-
       sia, they turn it into a colony, they encourage the genocide of the Russian people,
       they dream of wiping Russia off the geographical map. Therefore, both Islam and
       Russia have common enemies" (Islamskaya revolutsiya i russkiy patriotism.
       http://www.kontrudar.ru/).

[45]   G. Dzhemal is perhaps the greatest modern Russian metaphysician of Genon's
       style (and generally, he is a high-caliber intellectual). To be exact, uses Genon's
       scheme as a foundation (as the methodology rather than the entire ideology) and
       comes to somewhat different conclusions. According to Dzhemal, thre is no single
       primary Tradition. There are two different phenomena: the prophets' tradition and
       the priests' tradition. The former provides a vertical safety link with the Absolute
       (i.e., it is a rather positive pole of the Tradition, although no value judgments are
       applicable in this area). The latter conserves and kills the Revelation. A prophet is a
       revolutionary rekindling God's spark hidden in the 'clay' of man's body. Priesthood
       is interpreted as a consequence of entropy, imperfection of the human being. Within
       the framework of that system, the fullest tradition of Revelation is, of course, Islam.
       Rabbinical Judaism (unlike Biblical Judaism – but here, according to Dzhemal, one
       should distinguish the authentic-prophetic layer of the Bible and the result of the
       subsequent editions) is the priests' tradition and may not be evaluated positively.
       Only the Biblical prophets may be evaluated positively. However, according to the
       Muslim version of the Holy Scriptures, they are not 'Jews' but just 'monotheists' or
       even 'Muslims'. See a course of lectures given by G. Dzhemal in the Philosophy
       Department of the Moscow State University. The lectures were published in

Anti-Semitism shows in the ideology of EP-URP in the same two costumes – anti-Zionism and religious anti-Judaism – although in a less radical form. Niyazov constantly protests Israel's policies and expresses his support for the champions of the independence of Palestine, even for the most radical ones. Solidarity and the feeling of religious commonality is much more typical for Islam than for other religions in the world. Ideally, all Muslims feel their belonging to the common Umma (community) regardless of their state or ethnic identity. That's why the feeling of solidarity with the 'fighting and suffering Palestinians' is quite natural for the Muslim communities all over the world[E10].

On September 18, 2001, Abdul-Vakhed Niyazov and the co-chairman of the council of the Muftis in Russia Sheikh Nafigulla Ashirov gave a press conference devoted to the terrorist acts of September 11 in America. Having mentioned the principle "Look for the one who benefits from it", Niyazov said: "Who was the first to take advantage of the situation? Neither Americans, nor Russians, but the same Scharansky and Lieberman". Sheikh Ashirov added: "We know what country has a wide network of special services. They are Zionist special services. It was done not by Arabs or Muslims, but by those who have resources and who benefit from it"[46].

Religious anti-Judaism scarcely appears in the EP-URP materials. Rather, we may talk about a biased and suspicious attitude towards the Jews, but not ideologically formulated accusations.

We may end this chapter with the following conclusions. Anti-Semitism is a noticeable part of the ideology and propaganda of several large and influential parties in the Russian Federation. These parties belong to the three major ideological orientations: communist, National-Patriotic and Eurasianist. As a

---

Filosfskaya gazeta, Nos. 1-7, 9 and are available on the Internet on Dzhamal's personal site http://www.kontrudar.ru/.

[E10] That empathy alone does not explain the depth of the anti-Israeli feelings among the Muslims. Many other Muslim communities "fight and suffer", e.g. the ones in Kashmir or in the Philippines, but their plight has not attracted nearly as much attention as that of the Palestinians.

[46] *Kommersant*", September 19, 2001.

rule, they use anti-Semitic rhetoric in a simplified and 'moderate' form. When a party emphasizes anti-Semitic propaganda, it dooms itself to marginality and being squeezed out of the field of "big politics". In general, the situation is ambiguous. On the one hand, anti-Semitism is an essential part of the home-grown political tradition. On the other hand, in Russia, it is much more advan-tageous to exploit other forms of the people's xenophobia. Since the last fac-tor is pretty important, the Jews are not the most frequent target for hatred by politicians. Also, the Western stereotype, that open anti-Semitism is imper-missible in the rhetoric of a politician seeking popularity and respectability, seems to have penetrated Russia.

It is hard to say how the situation will play out. In our opinion, anti-Semitism will not disappear from the political arena all by itself. Yet, it may become a more influential political ideology only if the political context changes radically.

2   Radical Rightist Movements in Contemporary Russia

The radical rightist (ultra-nationalist and religious fundamentalist) political parties and movements deserve special discussion in our exploration of anti-
Semitism in Russia. Because of the Russian political tradition and mentality, it
is practically impossible to organize an ultra-nationalist movement that does
not promulgate anti-Semitic stereotypes to one degree or another. It is pretty
common even among the rank and file of the NBP, although its leaders officially renounced anti-Semitism. It makes its occasional appearance in the
NBP press too (more often in the regional newspapers than in the central
ones).

Since anti-Semitism is obvious in the ideology of these movements, we are
not going to pay much attention to it. Rather, let us consider the present
status of this part of the political spectrum.

At present, the radical rightist parties and movements are an integral part of
the political system in contemporary Russia. However, their position in the political spectrum is distinctive. On the one hand, the rightist radicals (nationalists and religious fundamentalists – both groups are widely known in Russia
as 'radical National-Patriots') do not conceal their goal of comprehensively
transforming society, including as a rule, changing the constitutional system
of the Russian Federation. The radicals balance on the brink of overstepping
the law and sometimes actually violate the law. They realize that the goals
they set can hardly be reached through 'normal' political efforts based on par-
liamentary methods and limited by federal legislation. That is why they rely on
alternative, extra-parliamentary activities. Some groups and their leaders do
little to conceal the possibility of gaining power through violence and revolutionary rhetoric plays an important role among almost all rightist radicals.

On the other hand, the nationalist organizations took part in the elections and
promoted their views, sometimes overtly extreme ones, practically without
any obstacles up until at least the late 1990s. Furthermore, radicalism was
the political norm during the first post-Soviet years. Violence was viewed by

society as a legitimate method of struggle on the part of both the authorities and the opposition. Radicals acted in every segment of the political spectrum and they promoted overtly extreme ideas that were an organic part of the political system in general. In fact, the entire political system was radical. Radicalism was not a marginal phenomenon, but rather part of the mainstream then. Hence, it was natural that the rightist radicals, ultra-nationalists and religious fundamentalists were free from inhibition. Even though their ideology and activity shocked, and caused anxiety among, many people, there was no real counter to the radicals on the part of the state or society in the early and mid 1990s.

Attempts by the authorities to counter the rightist radicals became systematic only at the end of 1998. Anti-Fascists rightfully criticized the government for its passivity, lack of political will and even open collusion with the radicals. There is no doubt that this state
of affairs seriously destabilized the situation inside the country and tarnished its image abroad. A tidal wave of activity of the nationalist-radicals resulted in a pessimistic, if not panicky, thesis about a 'Weimar Russia' analogous to Weimar Germany. That tidal wave took place against the background of general social instability in the country, popularity of revenge sentiments and government acquiescence.

By 2003, the situation drastically changed compared to what it was in the 1990s. Society became less radical and, generally, less politicized and the authorities began to pressure the extremists. However, it is easy to notice that the state opposition to the radical National-Patriots is largely situative in nature. Sometimes, specific actions by authorities caused serious doubts of both ethical and legal nature. The fact that by now the radical National-Patriots have largely lost their influence on society is only partly a result of the government's actions. To a larger degree, it is a result of the changes in society, in the political life of the country in general and the evolution of the extreme nationalists themselves in particular.

This chapter deals with the internal dynamics of the work of the radical rightist organizations in 1990 – 2003, firstly, and secondly, with consideration of the government's specific actions aimed at countering them. We will be especially interested in the latest events and in the present situation. As we cannot cover all spheres of ideology and activities, we will concentrate on a general description of the radical rightists' ideology and forms of organization, and discuss the issue of the popularity of their views in society and their extra-judicial activities. The state policies towards the radical rightists will be discussed in the last section of this chapter. The reader is referred to the reference books and analytical materials published by the Information and Research Center Panorama[47] for further details.

As a final preliminary comment, let us note that the political reality in Russia changes rapidly. It is certain that some of its details will be no longer valid within the several months necessary to prepare this book for publication. Some newspapers may cease to exist, parties may join coalitions, split or disappear from the political arena. Leaders may rename their own groups or join other groups. We ask the reader to be understanding about possible discrepancies between some details in the book and in reality by the time the book becomes available.

2.1   Radical Rightists in Contemporary Russia: Who Is Who

Classification Problems
The radical rightists, with all their ideological diversity, may be provisionally classified into several categories. Naturally, their classification may be based on several ideological parameters: their views on the ideal political order (monarchists, nationalist republicans, etc.), their ideas on the type of ideal nation-state (ethnic nationalists, super-ethnic imperial nationalists), their religious attitudes (RO fundamentalists, neo-pagans, secular nationalists), and their attitudes towards private property (from nationalist Bolsheviks and na-

---

[47]   Verkhovsky A., Papp A., Pribylovsky V. *Politicheskiy ekstremizm v Rossii*. Moscow: Institut eksperimental'noy sotsiologii, 1996; Verkhovsky A., Pribylovsky V. *Natsional-patrioticheskie organizatsii v Rossii*. Moscow: Panorama, 1996; Verkhovsky A., Mikhaylovskaya E., Pribylovsky V. *Natsionalizm i ksenofobiya v rossiyskom obshchestve*. Moscow: Panorama, 1998; *idem*, *Politicheskaya ksenofobiya: radikal'nye gruppy, predstavleniya liderov, rol' Tserkvi*. Moscow: Panorama, 1999.

tionalist socialists to the supporters of predatory nationalist capital), etc. However, even though any classification based on these parameters would be perfectly correct, such a classification would not help in drawing a big picture of exactly who are the radical nationalists in today's Russia. We can only reinforce what American researcher Walter Lacquer said. "Russian politicians move all the time and that will probably continue for a long time. Depending on the situation, people and groups belonging to the center move right, or vice versa, some rightists become moderate. <...> It is impossible and wrong, under such circumstances, to draw a clear boundary between 'extremists' and 'moderates'. Strange alliances are created and they will be created in the future. Hence, any attempt to classify them, as it is done by botanists, zoologists or chemists, is doomed to failure"[48].

Of course, despite the above-mentioned difficulties, we cannot give up completely on classification of the radical rightist groups. Otherwise, it would be impossible to form a general idea of the radical right wing in contemporary Russia.

To draw the most general picture of the radical rightist movement, we suggest, with some simplifications, to divide them into 'old' and 'new' right-wingers[49]. Such a division is based on the most general, informal traits related to their mentality and world outlook rather than on programmatic materials. The main parameter distinguishing the new rightists from the old ones is how revolutionary is their nationalism, not so much in terms of their programmatic goals, as in terms of their mind-set. As a rule, revolutionary conscious-

---

[48]   Walter Lacquer, *Black Hundred: The Rise of The Russian Extreme Right.* New York: HarperCollins 1993. A Russian translation was published in 1994.

[49]   Such a classification has already been described in the literature (see, for example, Verkhovsky A. Novaya oppozitsiya. In Verkhovsky A., Papp A., Pribylovsky V. *Op. cit.*, pp. 70-73). More importantly, it is perceived as an objective fact by the radical nationalists themselves (see, for example, Dugin A. Novye protiv starykh. *Limonka*, No. 1, 1994; Vanyushkina V. Russkie novye pravye. *Natsiya*, No. 2, p. 37, 1996). However, there is some confusion, because the term ' new right' is applied in western political science to at least two political movements: neo-fascism a la Julius Evola and Alain de Benoit and neo-conservatism a la Margaret Thatcher and Ronald Reagan. However, since these uses are unfamiliar to the Russian reader, the terms 'new right' and 'old right' are quite convenient and functional.

ness implies the formation of paramilitary groups, readiness for violence in real life, war mongering and an active incitement to inter-ethnic hatred propaganda.

Our comment above on classification based on a broad approach that takes behavior and mentality into account is crucial because it is practically impossible to differentiate among those organizations by relying on their usually trite political programs. This chapter will concentrate not on the relatively moderate 'old' groups (the Black Hundred[E11], RO fundamentalists) but on the 'new' right-wingers, nationalist revolutionaries, including nationalist socialists, nationalist Bolsheviks and open fascists.

Among them, RNU headed by Aleksandr Barkashov[50] has been the largest such organization for a long time.

Russian National Unity

RNU was formed during the period between September of 1990 (when the group headed by Aleksandr Barkashov and Viktor Yakushev left the National-Patriotic front *Pamyat* (Memory) of Dmitry Vasilyev) and October of the same year (when the A. Barkashov - V. Yakushev tandem collapsed). October 16, 1990, is RNU's official birthday.

RNU's ideology is a mixture of the traditional, Black-Hundred-style nationalism and open Nazism. RNU members profess aggressive anti-liberalism, anti-communism and anti-Semitism. They extol ideals of a Russian nation (the first version of RNU's program included an item on criminal prosecution for mixed marriages and use of eugenics[51]) and Russian spirituality (i.e. RO Christianity but in its 'original' form). Stylistic imitation of German Nazis by Barkashovites is obvious. The RNU insignia, which include a swastika, greeting with the raised right hand, a black uniform, etc., invite unambiguous asso-

---

[E11]   A reactionary movement formed in Russia circa 1900.

[50]   The official spelling of his name is 'Barkashev' with the e, but he himself prefers to spell it with an o. That's how his name is used in the literature and we keep that spelling too.

[51]   *Russkiy poryadok*, No. 8 (11), August 20, 1993.

ciations. Barkashov did not shy away from calling himself a Nazi and he spoke with reverence about Hitler[52].

RNU functioned as a paramilitary organization: its members wore uniforms, engaged in muscle-building sports, and trained to shoot guns. The group's leaders repeatedly claimed that its members were getting ready for a civil war[53].

RNU actively participated in the events of September – October of 1993. A Barkashov detachment was the most important unit among the ill-assorted forces defending the White House and was among the supporters of the Supreme Soviet dissolved by the President. The RNU members were the best trained fighters and they were responsible for the most crucial parts of the defense. On October 3, Barkashov personally led his people who attacked and captured the City Hall located on Kalinin Avenue.

RNU rapidly developed in the mid 1990s, but signs of an internal crisis began to show as early as 1998. By 2000, RNU split into several groups. The 2000 schism was accompanied by quarrelsome arguments among the leaders and, as a result, by a massive exit from the party. According to the best estimates, RNU membership at its peak fluctuated around 15,000 – 20,000 active members, with the number of its nominal members even higher. RNU local branches existed practically all over Russia and also in Ukraine, Belarus, Latvia and Estonia.

The RNU newspaper is "*Русский порядок*" (Russian Order). Its official circulation has fluctuated from 25,000 to 500,000 copies, but the paper has lately been published no more than once a year. The permit to publish Russian Order was revoked by a court on a technicality in 1999, but the paper was re-registered in Belarus in 2000 and began to come out again in 2001. (Accord-

---

[52]   See, for example, Mitrofanov A. Aleksandr Barkashov: "Ya ne fashist, ya natsist" [interview with A.Barkashov]. *Moskovskiy komsomolets*, August 4, 1993.

[53]   See, for example, Petukhov Yu. Nadezhda Rossii [interview with K. Nikitenko]; *Golos Vselennoy*, No. 3, 1994. Konstantin Nikitenko was RNU's Moscow regional leader at the time of the interview.

ing to an agreement between Russia and Belarus, the Belarus newspapers are distributed in Russia with no extra permit or registration and vice versa). Barkashov retained control over the paper after the RNU split. In addition to Russian Order, there are regional papers published by RNU in addition to papers published by groups formed after the split.

One may confidently state that RNU reached its peak in the mid 1990s. The heroic aura of the "White House defenders" attracted radical nationalists to RNU. Barkashovites were among the few people who managed to benefit from the 1993 crisis. However, internal stagnation, lame information policy and a passive approach to elections on the one hand, and the pressure from the central government on the other hand, caused RNU to enter a period of decline in 1999 – 2000[54]. After the split (or rather the series of splits), RNU has de facto ceased to exist as a single organization.

Some of its fragments claim the name and symbolism of the original organization. The relations among some of them may be tense. Even though they jointly participate in political and propaganda campaigns, their personal contacts sometimes deteriorate to the level of physical altercations. Various nationalistic publications are filled with unrestrained arguments among ex-comrades the include insults and accusations of various sins and crimes. A large amount of incriminating materials circulate freely. Such polemics begun during the RNU split are still going on in the press and on the Internet from time to time. Their presence has resulted in a massive exit of original members from the party.

At present, the two largest fragments of the former RNU are RNU-I and RNU-II. RNU-I has 1,000 – 1,500 members and its leader is Aleksandr Barkashov, the founder of RNU. Immediately after the split, most of the regional branches refused to recognize the authority of the former leader. Barkashov himself promulgated the idea of transforming the political movement into a 'military-religious fraternity' called the Barkashovite Guard. However, it soon became

---

[54]   For more details on RNU, see Likhachev V., Pribylovsky V. *Russkoe Natsional'noe Edinstvo*. Moscow: Panorama, 2001.

obvious that the renegades were unable to preserve a single RNU without Barkashov and the former leader returned the name RNU to a group of his followers.

Barkashov's major success was the resumption of the publication of Russian Order banned earlier. This let Barkashovites keep the name and status of a relatively well-known publication. However, the organization does not show much activity and manifests its existence only in leaflets distributed in the Moscow subway. The organization conducts some propaganda on the Internet too, but it does not keep up with "The Group of the Lalochkins" (RNU-II).

The brothers Evgeny and Mikhail Lalochkins are the leaders of RNU-II. They persuaded the leaders of the major regional branches of RNU to join their faction and they tried to keep control over the entire movement after expelling Barkashov and his followers. RNU-II has 2,000 – 3,000 members. The Lalochkin brothers head the RNU regional branches in St. Petersburg (Mikhail) and Voronezh (Evgeny). The leader of the RNU-II branch in the Russian Far East is Vladimir Shcherbakov who plays a generally prominent role in the movement as well.

The Lalochkin brothers' main achievement was setting up successful horizontal links with most of the regional groups and maintaining the party structure all over Russia. But to avoid accusations of ambitious plans, the brothers refused to become the RNU-II leaders and there were no alternative candidates. According to the initial plan, as soon as the links with the regional branches were restored, their representatives would meet and elect a new central council and its chairman. However, all they managed to do was hold several coordinating meetings with representatives of regional branches. RNU-II is an unstructured network of regional groups. The coordinating function of the St. Petersburg and Voronezh branches is minimal. The followers of the Lalochkins brothers have not been able to set up a stable cell in Moscow for a year and a half, which attests to their organizational weakness.

RNU-II conducts active propaganda. They support several web sites, including the original site that NRU-II managed to keep for itself. Besides, the

"Group of the Lalochkins" publishes newspapers either independently, or in collaboration with others ("*Evpaty Kolovrat*", "*Nashe otechestvo*" (Our Fatherland), and for a while "*Novaya sistema*" (New System) in St. Petersburg, "*Informatsionny byulleten VRO RNE*" (Information Bulletin of VRO RNU), "*Russky svet*" (Russian Light) in Ryazan, etc.).

Another major fragment of RNU is "*Russkoe vozrozhdenie*" (Russia's Revival) headed by Oleg Kassin (a coordinator of regional branches of RNU before the split) and Yuri Vasin (the head of the Moscow regional branch before the split). Taking advantage of the dissatisfaction that the local leaders felt towards A. Barkashov, Yu. Vasin and O. Kassin initiated the 2000 split. O. Kassin, who was the leader of the "coup d'etat", initially wanted to abandon RNU's symbols, uniform and radical ideology. However, he was not supported by most of the defectors who joined the Group of the Lalochkins (RNU-II). Hence, he, along with a minority of the regional branches rebelling against Barkashov, formed the "Russia's Revival" movement. RNU's regional branches in the Stavropol territory, in Perm, Kirovsk, Rostov, Kostroma and Tver regions and in Moscow joined Russia's Revival bringing the total membership to around 1,000.

Russia's Revival held a Founding Convention that adopted an eight-point star (without a swastika inside, which was a symbol of the Spas movement used in the ballots in the 1999 election). The color of the members' uniforms were blue instead of black. The new movement began to publish its paper "*Nashe mirovozzrenie*" (Our World Outlook) as well as regional papers in Tver and Perm. At the end of 2001, however, the movement had a crisis caused by internal discord about its future direction. O. Kassin wanted to create a more respectable image for his movement and repeatedly supported the Russian government's actions, whereas regional leaders, such as Andrey Dudinov (Stavropol) and Vladimir Noskov (Perm), viewed that as a deviation from the party line. As a result, Russia's Revival was also split.

At the end of 2001, Oleg Kassin joined the leadership of a party called *Vozrozhdenie* (Revival) created by businessman and State Duma member Evgeny Ishchenko. After the party's Founding Convention on February 16,

2002, E. Ishchenko became its chairman. Another State Duma member, Sergey Zagidullin, and O. Kassin became his deputies. The party does not publish its own news organ but articles by, and interviews with, E. Ishchenko are widely published, as for example in the newspaper *Krasnaya Zvezda* (Red Star) beginning in the spring of 2002. In its propaganda, Revival stresses a tough anti-immigration policy, a strong fight against crime, support for the military-industrial complex and domestic businesses and the use of anti-Western rhetoric.

Yury Vasin, in turn, joined the leadership of the National Revival Party *"Narodnaya Volya"* (People's Will), a successor to RAU.

The regional leaders of Russia's Revival who refused to follow Kassin and join "Ishchenko's Party" (Aleksandr Frutikov from Tver, Vladimir Noskov from Perm and Andrey Timofeev from Kostroma) dethroned Kassin as the movement's chairman. However, they could not keep the movement intact. Some regional groups kept calling themselves Russia's Revival, others joined the National Party of Great Russia, while V. Noskov and his newspaper World Outlook announced that they represented the Fraternal Order of Saint Iosif Volotsky.

Yet another group formed in Moscow and some other regions after RNU's split was *Slavyansky Soyuz* (Slavonic Union, SU). Its head is Dmitry Demushkin, its honorary chairman is Nikolay Kryukov, the former RNU chief of staff. SU claims to be the Moscow regional branch of RNU but it does not recognize Barkashov or the Lalochkins and it makes its own independent contacts with regional groups. SU's organ of mass information used to be the newspaper *Stenka* (Wall) which does not come out at present. SU's membership is around 200 people. Practically, it is not engaged in propaganda, being rather a paramilitary and athletic group. Its members are engaged in sports and guarding activities.

Another small group called *Svodny otryad RNE* (Joint Detachment of RNU) was formed in Moscow after the split. After trying unsuccessfully to establish contacts with regional groups, Joint Detachment then joined *Obyedinennaya Narodnaya Partiya* (Joined People's Party).

By and large, RNU was weakened after the split and it gradually disappeared from the political arena. Ex-Barkashovites have certain chances, such as possible registration or attempts to participate in elections, only within new groups (E. Ishchenko's "Revival" and S. Baburin's "People's Will").

National Bolshevik Party
Another major nationalist radical group is the National Bolshevik Party (NBP). Its leader is the well-known writer, Eduard Limonov. Since Limonov's arrest in April of 2001, the acting chairman of the party is Anatoly Tishin.

The NBP has some 7,000 members and branches in 51 regions. The first party congress was attended by party representatives from 38 regions. Additionally, the NBP branches are active in Belarus, Kyrgyzstan, Latvia, Moldova and Ukraine.

The newspaper *Limonka*[E12] was the main NBP publication between 1994 and 2002. It was published semi-weekly with its circulation fluctuating around 10,000 copies. Since the fall of 2002, the newspaper *Generalnaya liniya* (Fundamental Line) has become the official central party organ and it has kept *Limonka*'s format, circulation, periodicity and even its logotype. There are also a number of regional publications.

The NBP was formed gradually from November of 1992, when a group of radicals headed by E. Limonov and Andrey Arkhipov quit Vladimir Zhirinovsky's party and formed the Nationalist-Radical Party (that was later split into two groups: Limonov's and Arkhipov's), to November of 1994, when the first issue of *Limonka* came out. Officially, the party was born on November 28, 1994.

[E12]   The name *Limonka* is a play on words. It is based on the NBP leader's name. It is also a small hand-thrown grenade.

The characteristic feature of the NBP ideology is its pro-Soviet orientation and cultural (and to a smaller extent, etatist) rather than ethnic nationalism. The main party insignia consist of a black hammer and sickle inside a white circle against a red background.

An important part of the NBP activities is protection of the rights of the Russian people on territory of the former Soviet Union. NBP members (both from Russia and from local groups) actively participate in various events (sometimes illegal and often violent) aimed in their opinion at protecting the interests of the Russian diaspora in Latvia, Ukraine and Kazakhstan. Although such actions, as a rule, do not bring any immediate results, they attract public attention to the problem, which in the long run increases the party's popularity. The most known NBP actions were non-violent protests in Latvia (seizure of the bell tower of St. Michael's cathedral in Riga in 2001) and in the Crimea (seizure of the tower of the Sailors' Club in Sebastopol in 2000) as well as the support for the Russian separatists in Northern Kazakhstan (a failed rebellion of Cossacks in Kokchetav in 1997).

The NBP was registered as an inter-regional organization in early 1997 and re-registered on February 9, 1998. Despite its numerous attempts, the NBP has been unable to get national registration.

Although the NBP may hardly be called a mass party, it has managed to attain a certain niche in the political spectrum. Its bright style and successful propaganda substantially influence some of the Russian youth who do not always follow either nazi, or communist ideology.

The NBP's right radicalism is debatable: its ideology is inconsistent and leftist elements are perhaps even more noticeable than nationalist ones. One of several discussions about the party course's 'leftism' and 'rightism' broke out within the party itself at the end of 2002 on the eve of its IV congress. After A. Dugin, the NBP first ideologist, quit the party in 1998, the proportion in the NBP and *Limonka*'s left-right hodgepodge changed in terms of both style and ideas. The party became more leftist than nazi-oriented, it started to include more elements of anti-globalization, of Che Guevara's philosophy, of Trotskyism, as well as ideas of the European New Left and to include fewer elements of nazism, conservative revolution, traditionalism, Eurasianism and the New Right. However, the moving of the party to the left is just a trend rather than a final change of its position. The proportion of the right and left elements in the party may yet change, especially considering Limonov and his followers' eclectic views as well as the complete independence of the regional groups in choosing their ideological platform. While some regional groups are controlled by radical left-wing intellectuals, others are controlled by radical nationalists or even by racist skinheads.

The NBP had actively developed until the beginning of the 2000s, constrained only by external factors, such as the lack of national registration. At present, the NBP is the most radical party among the relatively large political parties. Apart from the NBP, only some versions of RNU have regional branches all over the country, but RNU is weakened by internal conflicts, whereas the NBP remains a centralized and vigorous party. However, the NBP is weakened by other factors, such as the arrest of its leadership and pressure from law enforcement agencies[55].

NBP chairman Eduard Limonov and a number of other NBP activists were arrested in April of 2001 after the purchase of several submachine guns by party members. The investigation claimed that the purchase had been ordered by Limonov himself. The trial began in Saratov (where the weapons had been bought) in September of 2002. In the following two years, the party's energy and resources were spent to a large degree on the defense of the jailed leadership (Limonov's lawyer was famous attorney Sergey Belyak).

NBP acting chairman Anatoly Tishin decided to use the persecutions of the party leadership to attract public attention and sympathies, which, we should add, the NBP does well. Various factors elicit a sympathetic rather than negative attitude towards the NBP in much of the media. The legal basis for Li-

---

[55]   The most detailed description of the NBP activities is written by Limonov himself. See, for example, Limonov E. *Moya politicheskaya avtobiografiya*. St. Petersburg: Amfora, 2002.

monov's arrest is questionable – it is unclear whether the investigation's theory about Limonov's participation in the purchase was substantiated enough. The circumstances of the purchase have all the earmarks of a frame-up – the persons who sold the weapons were not detained or identified, whereas the NBP members were arrested right after the purchase. At the very least, that proves the availability of timely information about the transaction, but perhaps, raises the possibility of a provocation. Another factor is the unselfish behavior of the rank-and-file party members – four of them went on a month-long hunger strike demanding an open trial, etc. So far as we can judge, the popularity and recognition of both the NBP and its leader in the country has increased due to Limonov's arrest and the advantage taken of it through the media. This conclusion is supported by the results of the additional Duma election held in the Nizhegorodsky region on March 31, 2002. Limonov ran in absentia, and although he lost, he got more votes than he did in all his previous attempts to run.

Yet, despite its skillful legal defense and attention to the media, the NBP is constrained in its actions, as it cannot continue violent actions for fear of affecting the course of the trial adversely. The NBP slogan "Jail Limonov, untie our hands!" attests to the party's somewhat passive behavior in the past two years in the expectation of the trial. Besides, some members quit the party after their encounters with the response of law enforcement (not always in the correct form, to put it mildly). On balance, the growth of the party's popularity and recognition did not translate into growing numbers of party members or even increased readership of the party newspaper.

Not only does the pressure on the NBP by the government hamper its activities in general, it also creates specific but very effective obstacles for the party. For example, the newspaper *Limonka* was banned on July 26, 2002; it is unclear if the party will have to move its offices to a new location, etc.

In 2002, the NBP launched a drive to increase its membership and the number of its regional branches up to the level required for national Russian registration. At present, this goal seems unrealistic. First, the NBP is essentially unable to meet the tough legal requirements imposed on political parties and there is no explosive growth in party building in sight. On the contrary, one may observe a certain membership outflow caused by fear of possible criminal or administrative prosecution. Some members were not ready to go through thick and thin without a real chance to win. Second, it would be harder for the NBP than for other political groups to use fake registration documents, because the authorities would check their documents very thoroughly and could use any excuse to deny it registration. And last, there is a great chance that the NBP will be banned altogether. A petition asking for NBP liquidation was filed in court, but the judge accepted party lawyer Sergey Belyak's arguments to postpone the case until resolution of the Limonov case. S. Belyak argued that the petition to ban the party was based on guilt of the party leadership and activists that had not been proved by that time. Since then (and before resolution of the Limonov case), a law against 'extremist activity' was passed, which significantly increased the probability of legal liquidation of the NBP.

Fundamentally, the NBP is in a complex situation. The arrest of its leadership and the powerful pressure from law enforcement organs would make it practically impossible for any political group to perform its functions satisfactorily. Although the NBP continues to function and even manages to use state harassment to gain popular sympathy, it cannot break out of its current boundaries. Hence, any future participation by the NBP in State Duma elections is out of the question.

As of today (June of 2003), realistically speaking, it is hard to predict the future of the nationalist Bolsheviks. On the one hand, the party has conducted yet another Founding Convention and is planning to apply for national Russian registration on the basis of the new law. More importantly, Limonov's lawyer has managed to secure a suspended sentence for his client. On the other hand, clearly, the NBP will not be registered, while the intense pressure by law enforcement and a possible ban may push the NBP out of legal political life.

In any case, even if the party totally disappears as a result of the repression or breaks into pieces as RNU did (which is very unlikely considering the release of its leader), one must admit that the NBP has been the brightest radical political project in post-Soviet Russia.

Other Radical Right Wing Groups

Apart from the NBP and RNU, other 'new' right wing groups have not been able to expand their activities to the national level. Nevertheless, some of them are rather conspicuous within that part of the political spectrum.

Among the groups that are still active, Aleksandr Ivanov-Sukharevsky's overtly racist *Narodnaya natsionalnaya partia* (People's National Party, PNP) is worth mentioning first. It has 500 – 700 members and its branches officially exist in 38 regions. Its official newspaper is *Ya – Russky* (I am Russian) (circulation of 15,000, periodicity – once or twice a month).

PNP's 'specialization' is its ability work with skinheads – teenage racists who shave their heads[56]. The skinheads represent a relatively popular movement in youth subculture. Their world outlook is based on aggressive racism and their main preoccupation is assaulting members of various minorities (natives of the Caucasus, African and Asian students, etc). Sometimes, these assaults become large pogroms. Their most infamous and bloody action was the Tsaritsyno marketplace pogrom in October of 2001. The skinheads are not a political movement proper, but radical nationalist parties recruit them as mercenaries. That does not always work though – the skinheads detest party discipline and avoid ideological jungles. They often believe that, unlike themselves, parties are merely talkers. PNP is one of the few nationalist parties working successfully with skinheads.

PNP deputy chairman Semyon Tokmakov is a skinhead who gained notoriety in 1998 by assaulting a black marine guard from the US embassy in Moscow.

---

[56]   For more details on the Russian skinheads, see, for example: Likhchev V. Britogolovye v Rossii. *Mezhdunarodnaya evreyskaya gazeta,* Nos. 39-41, 2001. Likhchev V., Pribylovsky V. Skinkhedy b'yut i ubivayut "neslavyan". *Russkaya mysl'*, No. 4385, November 15-21, 2001. Tarasov A. Skinhaeds ou naturel. *Neprekosnovennyy zapas*, No. 5 (7), 1999. The same author. Porozhdenie reform: britogolovye, oni zhe skinhedy. *Svobodnaya mysl'-XXI*, No. 5, 2000.

Tokmakov joined the party immediately after being released from prison in 1999 and brought with him a large number of skinheads. And the skinheads have become the main part of PNP since then.

PNP propaganda features radical nationalism, especially as far as the use of anti-Semitic and anti-Caucasus stereotypes is concerned. The party leader was sentenced to three years of prison in 2002 for inciting interethnic hatred but was immediately pardoned.

Another party actively working with skinheads is Yury Belyaev's *Partia Svobody* (Freedom Party, FP). It was known as *Natsionalno-respublikanskaya partiya Rossii* (National Republican Party of Russia, NRPR) before 2000 and it was formed as a result of the split of Nikolay Lysenko's party of the same name. FP is one of the main radical nationalist parties in the Russian North-West (Leningrad region, Pskov) and its headquarters are located in St. Petersburg. FP has been able to attract skinheads with the help of Andrey Grebnev who used to be the leader of the NBP St. Petersburg branch and joined Yu. Belyaev in 2000. At present, A. Grebnev is the editor-in-chief of the FP monthly *Nashe Obozrenie* (Our Survey); its circulation is 10,000 copies.

The fact that both PNP and FP have more actively worked with the skinheads in the last year or year and a half increases the recognition for both organizations. The young racists captured the media attention after several bloody pogroms in Moscow in 2001. Ivanov-Sukhrevsky and Belyaev took advantage of that interest, in fact hullabaloo, to gain popularity. That resulted in an influx of skinheads into both parties and helped their leaders exploit totally unrelated events, such as racist violence on the street, and the expectation of pogroms on Hitler's birthday (April 20, 2002), for self-promotion. On the other hand, this association with the skinheads weakens the parties. The skinheads have turned out to be unreliable and undisciplined party activists; only a minority of them can handle the routine work needed by a party. Even though the skinheads and radical nationalist leaders have the same ideological positions and view the world similarly, the difference in their mindsets is huge. A racist teenager would rather assault non-Russian appearing passers-by on the street than put posters on the wall or walk picket lines. And the obvious association of PNP and FP with skinheads scares older and more serious nationalists away from the parties.

Both PNP and FP would like to get national Russian registration but they have no chance. Realistically, each party has a few hundred members, most of which are juveniles, and less than ten active regional branches. Any real participation of PNP and FP in the political process is out of the question, but their propaganda poses a certain danger by influencing aggressive teenagers to spill their hatred on the street.

The most radical of all legal nationalist organizations – Konstantin Kasimovsky's *Russky natsionalny soyuz* (Russian National Union) – was prominent in Moscow and several other cities (St. Petersburg, Yaroslavl) in the mid 1990s. (We will use the acronym RNU-KK to distinguish it from another RNU, the Russian National Unity). RNU-KK has never had many members (it had 150 – 200 members in Moscow at its peak), but it is known for its active and aggressive propaganda. Their main periodical was the newspaper *Shturmovik* (Storm Trooper). In its best times, it was published weekly, but it was shut down by a court order in 1998 for its content, not on a technicality, as was the case, for example, with "Russian Order". In 1999, RNU-KK leader and Storm Trooper's chief editor K. Kasimovsky was sentenced to a suspended two-year prison term for inciting interethnic hostility.

After the sentencing, Kasimovsky resumed his political activities but more carefully. RNU-KK, known as *Russkaya natsional-sotsialisticheskaya partiya* (Russian Nationalist-Socialist Party) for a short time, is now named *Dvizhenie "Russkoe Deystvie"* (Movement "Russian Action", RA). The actual RA today is merely a group of ideologists, including first of all Kasimovsky himself plus Aleksandr Eliseev and Viktoriya Vanyushkina. They promote their views through the paper *Pravoe soprotivlenie* (Right Resistance), which is much less radical than Storm Trooper. After the confrontation with the law enforcement organs, Kasimovsky seems to have given up on his idea to seize power through a civil war. Now he modestly claims the laurels of the ideologist of the upcoming national revolution.

Uniting Right-Wing Radicals

Several attempts to unite radical nationalists were made in the 1990s. In 1992 – 1993, large unions of left-wing patriots (communists for Great Russia) and right-wing radicals, Ilya Konstantinov's National Salvation Front as well as Aleksandr Sterligov's Russian National Council appeared. These coalitions broke up after the October of 1993 crisis and the reform of the RF party system. So, despite all attempts by activists, the idea of a broad union of right-wing radicals has remained in the domain of theory.

The Coordinating Council of Radical Nationalist Parties (CCRNP) was formed in 1996. It included the NBP, PNP, Yu. Belyaev's NRPR, Georgy Shepelev's *Novoe obshchestvennoe russkoe dvizhenie* (New Social Russian Movement, NSRM), the Ukrainian *Partiya slavyanskogo edinstva* (Slavonic Unity Party) of Oleg Bakhtiyarov and a number of smaller groups. The main task of the Council was to determine the nationalists' platform in the 1996 presidential election. For all practical purposes, CCRNP ceased to exist after the election.

The idea of a broad union of right-wing radicals was revived in 2001 when a new law on the political parties strengthened the requirements for national registration, which is necessary to participate in the Duma elections. It became obvious that various right-wing radical groups would be able to meet the requirements for the numbers of members and regional branches only together.

The most successful attempt of unification in 2001 – 2003 was *Natsionalno-derzhavnaya partiya Rossii* (National Party of Great Russia, NPGR). The idea of a unified nationalist party was born in the spring of 2001 when it became clear that none of the existing National-Patriotic organizations by themself would be able to obtain national Russian registration. The initiative to create such a party probably originated from Stanislav Terekhov, the leader of the left-wing nationalist organization Union of Officers.

The first Memorandum concerning the creation of the Party's Organizing Committee was signed on May 18, 2001, by Yury Belyaev (Freedom Party, newspaper Our Survey), Dmitry Demushkin (Slavonic Union), Stanislav

Terekhov (Union of Officers and newspaper of the same name), Vladimir Selivanov (newspaper *Desnitsa* (Right Hand)), Aleksandr Aratov (newspaper *Russkaya Pravda* (Russian Truth)), Aleksandr Sevastyanov (League of Defense of the National Wealth, *Natsionalnaya Gazeta* (National Gazette)), Dmitry Rumyantsev (newspaper Wall), Andrey Arkhipov (Russian Project – Great Russia), Aleksandr Ivanov-Sukharevsky (People's National Party and newspaper I am Russian), Vladimir Avdeev (magazine *Ateney* (Athenaeum)). The memorandum called on the nationalist leaders to "abandon their ambitions and personal grievances for the sake of the common goal – Russia's salvation".

Later the document was signed by Viktor Korchagin (Russian Party of Russia), newspaper *Russkie vedomosti* (Russian Register)), S. Kucherov (information agency *Derzhavny soyuz* (Great Union)), Igor D'yakov (newspaper *Imperia* (Empire)), Vladimir Popov (newspaper *Era Rossii* (Russian Era)), Mikhail Kazmin (newspaper *Rubezh* (Boundary), Vladimir)), Stanislav Terent'ev (newpaper *Kolokol* (Bell), Volgograd), Oleg Kitter (newspaper *Alekc-Inform*, Samara), V. Mironov (newspaper *Peresvet*[E13], Krasnodar), Boris Mironov(former chairman of the Russian Federation State Committee on Printing), Grigory Trofimchuk (former RNU leader in Saratov, presently he is the editor of the newspaper *Natsionalny pod'em* (National Ascent) and the head of the Moscow Party of National Ascent). Initially, Aleksandr Chervyakov (magazine *Russky khozyain* (Russian Owner) and movement of the same name) worked with the Organizing Committee, but he did not sign any documents, was not a member of the Organizing Committee and soon moved away from NPGR activities. In the beginning of 2002, president of the Russian Federation of Hand-to-Hand Fighting Tadeush Kasyanov joined the Organizing Committee.

About half of the participants (I. Dyakov, A. Arkhipov, D. Demushkin and A. Ivanov-Sukharevsky) quit the Organizing Committee by the end of 2001 due to internal discord and A. Aratov and Yu. Belyaev quit at the beginning of

---

E13   Peresvet is a Russian monk who was a hero of the battle with the Tataro-Mongols in 1380.

2002. In reality, a broad coalition did not succeed. Committee members started ideological quarrels (neo-pagans bickered with RO fundamentalists, anti-communist nationalists with leftist patriots, etc). They could not forget personal ambitions, as the Memorandum demanded. Bad blood between some of the party's founders aggravated the situation.

The official publication of the NPGR organizing Committee was the newspaper Russian Front. It was published several times as special issues of the newspapers "I am Russian", "Union of Officers" and "National Gazette", their circulation varied between 1,000 and 10,000 copies.

The Founding Convention of NPGR was held in the Hotel Pines in the city of Korolev (former Kaliningrad), Moscow region. 216 delegates from 65 regions attended the Convention and they elected the NPGR Central Political Council (CPC). Its three co-chairmen were S. Terekhov (organizational issues, contacts with regions, charter committee), A. Sevastyanov (program and ideological platform) and B. Mironov (contacts with government officials and public groups).

Initially, NPGR was expected to become the largest group uniting radical nationalists and left-wing patriots since the Russian National Council and the National Salvation Front, but in the end, it became instead another organization including separate leaders and a few small or regional groups.

It obtained official registration in September of 2002. Having been shocked, democratically oriented journalists, anti-fascists and human rights activists publicized anti-Semitic and xenophobic statements made by NPGR leaders at the founding convention. They pointed out the illegitimacy of registering such a party on the basis of the Law on Political Parties and the Law on Counteracting Extremist Activity. Then the Ministry of Justice asked NPGR for clarifications, and the party leadership "dissociated themselves from some members' statements" (including two out of three co-chairmen). Justice Minister Yury Chayka said that his department would monitor NPGR, and if such statements were made again, the authorities would raise the question of withdrawing the registration. In January of 2003, NPGR got a warning from the Justice Ministry after the publication in Moscow News of an interview with Mironov containing anti-Semitic statements.

In the spring of 2003, NPGR lost its registration for a technical reason – the party could not register the necessary number of branches before the deadline. Other attempts to create a broad alliance of nationalist patriots have turned out to be even less successful. An alternative project to create a right-wing radical coalition called *Ob'edinennaya narodnaya partiya* (United People's Party, UPP) has completely failed too.

An organizing committee to create UPP was formed on August 2, 2001. The committee included a number of representatives of RO fundamentalist, nationalist and left-wing patriotic organizations: Alexey Romanov, chairman of the small right-wing radical movement *Bely mir* (White World); Igor Lavrinenko, leader of the fundamentalist group *Russkaya Falanga* (Russian Phalanx) and editor of the newspaper with the same name; A. Orlov, commentator of radio Resonance; Anatoly Makeev, elder of the Fraternal Order of Saint Iosif Volotsky; Evgeny Morozov, editor of magazine "Geopolitical Review".

The above-listed political and public figures as well as A. Serbo, a representative of the communists, signed the "Protocol on the Creation of the United Organizing Committee for the Joint Political Organization (Party of the Russian People)".

In Moscow, Vladimir Goncharenko, leader of the RNU Composite Detachment (one of the smaller groups formed after the RNU split), joined UPP. The party published a small circulation paper, *Narod* (People), had an Internet site but did not show any other activity. One may assume that currently the party does not exist. A. Romanov created the United People's Radical Movement on June 7, 2003.

Sergey Baburin's National Revival Party "People's Will" (formerly known as Justice and National Revival Party) also tried to serve as a union of nationalist patriots. The party's Founding Convention was held on December 21,

2001. Sergey Baburin (formerly the head of RAU) was elected the party chairman and Yury Vasin, Nina Zhukova, Vladimir Davidenko and Viktor Alksnis – his deputies. The newspaper Time formerly published by RAU became the new party's newspaper.

Initially, representatives of a wide spectrum of opposition forces – from D. Demushkin's radical nazi Slavonic Union to Ivan Rybkin's respectable Socialist Party – were involved in negotiations about joining Baburin's new party that positioned itself as social democratic and patriotic. In the end, the party turned out to be a rather restructured RAU joined by certain figures of both national patriotic and centrist orientation.

That same electorate is claimed by *Narodno-patrioticheskaya partiya Rossii* (People's Patriotic Party of Russia, PPPR) headed by Igor Radionov. The PPPR Founding Convention was held on February 23, 2002. The party's official publication is newspaper Patriot. Its goal is the social protection of the people and restoring Russia as a great power. Its leadership includes people well known in nationalistic circles, such as Vladimir Miloserdov, leader of the Russian Party.

By and large, we may conclude that the radical nationalist patriots have been unable to create a broad and flexible coalition similar to *Soyuz pravykh sil* (Union of Right Forces) created in the liberal democratic camp. Nationalist coalitions turn out to be weak and narrow. UPP will not get national registration, whereas NPGR seems to have lost its registration. If more stable, narrow and homogeneous groups, such as People's Will and PPPR, get their registrations, which they have a good chance of doing, their electoral successes are unlikely to exceed those of RAU or the Movement in Support of the Army (whose ideology and rhetoric is practically copied by PPPR) in 1999: 0.37% and 0.58%, respectively.

It is necessary to note another important detail: the largest and most serious organizations among all those listed above – People's Will of S. Baburin and PPPR of I. Rodionov – are also the most moderate ones. Perhaps, their very classification as right-wing radical groups is debatable. That is why Baburin's party was discussed in more detail in another chapter.

"Old Right-Wingers": Black Hundred and Orthodox Fundamentalists
The "old right-wingers" seem moderate compared to revolutionary minded "new right-wingers". The "old right-wingers" include RO Fundamentalist groups and neo-Black Hundreds. The prefix "neo" is used very tentatively here, as they follow Russian pre-revolutionary conservative ideology without any, or with very small, modifications. In this chapter, we are less interested in Black Hundreds, because their unlawful activities are much less aggressive than those of the "new" radical nationalists. Accordingly, their relations with the authorities are less contentious. The fundamentalists will be discussed in the chapter on religious anti-Semitism. Yet, for the sake of completeness, we will briefly describe the evolution of the old right-wingers' organizational forms in the 1990s.

When the Soviet regime fell, Black Hundreds seemed to hold a pretty strong position. They had a solid political history and claimed to have preserved continuity with pre-revolutionary Russian Nationalists via emigration and dissident groups. The "old right-wingers" were about the only group in 1991 that had a clear idea about their vision of the ideal Russia. From the late 1980s to the early 1990s, public consciousness went through changes favorable to the Black Hundreds: idealization of Czarist Russia, revival of the ROC, interest in cultural heritage of the Russian right-wingers.

However, the Black Hundreds' strength soon turned into their weakness. Several factors led to their decline: dogmatically narrow-minded ideology that they inherited from pre-revolutionary organizations, paranoid anti-Semitism, excessive attention to history at the expense of current problems, sectarianism, conservatism, and their unpreparedness to function in a substantially different political environment. The most active of their leaders left black hundredist groups, especially Dmitry Vasilyev's National Patriotic Front *Pamyat* (Memory) that forged cadres for the right radicals. They formed new organizations that, as a rule, were even more radical. They relied on the European fascist experience rather than on Russian pre-revolutionary conservatism.

Promising associations of both "new" and "old" right-wingers (flavored with the Soviet state patriotism), especially Aleksandr Sterligov's RNC, had completely disintegrated by the middle of 1990s. Memory, whose propaganda and actions greatly impressed journalists in the late 1980s – early 1990s and caused mass emigration of frightened Jewish citizens, became a tiny and insignificant group of D. Vasilyev's fans. In the past few years, Vasilyev's status was that of a political pensioner rather than a leader on a national scale or even a patriarch of Russian nationalism. The Memory leader died in July of 2003.

"Old right-wing" groups, such as Memory, Aleksandr Shtilmark's Black Hundred and various monarchist groups, continue to exist and have some influence on a certain sector of the population, but they are going through a deep crisis. By and large, they occupy the margins of the political process in the country. The only sphere of public life where they are strong is quasi-religious RO organizations. In practice, quasi-religious public life consists of such groups as *Soyuz pravoslavnykh bratstv* (Union of Orthodox Brethren, UOB), *Soyuz pravoslavnykh grazhdan* (Union of Orthodox Citizens, UOC), *Soyuz Khristianskoe vozrozhdenie* (Christian Revival Union, CRU) and more recently *Soyuz pravoslavnykh khorugvenostsev* (Union of Orthodox Gonfaloniers, UOG) and the party *Za Rus' Svyatuyu* (For Holy Russia). Most of the popular Orthodox publications (newspapers *Russky Vestnik* (Russian Herald), *Rus' pravoslavnaya* (Orthodox Russia) and the magazine *Russky dom* (Russian Home)) stand on positions of "old rightist" fundamentalist nationalism.

The RO fundamentalist groups do not carry out much political activity. They organize certain public events like religious processions, historical-theological readings, etc., and not much else. However, the heat of xenophobic emotions, primarily anti-Semitic ones, at UOB/CRU/UOG events generally reaches a high level. For example, these organizations held a rally in front of the Israeli embassy in Moscow on April 20, 2002 (i.e. on Hitler's birthday), protesting the Israeli policy in the occupied territories. The specific pretext for the rally was the confrontation between the Israeli Army and Palestinian gunmen taking refuge in the Church of the Nativity in Bethlehem. The very idea that the Jews might storm a Christian holy place outraged fundamental-ists. During the rally, UOB and UOG leader Leonid Simonovich and CRU chairman Vladimir Osipov repeatedly made extremely anti-Semitic remarks in the Christian anti-Judaism vein: the "zhids" are "visible demons", "Satan's children", "God's enemies", etc. The fact that the day of the rally was now chosen by accident is supported by the title of Simonovich's article describing the rally – "The Leader's Birthday"[57].

UOC (leader – Valentin Lebedev), on the other hand, gradually acquires a re-spectable reputation. In the spring of 2002, UOC jointly with the State Duma's pro-President faction "People's Deputy" and Gennady Raykov's centrist "People's Party of RF" conducted a series of protest actions against the es-tablishment of Catholic dioceses by the Vatican in Russia. Even though a xenophobic tension showed at UOC meetings, the very fact of cooperation with authorities proves that V. Lebedev has distanced himself from the radi-cals and become a "respectable politician". Lebedev's evolution may be fur-ther illustrated by the fact that in 1999, he ran for the State Duma on the same ticket as Barkashov and Tokmakov, whereas at a meeting in 2002, he did not give the floor to any of his radical comrades (Osipov and Simanovich tried to make their way to the microphone).

Some of the UOB/CRU/UOG activities attract many activists, although that pertains more to religious processions on anniversaries of Czar Nicholas II's murder, for example, than to anti-Israel rallies. However, this group of RO fundamentalists practically does not conduct any active propaganda in the print media or on the Internet. It prefers to channel its energy into prayers ca-pable, in its opinion, of miraculously changing Russia's future.

On the other hand, the more radical Fraternal Order of Saint Iosif Volotsky (elder – Anatoly Makeev, ideologist – Ruslan Bychkov) is engaged in very ac-tive propaganda in the media. The Order publishes three newspapers of its own, *Tsarsky Oprichnik* (Czar's Guardsman), *Prosvetitel* (Enlightener) and

---

57   Simonovich A. Den' rozhdeniya vozhdya. *Era Rossii*, Nos. 11-12 (79-80), June, 2002; Nos. 13-14 (81-82), July, 2002.

Russky partisan (Russian Partisan) and books. Just in 2002, it published "Parallel Orthodoxy" by A. Makeev, "Introduction to the Philosophy of Riot" by R. Bychkov and the collection of papers "Skinhead Russia". It also has a strong influence on a number of newspapers that technically do not belong to the Order: *Era Rossii* (Russian Era) in Moscow, *Oprichnina* (Czar's Guard) in Novgorod, *Mirovozzrenie* (World Outlook) in Perm. The Order's ideologists and publicists rather successfully combine neo-Nazism with RO fundamentalism abundantly mixed with anti-Semitism and, strangely enough, with some elements of new left-wing philosophy in their propaganda. Unlike most of the other RO Nazis who just use an eclectic mixture of various elements, they manage to synthesize them.

Being in a deep intellectual and ideological crisis, the RO public senses new elements in the Order's ideas, such as the thesis on an RO revolution as the only way to overcome the "alienation" of the modern world. They think that the Order's ideas can overcome the crisis caused primarily by the lack of adjustment of the traditional RO teachings to the contemporary environment. However, the adoption of the Order's ideas by the wide Orthodox-patriotic public is impeded the fact that most of the Order's brothers are outside the jurisdiction of the ROC Moscow Patriarchy (MP) either belonging to the "catacomb church", or living abroad. That allows them to criticize the "decadent" elements in the ROC MP and in contemporary Christianity as a whole sharply and consistently and offer as an alternative a "parallel Orthodoxy" by analogy with "parallel" (informal) Islam. However, that makes their propaganda unacceptable for most of the RO fundamentalists. The Order's ideology and propaganda are of a sectarian character and they have no chance of being accepted by the broad masses, or even by their targeted group: the RO fundamentalist nationalists.

The party For Holy Russia was created with the ambition of gaining wide popularity. Its Founding Convention was held on December 1, 2001, near Moscow. The Party chairman is Sergey Popov, his deputies are D. Merkulov, I. Shatalov and I. Starikov, the chairman of the bureau of its central council is Aleksey Kuimov. Partly, the party is UOB's political arm; partly, it was created from scratch. There is a public organization bearing almost the same name as the party For Holy Russia – Holy Russia. The organization concentrates on founding RO brotherhoods, folklore groups and martial arts groups (in RO parishes!) but is not involved in politics.

The party has enjoyed certain organizational successes and it conducts an active propaganda campaign on the Internet and in the print media (newspapers *Pravoporyadok* (Law and Order), *Serbsky krest* (Serbian Cross)). However, an organizational breakthrough expected by the party leadership has not occurred despite the blessings of elders prominent in the church hierarchy. The party For Holy Russia got national Russian registration in October of 2002. At present, there are negotiations going on about forming an electoral bloc including For Holy Russia, Leonid Ivashov's *Voenno-derzhavny soyuz Rossii* (Military Union for Great Russia), Aleksandr Martynov's *Soyuz Kazakov Rossii* (Cossack Union of Russia) and a number of other groups. The bloc's potential name is *Derzhavny soyuz Rossii* (Union for Great Russia). If the bloc participates in the State Duma elections of 2003 in that composition, the results are unlikely to be better than those of an ideologically similar coalition named *Russkoe Delo* (Russian Deed) in the 1999 elections - 0.17%.

Although "old" right-wing radicals use and condone unrestrained extremist and xenophobic (mainly anti-Semitic) rhetoric, their mindset is such that the ideological extremism very seldom turns into action. That's why the next section discussing the right-wing radicals' activities (taking part in elections and illegal actions) is primarily concerned with the "new right-wingers".

2.2   Activity of Right-Wing Radicals: Defeats in Elections and Successes in Crime

Right-Wing Radicals in Elections.
Electoral statistics is a source of important information on the popularity of the right-wing radical organizations in society and their chances of coming to power using constitutional means. The State Duma of 1993 – 1995 had just one radical right-winger in the fullest sense of the word. It was NRPR chairman Nikolay Lysenko who won in a single-mandate district in the Saratov region. Not a single radical has been able to repeat his success in the following elections on the national level.

A candidate supported by the overtly Nazi movement RNU ran for the State Duma during the runoff elections on October 30, 1994, in the Mytischy majority district. Aleksandr Fedorov got 5.92% of the vote and placed sixth out of the 12 running. His result has happened to be the best for an RNU candidate on the national level since then. However, the RNU leadership expected a victory then, and, after Fedorov's defeat, claimed that he was not the movement's official candidate. Having been offended, Fedorov in fact withdrew from RNU and set up his own organization named *Russkoe patriotihceskoe narodnoe dvizhenie* (Russian Patriotic People's Movement, RPPM) since 1998.

Several National-Patriotic groups made equally unsuccessful attempts to participate in the 1995 State Duma elections. The only really radical organization listed on the ballot was N. Lysenko's NRPR which got 0.48% of the vote. A number of right-wing radical candidates ran in single-mandate districts. Their results were very disappointing too.

RNU candidates ran in two Moscow districts (Yury Kapralny in the University district number 201 and Larisa Dementyeva in the Babushkin district number 192), in the Kaluga region's Dzerzhinsky district number 85 (Aleksandr Ushakov), in the Stavropol territory's Vladimirsky district number 55 (Andrey Dudinov).

Yu. Kapralny got 0.62% (16th place out of 17 candidates), L. Dementyeva — 2.53%, (9th place out of 23) A. Ushakov — 1.43% (13th place out of 15 candidates), A. Dudinov — 1.51% (14th place out of 20).

Former RNU member Aleksey Vedenkin ran in the Moscow region's single-mandate Lyubertsy district number 107 and got 1.93% (12th place out of 14). NBP leaders E Limonov and Aleksandr Dugin ran for the State Duma in single-mandate districts and were unsuccessful too.

The Presidential election in 1996 was a complete failure for the right-wing radicals too. An ad hoc committee tried to put A. Barkashov on the ballot. RNU members actively gathered signatures in his support, but the RNU leader announced in April that he had no intention to run and did not submit the signatures to the Central Election Commission. Barkashov's pretext for withdrawing his candidacy was the allegation that some other registered candidates submitted fake signatures, and the RNU leader did not want to equate those candidates' "dead souls" with his supporters. In reality, however, either Barkashov did not get the necessary million signatures, or even if he did, which is theoretically possible, he realized that his chances for success or for any respectable result were next to nothing.

Other right-wing radicals comprising CCRNP tried to determine their candidate for the upcoming presidential elections. After a short period of uncertainty (at first, they even stated that they supported the candidacy of then-President B. Yeltsin), CCRNP announced their nominee for the presidency – legendary weight lifter, writer and public figure Yury Vlasov. Although Yu. Vlasov managed to submit the required number of signatures in his support to the Central Election Commission, his election results were a complete disaster - he got only 0.25% of the vote.

By the State Duma elections in 1999, the main nationalist-radical groups – RNU and the NBP – failed to get national registration despite their numerous attempts. Hence, they could not run in federal districts. The NBP tried to join Viktor Antipov's Working Russia and Stanislav Terekhov's Union of Officers. At first, their coalition was called the Front of Working People, then Stalin's

Bloc, but the NBP representatives were not included in the bloc's list of candidates.

Members of the RNU leadership were included in the party list of the movement Salvation whose registration was invalidated by a court decision right before the elections. "Russian Deed", a right-wing radical list close to the Black Hundreds, ran in federal districts and it gained 0.17% of the vote.

Additionally, A. Fedorov's RPPM and the radical Orthodox-monarchistic movement *Za Veru I Otechestvo* (For Faith and Fatherland) of Father Nikon (Belavenets) registered their own federal candidates, but they could not open an electoral bank account before the deadline and therefore could not participate in the elections.

Several RNU members were nominated in single-mandate districts, but some of them did not advertise their party affiliation. According to official and unofficial information about such candidates, 15 candidates listed their RNU affiliation; 7 of them applied for registration; 3 (in Karelia, the Voronezh region and Kaliningrad) were denied registration.

The RNU candidates results in 1999 were as poor as four years earlier. Andrey Dudinov (Stavropol District 55) won 3.4% of the vote, Sergey Galkin (Kavminvody District 53, Stavropol territory) – 4.03%, Nikolay Dengin (Kirov District 92) – 1.26%, Andrey Eremin (Volzhsky District 68, Volgograd region) – 3.1%.

NBP candidate Anatoly Tishin got 2% of the vote in the Mytischy District of the Moscow region.

Other radical nationalists running in single-mandate districts got approximately the same results. For example, leader of the Russian Party Vladimir Miloserdov won 1.15% of the vote. Igor Artemov, the leader of the Russian National Union, got the best results – 14.94% of the vote in the Vladimir region. Nikolay Bondarik, a Nazi from St. Petersburg, got 6.08%. Both candidates mounted very active and expensive campaigns but lost the election despite relatively broad support.

In the presidential election in 2000, the right-wing radicals did not even nominate their own candidate. Rather, they called on the people to vote for others (for Vladimir Putin and Aleksey Podberezkin, in particular), or against all of the above[58].

As of this writing, the most recent elections in which the right-wing radicals actively participated were the elections to the St. Petersburg City Legislature in the end of 2002. The results were very graphic. The three NBP candidates got between 1.2% and 1.4%; the two FP candidates got 0.11% and 0.68%. N. Bondarchuk was supported by 0.85% of the voters.

By and large, we may state that right-wing radicals do not enjoy broad electoral support in Russia today. This is related to both objective (the country is tired of radicalism; people want a stable life; negative associations related to the WWII still exist) and subjective (lack of sound financial sources; the low level of propaganda carried out by nationalists; an initial orientation towards a non-parliamentary strategy) reasons.

Illegal Activities of Right-Wing Radicals
Winning an election has never been the main goal for right-wing radicals. Nationalistic organizations in Russia are not oriented towards elections. On the contrary, nationalist-socialists and other right-wingers prefer the types of activities explicitly covered by the Criminal Code[59].

---

[58] For a more detailed description of the results of the 1999–2000 elections for the right-wing radicals, see Verkhovsky A., Mikhaylovskaya E.., Pribylovsky V. *Natsional-patrioty, Tserkov' i Putin. Parlamentskaya i prezidentskaya kampanii 1999-2000 gg.* Moscow: Panorama, 2000.

[59] A mere listing of the illegal actions carried out by nationalist-radicals would take a lot of space. The entire book Likhachev V, *Natsizm v Rossii.* Moscow: Panorama, 2002, is practically devoted to a detailed description of such facts. See also Likhchev V., Pribylovsky V. Banditstvuyushchie "patrioty" i patriotstvuyushchie bandity. *Russkaya mysl',* No. 4250, December 17-23, 1998; *Russkaya mysl',* No.4251, December 24-30, 1998; Mendelevich E. *Svastika nad gorodom pervogo salyuta.* Orel: Tsentr podderzhki maloy pressy, 1998; *Natsistskie igry.* Moscow: Pik, 2000;

Almost all right-wing radicals – from RNU to the Black Hundreds – form paramilitary groups, which shows their non-parliamentary orientation. Officially, those groups are referred to as "military-patriotic clubs," sports groups etc., but their hierarchical structure, military uniforms and other details clearly show that they are paramilitary units. Naturally, members of these detachments have not been idle, and what they have been doing has not been limited to legal or semi-legal guarding functions. During the 1990s, right-wing radicals were constant characters in the criminal chronicles, accused of various crimes — from illegal weapons possession to murders and blackmailing. RNU members especially distinguish themselves in those ways.

The contrast between the outward "toughness" and the everyday party routines has often depressed rank-and-file party members. Hence, it is no surprise that despite the leadership's emphasis on "respect for law", Barkashov's militants have often resorted to violence against their political opponents and "enemies," as identified by their ethnicity. The cases, in which Barkashov's political opponents and members of ethnic and religious minorities are beaten up, are numerous. But often the crimes committed by the Nazis had no "ideological" grounds. Barkashovites got too involved in the role of the semi-demonic "fascists," portrayed in Soviet movies, and turned into vicious murderers, hired killers, burglars, racketeers and sadists.

Clearly, a large number of illegal actions can be explained mostly by the mentality of RNU members. They are aggressive and prone to violence. On the one hand, the RNU leadership has tried to keep rank-and-file members away from actions that could instantly implicate the movement; but on the other hand, the leadership has attempted to maintain their smoldering hostilities. "We believe that the bright day will come when our iron fist will get tight", says the party anthem. Barkashovites impatiently waited for the leadership's sign indicating that it was time to start. The most impatient ones broke loose and

---

Khinshteyn A. Shest' mgnoveniy russkogo fashizma. *Moskovskiy komsomolets,* December 5, 1997.

committed foolish actions. The more patient ones made and purchased weapons.

A mere enumeration of criminal actions committed by Barkashovites would take many pages. Entire regional branches of RNU have turned into criminal entities. Barkashovites from all over Russia and abroad were accused of terrorism (Perm, Vladivostok), murders (Orel, the Maritime Territory, the Moscow Region, Belorus), assaults (Kostroma, Omsk, Orel, Ekaterinburg, the Moscow Region), burglaries (Saratov, Latvia), weapons possession (the Moscow Region), racketeering (Kostroma, the Sverdlovsk Region), pogroms (Rostov-on-Don, the Krasnodar Territory), and inflaming interethnic hostility (Kaliningrad, Karelia, Orel, Krasnoyarsk, Tomsk, Estonia). When the local leaders were incriminated in illegal actions, the RNU leadership hastily disowned the regional branches. Thus, the RNU leadership refused to recognize the Orel and Vladivostok organizations as their branches after the arrest of the local leaders. However, if the crimes were committed by rank-and-file members, the leadership either ignored such facts, or tried to call in question the actual participation of the RNU comrades in the crimes, or hastily claimed that the perpetrators had nothing to do with RNU or had already been expelled from it. RNU copied that style from "Memory". However, similar methods are typical for more than radical political entities. Many security agencies require that a newly hired employee file both a job application and a resignation letter (undated, of course) simultaneously, in case of unforeseen circumstances.

The same characteristics – guarding functions gradually turning into banditry – were typical for almost all Russian right-wing radicals, such as members of the Russian Party, NRPR or RNU. Beating up 'non-Russians' and carrying out pogroms are simply the main preoccupation and the purpose of existence for skinheads – members of the disorganized right-wing radical racist subculture. There were outright terrorist right-wing radical groups in Russia, too, like the Werewolf Legion or Heaven's Aryans. The still unknown perpetrators of the terrorist acts against synagogues may be added to the same category. Yet, the right-wing terrorism has not become as wide spread in Russia as it has in Europe.

Illegal activities of National Bolsheviks are somewhat different. Crimes committed by NBP members are of a more ideological nature. Often they are mischievous acts against political opponents or embassies of various countries, which is an NBP hallmark, or symbolic attacks on individuals. The National Bolsheviks would prefer to toss a bottle with paint, or a Molotov cocktail at worst, at an embassy building, an egg at the face of a political opponent, or to slap the ex-president of the USSR with a bunch of flowers for "wrecking the country," rather than beat up a person with a non-Russian appearance.

However, the National Bolsheviks have not limited themselves to simple hooliganism, as they realize that a tossed egg cannot hasten a national revolution. Using a rational analysis of the situation in the country, the NBP leadership concluded that the only way to overcome the national passivity and political indifference of the population is to play "the Russian card" in the post-Soviet space. The internal party bulletin NBP-Info (No. 3, 1999) published the "Second Russia" project, which envisioned specific actions targeted against some post-Soviet countries with sizable Russian-speaking minorities — Kazakhstan, Ukraine and Latvia. Actions against those countries could vary in nature including gaining control over some of their territory. The creation of a "Second Russia" was meant to be just the first phase of a national revolution in Russia proper: "Create a second Russia and then move against the first".

After Limonov's arrest, one could suspect that the National Bolsheviks were quite serious about statements like, "Let us organize revolts on the territories that we like and that are of vital importance to the National Bolshevik empire. Basically, we are talking about Southern territories given away to CIS[E14] states. <...> There is only one state precisely fit for establishing a guerilla base for the Russian liberation movement. That is Kazakhstan. <...> Obviously, that is where guerillas should be sent[60]". Limonov wrote in one of his books in the spirit of the "Second Russia" project: "We should not start a rebellion in Moscow for many reasons. First of all, the spark of the rebellion

---

[E14]   CIS stands for the Commonwealth of Independent States (formed after the disintegration of the Soviet Union; Lithuania, Latvia, and Estonia did not enter the CIS).

[60]   NBP-Info, No. 3, 1999.

must be outside Russia. <...> One has to understand that starting a conflict <...> is not an end in itself, but merely the first necessary step of an armed rebellion aimed at changing power in Moscow"[61]. The fact that Limonov and his comrades were arrested in the Altay Territory near the Kazakhstan border takes on a completely different meaning in light of the quotations above.

While Limonov's trial was in full swing in Saratov, the reminiscences of Artem Akopyan, one of the National Bolsheviks who visited Altay, were published in several issues of one of the capital's newspapers[62]. According to the reminiscences, the NBP members were at least conducting reconnaissance on the Russo-Kazakh border. However, one should not draw a firm conclusion regarding the fairness of the accusations against Limonov and his comrades on the basis of the newspaper article. Besides, a statement by the NBP Central Council was published next to the article claiming that everything reported by the author of the article was a fabrication. However, there are no obvious discrepancies or exaggerations in the text. Furthermore, Akopyan's information seems conceivable for a different reason. Limonov himself did not conceal the fact that he went to Kokchetav with a group of his party comrades to take part in a failed separatist riot by Northern Kazakhstan Cossacks in 1997. It is likely that the statement by the NBP Central Council was caused by the fact that the investigation into Limonov's case was still in progress at that time, and any careless word might give more ammunition to the law enforcement agencies to prove Limonov's guilt. That did not help: Akopyan testified at the trial as a key prosecution witness. However, his testimony concerning Limonov and his comrades' preparations for sabotage and terrorist actions in Kazakhstan contained a lot of rubbish. Perhaps, having taken the first step by saying "we moved back and forth across the border" and pressured by the law enforcement agencies, he had to go on by saying "we prepared terrorist acts" even if that was not true. These sketchy facts do not allow us to draw a conclusion on whether the National Bolsheviks were preparing for any actions in Kazakhstan, or on whether all events preceding Limonov and his comrades' arrest were a chain of random events or / and a result of a provocation.

---

[61]   Limonov E. *Anatomiya geroya,* pp. 465-472. Smolensk, 1998.

[62]   Akopyan A. Kak ya delal revolyutsiyu v Kazakhstane. *Stringer,* No. 2, February, 2002, No. 3, March, 2002.

In our opinion, even the outcome of the trial will not let us answer that question.

All of the above pertains only to the 'new' right-wing radicals – nationalist socialists, National Bolsheviks and racists. The 'old' right-wingers – black hundreds and RO Christian fundamentalists – generally have not been involved in extremist activities. Perhaps, the only exception was a small monarchist group in the city of Vyshny Volochok in the Tver region. Its leaders, Aleksandr Sysoev and Evgeny Kharlamov, attempted to start a RO Christian revolution by storming the city police building and killing three policemen[63].

2.3   State Policy on Nationalist Radicals

After a long period of passivity and indifference even towards overt law-breaking, politicians started to counter nationalist radicals in the late 1990s[64]. Since 1998, the government's pressure on radicals has sharply increased. In the past two years, this "tightening the screws" has occurred in the context of a more general change in the political life of the country and it appears quite natural in the new environment.

Registration Denial
Initially, nationalist radicals encountered difficulties in their activities when they tried to obtain national Russian registration. The registration was necessary for taking part in the State Duma elections in federal districts. In the latest state Duma elections in 1999, the registration had to be obtained at least a year in advance, i.e., no later than December 19, 1998.

---

[63]   This little known story is described in: Krovavaya Paskha. *Oprichnina*, No. 11, 2002. From time to time, Sysoev published articles in the spirit of religious anti-Semitism in Orthodox patriotic newpapers. See, for example, Sysoev A. Pravda o blagodatnom ogne. *Oprichnina*, No. 9, December, 2001.

[64]   We are not discussing the issue of whether the existing legislation is adequate to oppose nationalist extremism and neo-nazism. On the legal aspect of the issue, including the new Law to Counter Extremism, see Verkhovskiy A. *Gosudarstvo protiv radikal'nogo natsionalizma. Chto delat' i chego ne delat'?* Moscow: Panorama, 2002.

Since only two nationalist radical organizations — RNU and the NBP — had truly national scope, the following discussion deals only with those two organizations. RNU held a national Russian convention required for registration in February 1997. By the end of that year, the Justice Ministry managed to deny RNU registration twice under different pretexts. First, having found a number of technical glitches, the Justice Ministry sent back the RNU charter for revision. After the resubmission, the Justice Ministry ruled that the registration procedure had been violated, because amendments may be added to a charter only by the convention rather than the Central Council, even though the convention delegated its powers to the Council. Barkashovites decided to appeal the Justice Ministry's decision in court. On January 5, 1998, the Tagansky district court denied the appeal, confirming that any amendments in the charter could be made only by the convention. On April 22, 1998, a Moscow city court refused to reconsider the ruling of the Tagansky district court.

Significantly, the Ministry's lawyers did not even try to prove that the RNU program and propaganda materials violate the RF Constitution and federal legislation, or that the use of the swastika in the party's emblem is illegal. They could have stretched the law on "Immortalization of the Soviet People's Victory in WWII" of May 19, 1995, or other administrative violations. Instead, they found technical glitches to find fault with the movement's charter. But Justice Minister Sergey Stepashin stated that if RNU would continue its attempts to register, denial would be based on essence rather than form.

The NBP's situation followed the same pattern. The party held its all-Russian founding congress on October 1 – 2, 1998. On November 6, 1998, the Justice Ministry denied the party registration finding faults with the charter and allegedly forged records of regional branches. On November 14, the NBP hastily held a second special national congress to make all necessary modifications in the charter. On December 18, the Justice Ministry denied registration again. On August 18, 1999, the Tagansky district court rejected a complaint against the Justice Ministry.

The government's pressure on RNU was not limited to denial of national registration. The party leadership chose an overt conflict with the central government, which resulted in lengthy legal battles.

Still trying to get national registration and participate in the elections, RNU decided to hold its second all-Russian congress, which was supposed to make all necessary changes in the charter. The congress was scheduled for December 19, 1998. However, Moscow Mayor Yuri Luzhkov made a decision to ban the congress. It seems as though Yury Luzhkov's passionate anti-fascist fervor was related to the beginning of the election campaign and the Mayor's image during the campaign was supposed to be that of a respectable but tough person, a democrat to a degree, balancing patriotism with anti-fascism. A wave of public protest was instigated to allow the authorities to ban the congress[65]. After the rallies of indignant anti-fascists facilitated by the authorities, the government of Moscow passed a resolution on December 15 to ban the congress on the pretext that it "posed a threat to peace and security of Muscovites" (Resolution No. 951, of December 15). Luzhkov declared that "gatherings of this sort cannot be held in Moscow now or ever in the future[66]".

Obviously, the legal basis of the ban was problematic. The RNU local branch operated in Moscow legally and, according with its registered charter, the organization was entitled to conduct its activities in the city. Therefore, there were no legal grounds to ban the congress. Using this argument, A. Bakashov declared his intent to appeal to the prosecutor's office with a complaint against the Moscow Mayor's illegal decision[67]. Even Vladimir Putin, who was the FSB Director at that time, doubted the legality of the Moscow government resolution. "As long as they (Barkashovites) function within the framework of

---

[65]   A verbal communication from chairman of the Moscow Anti-fascists Center E. Proshechkin. See also Deych M. Yuriy Luzhkov v interesnom polozhenii. *Moskovskiy komsomolets*, December 15, 1998.

[66]   Babichenko D. Moskva zapretila s"ezd chernorubashechnikov. *Segodnya*, December 16, 1996.

[67]   *Ibid.*

existing legislation, they are entitled to hold their legal meetings. Law enforcement agencies should not stretch the law, let alone break it[68]".

The Moscow prosecutor's office responded on December 16, 1998. It stated that nothing illegal had been found in the Moscow government's resolution. The sports complex "Ismailovo," where the congress was supposed to be held, had been hastily closed down for repairs related to the "dangerous conditions of its chairs."

After a hue and cry was raised, the RNU headquarters were promptly kicked out of Terletsky park on the technical ground of not complying with fire safety regulations. At the same time, tax police began to check RNU's security units looking for any violations. Businessmen who used Barkashov's security guards got suggestions to let them go.

On January 18, 1999, RNU filed a lawsuit in a Moscow city court asking to cancel the ban on their congress. On February 11, the court denied the petition. Moscow government's lawyer, Alexander Tarasenko, succeeded in proving that the aims stated in the charter contradicted the real activities of the movement.

In January 1999, the Moscow government ruled that RNU emblem was a "nazi" one. This justified fining Barkashovites for carrying their badge and sleeve band, or for disseminating their newspaper, under the Moscow law of January 15, 1997, "On Administrative Responsibility for Producing, Disseminating and Displaying Nazi Symbols in the Territory of the City of Moscow". It is worth noting that a year earlier, in February of 1998, the Moscow prosecutor's office had already examined RNU symbols at the request of the Moscow Anti-Fascist Center for the purpose of categorizing them as nazi ones. At that time, a commission of experts studied the matter. According to a report written by the Institute of World History of the Russian Academy of Sciences, only the symbols of Germany of 1935 — 1945 could be correctly referred to

---

[68]   Amelina Ya. Zapret s"ezda RNE ne zakonen. *Ekspress-Khronika*, December 21, 1998.

as nazi symbols, i.e. a "black, diamond-shaped swastika inscribed in a white circle against a red background." Therefore, the commission stated that within the framework of this law, RNU emblems cannot be considered as nazi symbols"[69].

The resulting situation was paradoxical: the authorities seemed to be unable to clearly explain and justify the necessity of countering nazis, even though this necessity was obvious to everybody, including the authorities themselves and society at large. Instead, they used excuses like "dangerous conditions of the chairs" or "violations of fire safety regulations". The fact that the police were instructed to detain nazis rather than "persons of Caucasus nationality" did not create the impression that the occurring actions were legitimate. It was abundantly clear that the city authorities were driven by political rather than legal motives.

In February of 1999, staff of the Moscow prosecutor's office reinforced with a special police unit, searched RNU's Moscow premises, including those that were registered by fake organizations (for instance, parishes of the True Orthodox Church)[70]. According to the RNU Central Council, more than twenty searches were carried out in offices and apartments of RNU activists.

On March 26, 1999, the RF Supreme Court heard the appeal of the decision made by the Moscow city court of February 11, which ruled that the ban on the RNU convention imposed by the Moscow city administration was legal. The appeal was filed by the RNU leadership. Their lawyers argued during the hearing that any restrictions on the activity of a political organization may be imposed only on the basis of Federal Law "On Public Organizations". According to this law, regional authorities have no right to introduce such prohibitions; and the Mayor' s administration "was driven by a number of emotions",

---

[69]   A letter to E. Proshechkin on the letterhead of the Moscow Government Administration of March 3, 1998, signed by I. Shilov, head of the department in charge of the law enforcement agencies. (Xerox copy in the author's archive.)

[70]   Sudovtsev G. Oskvernyayut khramy. *Zavtra*, No. 10, March, 1999; see also: "Zayavlenie Tsentral'nogo Soveta RNE", March 3, 1999. (Xerox copy in the author's archive.)

namely, by letters from anti-fascist and human rights organizations that are themselves the "targets of a lawsuit". However, the court denied the appeal by referring to Federal Law "On the Status of the Capital".

Banning Existing Organizations

On March 3, 1999, Moscow Prosecutor Sergei Gerasimov filed a lawsuit with the Moscow city court aimed at invalidating RNU's Moscow registration. According to the materials gathered by the prosecutor's office, "RNU activities are inconsistent with the charter requirements and goals of the organization, requirements of the RF Constitution, federal laws and other administrative ordinances". On the same day, the Moscow City Duma passed the bill in the first reading on the responsibility for producing, disseminating and displaying "any images resembling the nazi swastika".

On April 16–19, 1999, a session of the Butyrsky district court of the city of Moscow was held in the clubhouse of Severny settlement to consider a petition by the Moscow Prosecutor. Barkashovites were accused of violations, such as disseminating their newspaper in inappropriate places, involving minors in political activities, as well as spreading their activities onto a neighboring district, the Moscow Region. It is not hard to notice that once again, the accusations against RNU were of technical nature only. On April 19, Judge Marina Golubeva ruled that the RNU Moscow Regional Branch be liquidated as a legal entity.

On April 22, the court invalidated the publication permit of the Russian Order newspaper. Initially, the State Committee on Press argued that the newspaper had not been published for more than a year. After RNU representative S. Poluboyarov presented to the court documents showing that the last year's (the latest) issue had been constantly updated, the State Committee on Press modified its accusations. It turned out that the editorial board and the founder of the paper had not filed either the charter or an agreement substituting the charter after the registration (in 1991!). The petition of the State Committee on Press was approved.

Despite the lack of its own registration, RNU attempted to take part in the elections as part of the registered national movement Salvation. The list of candidates of the movement in federal districts approved on October 18, 1999, was headed by A. Barkashov.

As soon as the list of candidates was submitted, the Justice Ministry filed a petition with the Supreme Court to invalidate the registration of Salvation. The suit was based on the fact that Salvation submitted invalid information on its regional branches in process of its registration. Ten of them were not found during verification. Despite the technical nature of the complaint, it was obvious that the reason for Salvation's problems was Barkashov. Justice Minister Yury Chaika stated that, "persons sharing fascist ideology cannot become members of the Legislature[71]".

A week after the filing of the petition by the Justice Ministry, the RF Supreme Court dismissed it for two reasons. First, there were no legal grounds: not a single warning had been issued. Second, the Justice Ministry should have petitioned a lower court. The Supreme Court could have suspended activities of the organization only if these activities had violated the law. The Ministry's blunder - registering a fictitious organization - should have been corrected in the lower court.

On November 2, 1999, the federal list of the Salvation movement was registered by the Central Election Committee. The Justice Ministry, in turn, filed a complaint with the Zamoskvoretsky district court of the city of Moscow. On November 9, 1999, the first hearing was held. To please the Justice Ministry, all pending cases were put aside. Normally, it takes several months between filing a complaint and the trial. (For example, The NBP's complaint against the Justice Ministry was filed in December of 1998 and the case was heard only in August of 1999). On November 12, the court invalidated federal registration of Salvation, because the number of its regional branches was insufficient.

---

[71]   Kamyshev D. Barkashov voydet v kazhdyy dom. *Kommersant"* , November 3, 1999.

On November 16, 1999, Salvation was sued for forgery of certain documents. The investigation carried out by law enforcement agencies revealed that Salvation submitted falsified data on the number of its regional branches in the process of its registration in 1998.

Salvation lawyers tried to appeal the decision of the Zamoskvoretsky district court that invalidated the movement's registration, but on November 24 the Moscow city court agreed with the lower court.

On November 25, a session of the Central Election Commission unanimously removed Salvation from the ballot. On November 29, Salvation representatives appealed the decision of the Central Election Commission to the RF Supreme Court. On December 3, the Supreme Court dismissed the appeal. On December 16, 1999, the Appeal Board of the Supreme Court affirmed the legality of the invalidation of the Salvation registration.
Salvation appeared on the ballot in the elections on December 19, but it was crossed out by hand.

The victory of the government over the nationalist radical movement clearly proved two points. First, it became clear that, given a certain political will, existing legislation is quite adequate to counter nazis. But on the other hand, the story of banning the RNU congress, invalidating its registration in Moscow and keeping Salvation away from the elections made it equally clear that bureaucrats have no political judgment and no ability to respond to extremists in a clear and meaningful way. Rather, it showed their penchant for backstage manipulations.

Beating RNU by the government caused a crisis in the movement and its split. The position of "Extremist Organization Number 1" was gradually taken over by the NBP, and soon it was its turn to face the authorities and law enforcement agencies.

In March 2001, local Barkashovites approached Saratov NBP activists with an offer to sell several assault rifles. The deal went through and on March 10, National Bolsheviks bought two rifles, and then four more. The National Bolsheviks who tried to bring the rifles from Saratov to Ufa were arrested. The circumstances of the case give reason to guess that Barkashov's people were provocateurs[72]. The Barkashovites were not even detained. The arrested were the leader of the Vladimir NBP branch Nina Silina and several party members from Nizhny Novgorod and Saratov: Oleg Laletin, Vladimir Pentelyuk and Dmitry Koryagin. A wave of searches swept NBP offices, the party activists' residential apartments in Moscow and other regions in late March.

On April 7, 2001, FSB arrested Eduard Limonov on a bee farm twelve kilometers away from the village of Bannoye of the Ust-Koksinsky district of the Altai territory. According to eyewitnesses, about a hundred people were involved in the detention. Along with Limonov, one of the founders of the *Limonka* newspaper, Sergei Aksenov, was arrested. On April 9, both National Bolsheviks were moved to the Lefortovo prison on charges of "organizing an armed criminal group". Limonov was suspected of preparing an armed riot in Northeastern Kazakhstan aimed at setting up an autonomous Russian republic there. Latysheva M. O. On the role of the Russian National Unity in Limonov's arrest, http://www.agentura.ru/press/latysheva/limonov/

Originally, Limonov and Aksenov were charged under Article 222, Section 3 of the RF Criminal Code ("illegal acquisition, storing, and transportation of firearms"). On September 6, 2001, Limonov was additionally charged under Article 205, Section 3 ("terrorism committed by an organized group"), and Article 208, Section 1 ("establishing and commanding an illegal armed formation") of the RF Criminal Code. On November 28, 2001, Limonov got yet another charge under Article 280, Section 2 of the RF Criminal Code ("public calls for changing the constitutional system of the Russian Federation made through the mass media").

Limonov believed that his arrest was an FSB provocation. In any case, even if the rifle deal was not staged by special services, Limonov's involvement in purchasing rifles was eventually proved only after the testimony of one of the

---

72   Latysheva M. O. On the role of the Russian National Unity in Limonov's arrest, http://www.agentura.ru/press/latysheva/limonov/

suspects (the other suspects denied it). All other charges were eventually dismissed.

On August 9, 2001, the department of the Justice Ministry for the Moscow Region sent a petition to the regional court asking for a termination of the NBP activities on a formal pretext. The justification for the petition was the fact that the party lost its legal address, because the organization that had provided the address - the Association of the Veterans of Afghanistan in the town of Electrostal - had been liquidated.

Bureaucrats of the Justice Ministry sent mail to the former legal address requesting submission of information on NBP activities. The absence of answers became a formal pretext to sue the party. During the hearing, evidence proving that the party existed and had repeatedly filed applications for a national registration was presented. On September 27, 2001, the Moscow regional court sided with the NBP, dismissed the Justice Ministry's petition claiming that Interregional Public Association "National Bolshevik Party" ceased legal activity, and refused to remove this organization from the state register of legal entities. Representatives of the Justice Ministry appealed the decision of the Moscow regional court to the RF Supreme Court, but the latter left intact the decision of the Moscow regional court on November 19, 2001.

On January 9 – 10, the Moscow regional court held a hearing and dismissed another petition to liquidate the NBP filed by the Moscow regional prosecutor's office. The prosecutor's office claimed that the NBP violated Article 16 of Federal Law on Public Organizations banning activities of associations whose goals or actions are aimed at violent change of the constitutional system of the RF. Representatives of the prosecutor's office presented the Limonov case as evidence. However, the court agreed with NBP lawyer Sergei Belyak's arguments that the court must not make decisions on the basis of materials of an unfinished case. Furthermore, the use of such materials is a gross violation of the principle of confidentiality of investigation. The court suspended the prosecutor's office case until the criminal case against Limonov was finished.

By March of 2002, the investigation of the Limonov case had been completed. By July of 2002, the NBP newspaper Limonka was banned. The NBP started to publish a new newspaper, registered in advance, titled *General-naya Liniya* (Cardinal Line). They kept the design, including the font and the large title on the front page, as well as the numbering system of Limonka's issues.

In September of 2002, the trial of Limonov and five party activists started. The prosecutor asked the court to sentence the NBP leader to 14 years in prison. But due to defense lawyer Belyak's brilliant speech, the defendants were found guilty only of "illegal acquisition, storing, and transportation of firearms". On March 14, 2003, Eduard Limonov was sentenced to 4 years in prison. The other defendants got even shorter terms. On June 18, 2003, a closed court session held in forced-labor camp number 13 of the city of Engels granted Limonov's early release from prison.

Current Situation and Future of the Right-Wing Radical Movement
Right-wing radicals acted without any restraint in Russia for a long time. They called for changing the constitutional system and constantly violated Russian legislation. Yet, practically they had not faced any significant opposition from authorities or law enforcement agencies up until the late 1990s. There was an opinion that existing legislation did not allow for curbing extremist activities and propaganda.

The events of 1998 – 2002 demonstrated that given political will, current legislation is adequate at least to keep radicals out of election participation and to prosecute the most extreme and bold nazis. Yet, the same events revealed another side of the problem. The government fought extremism using formal excuses and only when it was advantageous in the current political situation. Of course, the relation between the government and right-wing radicals is part of the global problem of the current state of legal standards in the Russian Federation. A law is implemented fully and efficiently only when the authorities want it to be, and it is applied only against those who somehow displease them.

Inconsistent as they are, and not always competent and often with doubtful legal justification, the government's actions still bring results. The direct pressure on the NBP gradually makes the "loosest" party check its own actions and propaganda. If the most consistent and uncompromising National Bolsheviks still try to continue their activities under such conditions, then they will obviously have to resort to extra-parliamentary methods. The banning of the RNU convention, shutting down of its newspaper and pressuring its Moscow organization were also not the final reasons for the crisis and split of RNU. Now, RNU has no chances for revival as a unified organization and for participation in the political process. Moreover, it does not have any chances even for transformation into an underground extremist group, while the NBP does. With the passage of the Law on Counteracting Extremist Activity and, to a larger degree, with the growing realization of the necessity to do so on the part of the bureaucrats, one may expect stronger actions by the state against the most radical organizations, such as the NBP, as well as actions towards "taming" moderate nationalists, such as UOC.

However, a certain pressure by the state on the right-wing parties and movements notwithstanding, it was not that pressure per se, but other factors that caused the decline of the National-Patriotic organizations. Subjective factors undoubtedly played a certain role. Even the new Law on Political Parties that encourages party activities could not make the right-wing radicals form a powerful national organization, although there have been several attempts to do so in the last year. All such associations have come out flabby, eclectic, and more narrow than they were initially meant to be. No broad unification of the radical nationalists has happened, while the parties trying to assert their independence are too weak and small in numbers to hope for success.

On the other hand, we should note that the new law has not become the sieve needed to filter out minuscule groups. Despite the increased number of quantitative parameters required for registration, the requirement are still of a technical, bureaucratic nature. In reality, nobody verifies the submitted data unless a special need arises.

The current crisis of the right-wing organizations is caused by reasons of both objective and subjective in nature. Objective reasons for the right wing crisis include the general socio-ideological climate in society and the high level of consolidation of society around the present President. Besides, the political elite has appropriated right-wing radicals' slogans potentially attractive to the masses of people and skillfully utilized them for their own public relations purposes, which has deprived the radicals of their main weapon – the ability to criticize the government.

Subjective reasons for the right wing crisis include extremely low levels of propaganda, a primitive ideology, the lack of a creative approach to the main contemporary problems, recycling of ideological clichés irrelevant to the current situation, personal ambitions of some leaders, etc.

This situation creates very uncomfortable conditions for the existence of the right-wing radical political organizations. It strips them of the slightest chance for success, at least in the near future. And the old nationalist organizations keep losing the support of society.

However, the arguments above do not mean that the agenda of nationalism and xenophobia loses its relevance for Russian society. New problems come up. Teenagers' nationalist activity manifests itself now not in participating in the work of political parties, which is mostly boring and futile, but in street assaults and pogroms against "enemies" chosen on the basis of ethnicity. The level of xenophobia and nationalism in the contemporary Russian society is expressed not in the electoral support for the nationalist parties, but in people's relating positively to the perpetrators of pogroms and in their demands for repressive steps from the government towards "illegal immigrants".

This knot of ethno-demographic and social problems gets tighter. This author is pessimistic about the short-term future. The situation will worsen, the level of xenophobia will rise along with the number of victims of the street fights. The authorities will play footsy with such attitudes because of their popularity in society, and that is fraught with serious problems down the road for Russia as a multiethnic country. The current situation makes it problematic to solidify the notion of *Rossiyane* (inhabitants of Russia), which is a necessary condition for the stability of society. The country's consciousness still attaches a lot of significance to ethnicity, whereas the tensions among ethnic groups grows and sometimes turns into open violence. Only a deliberate and consistent policy by the government in various spheres – from law-enforcement to education - may improve the situation. So far, one cannot see any sign even of understanding this problem by the highest echelons of the power structure.

II   Propaganda

1   The Anti-Semitic Press: What Is It?

1.1   General Overview of the Nationalist and Communist Press

It is known that the printed word possesses qualities that are indispensable for political propaganda and persuasion. We know that "the 'Spark' kindled a flame[E15]" and many revolutionary leaders, both on the left and on the right, started their activities as newspaper editors. But the situation in the field of propaganda has definitely changed since then. There have appeared much more effective and advanced forms for influencing the mass consciousness. However, the radical nationalists practically have no chance to access radio or TV in Russia now. The printed word for them is the main, if not the only, way to bring their ideas to people. Yet, with the advances of computer publishing and duplicating technology, almost everyone may publish several hundred copies of a flyer. As a rule, when anti-fascist minded journalists talk about neo-nazism, anti-Semitism and extremism, they illustrate their stories with horrible quotations from precisely such "publications". What does the radical nationalist press consisting of one hundred to two hundred newspapers look like?

In this chapter, we will concentrate on several issues. First, we will see how widely radical nationalist publications are distributed. We will discuss their circulation, periodicity and the regions of their distribution. Separately, we will discuss the darkest question – their funding source. Second, we will consider the contents of the nationalist propaganda: what subjects are discussed in these publications, what role is played by xenophobia in general and by anti-

---

[E15]   The expression "The spark will kindle a flame" is part of A. Pushkin's poem dedicated to the Decembrists, Russian Army officers who plotted to overthrow the Czar in 1825. Their plot failed and they were exiled. In 1900, the socialist revolutionaries who founded the newspaper *Iskra*, the Spark, used that line as a motto for the newspaper. The author alludes to the fact that *Iskra* kindled the revolution of 1917.

Semitism in particular. And finally, the last question for us will be the position of the state towards radical publications.

To begin with, let us try to draw a general panorama of the radical nationalist publications along with a brief look at their characteristics. The most popular and influential radical publication is certainly the newspaper *Zavtra*, (Tomorrow, editor-in-chief – writer Aleksandr Prokhanov). Its circulation is 100,000 copies; it is published weekly. Tomorrow maintains a mixed audience including communists and nationalists of various ideological persuasions. It would be impossible to create a consistent ideology from the articles published in the newspaper – it is eclectic by definition. On the one hand, its eclecticism allows it to maintain the interest of a wide readership. On the other hand, it makes the newspaper incapable of influencing the course of elections, for example, because there is no consistency in covering various candidates. The newspaper may waver between enthusiastic support and outrageous maligning of certain political figures. Tomorrow creates an emotional setting, not an ideology. The editorials written by its editor-in-chief are expressive sketches with elements of satire, grotesque, and a lot of emotions. Prokhanov makes the reader hate or love, be indignant or delighted, angry or sympathetic (obviously, the negative emotions are applied more actively than the positive ones). However, it is impossible to understand what kind of state system is being advocated by the newspaper.

The same applies to the second most popular left-wing nationalist newspaper Duel (editor-in-chief - Yury Mukhin, circulation – 12,000 copies, published weekly). Duel occupies a narrower niche of the left-wing nationalism and it does not enjoy any prestige among right-wing nationalists. However, since the traditions of soviet patriotism and nostalgia for the USSR merge in society with painful social and ethno-demographic problems associated with the R. F.'s present structure, an eclectic mix of some elements of the soviet ideology with a superpower's nationalism is pretty common among the population.

Both Tomorrow and Duel attach a lot of importance to negative materials that create an "image of an enemy" on an emotional level. Because of pro-communist leanings of these publications, the notion of an enemy is viewed primarily in social terms, and only afterwards in ethnic terms. Anti-Semitism plays a large role in Duel in the form of stories about how Jews ruined the USSR, about their atrocities in the Middle East, or how they first fostered Hitler, set him against the USSR and then invented the Holocaust in order to discredit the ideas of nationalism, and make the world feel guilty and thus untie the Jews' hands in Palestine. Duel is the main publication in Russia pursuing the mythology of Holocaust revisionism. For Tomorrow, the Jewish issue is less prominent, although it constantly comes up in the newspaper. The Jewish issue is shaped in Tomorrow either as a social or a religious one. In that sense, the following two articles published in the same issue of the newspaper are typical[73].

In the editorial "Let us look for Himmler among SPS[E16] members", Prokhanov writes: "Russian big capital, or small capital for that matter, does not exist at all. A Russian is penniless, flat broke now... Presently, big capital in Russia is Jewish and it was unjustly gained. And that capital has a huge temptation to establish a dictatorship to push Muslim capital, but mainly to put down the growing protest of the fleeced indigenous people". In the same issue, Mikhail Nazarov theorizes in an article titled "Fascism from Shulkhan Arukh[E17]" on the subject of "hatred towards the people" by the Jewish religion, its cynicism, brutality, vileness, amorality, etc.

However, anti-Semitism cannot be the main, or even the most important, topic for such publications aiming at a wide audience. Unlike nostalgia for the Soviet empire or a rejection of the West and democratic institutions, anti-Semitism does not perform a consolidating function even among the nationalists. "Caucasus-phobia" and "America-phobia" are definitely present on the pages of these publications as well, but these topics are not the main ones for their authors.

---

73   Zavtra, No. 30 (453), 2002.
E16   SPS is the Russian acronym of Soyuz pravykh sil (Union of Right Forces, URF), a liberal political party advocating free market reforms, among other things.
E17   Shulkhan Arukh is a compilation of Jewish Law as of the 16th century.

The nationalist press proper is directed towards a significantly more narrow audience. Since such publications aim at the already convinced nationalists, the purpose of their materials is not to persuade the reader to hate, but rather to maintain his level of hatred. There is a certain category of readers who need papers describing the horrible details of the 'zhido-mason' conspiracy or endlessly repeating the stories of schoolgirls raped by the people from the Caucasus, as if these stories were an addictive drug. The overwhelming majority of the radical nationalist publications target precisely this audience. Their circulation is small and they come out very infrequently (we will list the most conspicuous ones below), but they have a stable group of ardent fans whose financial support allows the publications to exist. Any materials of a positive nature are practically absent here. The main part of these newspapers is aggressive xenophobia, primarily - anti-Semitism followed by "Caucasus-phobia" and "West-phobia".

Among the newspapers fitting the characterization above, we may mention *Nashe otechestvo* – Our Fatherland, *Novaya sistema* – New System (both are published in St. Petersburg), *Era Rossii* – Russia's Era, *Russkie vedomosti* – Russian Register, *Russkaya Pravda* – Russian Truth (Moscow), *Kolokol* – Bell (Volgograd), *Slavyanin* – Slav and *Slavyansky nabat* – Slavic Alarm Bell (Vologda), "Aleks-Inform" (Samara), etc.

Our Fatherland (editor-in-chief – Evgeny Shchekatikhin, circulation fluctuates from 5,500 to 10,000 copies, periodicity – twice a month, earlier – three times a month) is the flagship of the domestic anti-Semitic press. Radical, brazenly anti-Semitic articles take much of the printed space. The expressions that the editor and authors use in their writing about Jews are simply shocking. It is embarrassing to quote the newspaper, but to substantiate our point, we shall provide a few statements. "The zhids' power does to the indigenous Russian population whatever it wants. If the zhids-oligarchs are thirsty for Russian blood, they drink it; if they want to kill someone, they kill him[74]"; "The slogan

---

[74]   Vladislavov St. Pust' slugi okkupatsionnogo rezhima ne stanovyatsya na puti russ-kikh patriotov. *Nashe Otechestvo*, No. 177, June, 2002.

'Death to the zhids!' is becoming quite timely[75]; "the way out of the present situation is to fire all zhids from the positions of power[76]"; etc.

A standard text at the end of each issue acknowledging financial support of the newspaper ends with this sentence: "Let the AIDS-carrying zhido-masonic plague vanish from the Russian land!" The newspaper flashes expressions such as "despicable zhids", "a pack of Jewish rats", "there is no limit to the zhids' obnoxiousness and their pathological perversion!", "the zhids' irreparably defective, wildly tribal mentality[77]".

The same themes and practically the same expressions were utilized in the presently closed Vologodsk newspaper Slav (editor-in-chief - Vladimir Popov not to be confused with his Novosibirsk-Moscow namesake who is the editor-in-chief of Russia's Era).

Similarly unrestrained anti-Semitic propaganda not supported by any logical arguments is contained in all publications listed above. For example, the editor-in-chief of the Samara newspaper Aleks-Inform[78] in his editorial states that "the zhids confuse us with their slogan 'Liberty, Equality, and Fraternity'". The author mockingly calls URF "the Union of Filthy Zionists"[E18]; Zionism in his words is "super-fascism beyond comparison with Hitler, the Jews way outstrip him". The author calls Zionism the "main enemy" and those who deny that – "sold-out kike-lovers". The same issue contains a sample of anti-Semitic expressions attributed to prominent figures of various centuries from Cicero ("the Jews belong to the dark and repulsive force") and evangelist John ("they are children of lies and their father is the devil") to Dostoevsky ("the zhids will destroy Russia") and Duhring ("... solving the zhid problem is a duty of all countries. The zhids threaten not this or that nation separately, but the entire mankind").

---

75 Nashe Otechestvo, No. 178 (editorial).
76 Nashe Otechestvo, No. 176, May, 2002 (editorial comments on the article "Ritual'noe beschinstvo zhidov" by Zenkin A.)
77 All examples are taken from a single issue of the newspaper: No. 176, May of 2002.
78 Kitter O. Kommuno-sionizm. Aleks-Inform, No. 20, 2002.
E18 The Russian acronyms for the Union of Right Forces and the Union of Filthy Zionists are the same.

Another article in the same issue is titled "How to Expel Occupiers" written by Yu. Slobozhaninov. The author claims that "our country has been captured by a Zionist-Caucasian gang". The main enemy of the Russian people is the Jews, because the "hatred towards the people is fostered in Jews by Judaism, Talmudism, Zionism, and Freemasonry". The author uses boldface to highlight his conclusion: "The Jews do not belong in human society, because they have adopted crimes against mankind as their national practice. In Russia, for example, they have exterminated about 200 million people since 1917".

Probably, it does not make sense to characterize all these newspapers in detail. Quotations similar to the ones above can be easily found in any issue of such publications. It is interesting that radical anti-Semitism that is pathological in itself gradually morphs into decidedly schizophrenic concepts.

For example, the author of an article in issue 21 of the newspaper New System (editor-in-chief - Tamara Mishchenkova, circulation – 6,000 copies, published once in 2 – 3 months) begins with declaring the fact of Jewish conspiracy ("having reached power in Russia, the Jews sent agriculture back 140 years"). At the end, he says that Jews promote a pernicious meat diet to make "goyim" die, among other things, from Mad Cow disease – which is nature's normal reaction to cruelty, because the "anti-material body of the Earth has a cow's shape". Perhaps, that article is worth quoting: "Section V, paragraph 5 of a memo to the delegates of the World Zionist Congress simply says that a goy's blood must be acidic, not alkaline. Acidic blood is poisonous, killing him. Only alkaline blood is normal and only vegetarians have it. The same memo, Section X, paragraph 2 has a recommendation to "advertise eating meat" as the main product oxidizing blood and "avoid mentioning the fact that the ancient Slavs did not eat meat. As a result, the vegetarians make up only one fifth of the population of the earth[79]".

---

[79]   Having taken power, the Jews lowered the productivity of Russian agriculture back to the level of 1860. *Novaya sistema*, No. 21, 2001. The article is not signed, but judging from her inimitable style, it could be written only by the newspaper's editor-in-chief Tamara Mishchenkova.

This rambling train of thought is a rule for the rabid anti-Semites rather than a funny exception. The newspaper Russia's Era (editor-in-chief - Vladimir Popov not to be confused with his Vologotsk namesake, circulation fluctuates between 2,000 and 5,000 copies, periodicity – twice a month) arrived at the conclusion that the Jews are descendants of the "bald marsh apes[80]".

However, this panorama of the radical press is not limited to publications pre-occupied with the Jewish question and with xenophobia in general. Russia's Era exploits the Caucasian theme no less than the Jewish one; the presently banned Russian Register used to write about the "Zionist-Caucasian mafia" as an integrated entity. Most of the party-affiliated publications obviously differ from the above-mentioned papers, simply because they have to provide some positive concepts and promote their ideology in addition to negative materials. Since by definition a political party tries to spread its ideology as widely as possible, xenophobia and other repulsive materials, like the ones quoted above, occupy less space in party publications.

The most radical newspapers are published by these parties: the NBP (Li-monka, Smerch – Tornado), PNP (I am Russian, Izhevskaya diviziya – Iz-hevsk Division), RNU (Russian Order, Russky svet – Russian Light, Evpaty Kolovrat[E19]), National-Patriotic Front Memory (Memory), the Black Hundred (the Black Hundred), the movement RA (Right Resistance), NPGR (Russky Front – Russian Front, Natsionalnaya Gazeta – National Gazette), etc.

In the 1990s, the most widely distributed newspaper was RNU's Russian Or-der (editor-in-chief – Sergey Poluboyarov, the circulation reached 500,000, the newspaper was distributed free of charge). Russian Order has also the dubious distinction of being the most boring nationalist newspaper. Lately, the paper has been published once a year and then RNU activists distributed it to the population for months. The main enemies portrayed by the paper are the "world plutocracy", "Zionist globalism", "Jewish theomachist civilization", while

---

80   See, for example, Era Rossii, No. 12 (80), June,2002.
E19   A legendary Russian hero who fought the Tataro-Mongol invaders in the 13th cen-tury.

the main positive values are RO Christianity, race, national identification, discipline, and order. Black-hundredist newspapers – Memory and the Black Hundred – that come out very sporadically, too, but have a much smaller circulation, languidly expose the "zhido-masonic conspiracy" and castigate "mankind-hating, satanic Judaism" as well (besides, Caucasus-phobia is present in the Black Hundred also). However, they put much more stress on the "positives": Russian history, culture, literature, spirituality, RO Christian values and authorities.

The most radical, yet bright and unique, party newspaper was Limonka (now titled Fundamental Line, circulation fluctuated around 10,000, periodicity – once every two weeks, editor-in-chief – Aleksey Volynets and earlier – Eduard Limonov). The xenophobia of the Limonovites is directed against the West and the values of the contemporary European civilization, against America, against various peoples (Croatians, Ukrainians, Crimean Tatars, Finns, practically any people) and religions (Catholics, Protestants, sometimes even against the RO Christians, various sects, etc). That xenophobia is expressed in lengthy articles (for example, a series of articles "There are bad peoples!" by Limonov or articles explaining why it was necessary to deport the Crimean Tatars, the Chechens or how the Finns misbehaved during the Russo-Finnish war written by A. Volynets under the pseudonym Viy) as well as slogans like "Kill the Yankee!". A larger theme for Limonka is social hatred towards the rich ("Eat the rich!", "Kill a capitalist!"), the bureaucrats, policemen, journalists, the institution of family,… Unlike many other publications, the National Bolsheviks avoid exploiting anti-Semitism when they describe social problems. Moreover, they position themselves as a party that is not anti-Semitic, which obviously does not quite agree with reality: certain strong anti-Jewish and / or anti-Israeli passages have appeared in the NBP newspaper.

RA's newspaper Right Resistance (circulation – 1,000, periodicity – once every two months, editor-in-chief – Konstantin Kasimovsky, earlier – Aleksandr Eliseev) also intentionally got rid of anti-Semitism. Its predecessor, the newspaper Storm Trooper published by the same people was very aggressive and unrestrainedly anti-Semitic. In order to avoid old mistakes and not to provide a pretext for being banned, Right Resistance tries to stay away from anti-Semitism, (which is not always successful though[81]), and even demonstratively supported Israel in its policies on the occupied territories. The main target of xenophobia for the editorial board and the authors of Right Resistance is the Muslims and Caucasian peoples.

In terms of rhetoric, the most radical party newspaper now is I am Russian (founder – Aleksandr Ivanov, executive editor – O. Yaroshenko, circulation – 7,500, periodicity – twice a month). The PNP newspaper pays equal attention to Caucasus-phobia and anti-Semitism. This article[82] resembling many similar ones is characteristic in this respect. It says that "Yeltsin's zhidocracy" intentionally developed an "openly anti-Russian criminal immigration policy ". The concepts of this policy were "conceived by two Jews: Yeltsin's advisor on ethnic issues Emil Abramovich Pain and his deputy Vladimir Izievich Mukomel. This policy is nothing but a capture of the Russian land by foreign occupiers without a war".

The religious publications take an important part in the whole group of the radical nationalist periodicals. Anti-Semitic materials are frequently published in religious publications with these two target audiences: RO Christian fundamentalists and some Neo-Pagans. Naturally, these materials are mostly of an anti-Judaic character. Actually, it is hard to say to what degree their position may be labeled as anti-Semitic in the proper sense of that word. Strictly speaking, anti-Semitism is part of a political ideology, but within the framework of the Christian outlook, the nature of anti-Semitism is presumably related to contention in the heavenly rather than in the earthly world.

Neo-Pagan nationalist publications target a pretty narrow audience. The main ones come out rather infrequently (Aleksandr Aratov's Russian Truth – several times a year, circulation – 3,000; Roman Perin and Oleg Gusev's Za russkoe delo, For Russian Cause published in St. Petersburg, circulation –

---

[81]   See, for example, Lavrinenko I. O evro i evreyakh. *Pravoe soprotivlenie*, No. 1 (8), March, 2002.

[82]   Baryshenko V. O prestupnoy immigratsionnoy politike. *Ya – Russkiy*, No. 11 (93), June, 2002.

5,000). They are usually devoted to the internal debate on whose reverence for the native gods is more authentic or to criticism of Christianity. Anti-Semitic arguments play an important role in the anti-Christian polemic. The following quotation from the leading anti-Semitic publication of the Pagan brand – Russian Truth – is typical: "Christianity is a religion specifically invented by the Jews for the slaves. Judeo-Christianity is a Jewish religion imposed with force on peoples of the world, with fire and sword. Animal hatred for the traditional Pagan religions is … the foundation of Judeo-Christianity. Read the Jewish Bible, especially the Old Testament. It teems with Jewish chauvinism and hatred for anything non-Jewish[83]".

The nationalist publications related to RO Christianity have a much wider distribution. The include Rus pravoslavnaya – Orthodox Russia (St. Petersburg, editor-in-chief – Konstantin Dushenov, circulation – 30,000, periodicity – monthly), Russian Herald (editor-in-chief – Aleksandr Senin, circulation – 50,000, periodicity – once or twice a month), the magazine Russian Home (editor-in-chief – Aleksandr Krutov, circulation – 50,000, periodicity – monthly). They promote RO Christianity as a positive, universal and ideal model of religion, world outlook, culture, politics, ideology, morals and everyday life. And they criticize secular liberalism, secularism, various competing religions (practically all of them – from the Catholics to the Satanists), and the Jews especially as negatives.

Anti-Judaism occupies an important place in the RO Christian tradition. Any fundamentalist interpretation of the teachings of the Eastern Church implies a set of anti-Semitic theses: "the Jews crucified Christ", "the Jews are enemies of Christianity", "the Jews wait for their Messiah who is the Antichrist", or even "the Jews commit ritual murders", etc. As an illustration, let us provide a quotation from an issue of Orthodox Russia[84].

It is a standard of the Christian tradition to equate the Jewish Messiah with the Antichrist, which is once again mentioned in the article "He is already on

---

[83]   *Russkaya Pravda*, No. 24, June, 2002.
[84]   *Rus' pravoslavnaya*, Nos. 5-6, May-June, 2002.

the way" by G. Aleksandrov. He writes: "The Church's doctrine clearly states that the coming Antichrist and the Jewish Messiah are the same". Then, the author provides quotations from the Church's Fathers supporting that position. After that, he tells the readers about the closeness of the "Catholic and Jewish Messianic aspirations". For example, the Vatican has recently released an official statement that the Messianic aspirations of the Jews are not futile... Answering a question from Jews: "Ought one to presume that the Messiah, perhaps, has not come yet?", a papal representative answered: "The Catholics should not presume that, but the Jews could". Aleksandrov draws this conclusion: "The Vatican's official admission of the legitimacy of the Jewish Messianic aspirations seems especially disgusting. What is that but not an open conspiracy of the precursors of the Antichrist? They become more active and overt in preparing mankind for the enthronement of their terrible master?".

It is significant, however, that anti-Semitic propaganda of the RO Christian fundamentalist publications is not limited to the strictly religious issues: the authors gradually move from religious issues to social ones. In the article "Love Cannot be Forced" in the same issue of Orthodox Russia, Vyacheslav Prokofyev writes about the "Jewish, openly pro-Western, anti-Russian and anti-Orthodox newspaper *Izvestiya* (News)". Having listed several articles published in the News, the author writes: "What? By the way, it is significant that all quotations listed above were written by Jewish authors. Why don't they care about the problems of their own synagogue? No, not likely. They long for lecturing the RO Christians on how they should live". Another page of the same paper shows a caricature of a person with distastefully exaggerated Jewish facial features, in a kippah with a star of David and a caption that reads: "The Kremlin speech writer". A photo next to it shows a nationalist picket: two girls hold a sign "No to the zhids' fascism".

More radical newspapers of the Christian fundamentalist movement (such as Czar's Guardsmen, Czar's Guard, Czar's Guardsmen's Paper, Russian Partisan, Enlightener, etc) may allow themselves to use even more radical anti-

Semitism up to the statements that the "zhids are visible demons[85]", Hitler was almost a Christian saint because he slaughtered Jews and to kill Jews is good and right[86]. It is true, however, that most of such publications criticize the Moscow Patriarchy for its being "pro-zhid" and their authors belong to alternative denominations, such as the "Catacomb Church" and the "Karlovatsky Council". A general principle that works here is as follows: the more radical a publication is in general, the more aggressive and radical its anti-Semitism. It goes without saying that such views do not have many chances to become popular even in the Christian Fundamentalist community; their circulation is under a thousand copies.

Having seen a wide panorama of the radical nationalist publications, we may conclude that, for both objective and subjective reasons, these newspapers occupy a small niche on the publishing market. How do they exist without a wide readership and, quite logically, without much interest from advertisers? Let us discuss this question in detail.

1.2   "Nazi Gold"

While discussing the problems of the anti-Semitic press, one can often hear the following argument. "Yet someone gives money to those newspapers! Someone profits from that!". An odd notion of "Nazi money" is in very wide circulation within the anti-fascist community. That is as amusing to the nationalists as the anti-Semitic claim that Jewish organizations control the coun-

---

[85]   Bychkov R. Tysyachelentnyaya imperiya. *Era Rossii,* No. 1 (69), January, 2002.

[86]   See, for example, *Russkiy partisan"*, No. 14, March, 2002, published by the Fraternal Order of Saint Iosif Volotsky entirely devoted to the Jewish issue. The following quotation is typical: "Comrade, bring closer the day when broken glass of the Jewish homes and stores will crunch under the pogromist's boot, when the last synagogues will vanish in ruins, when cheerful smoke will rise over the crematorium ovens of new Auschwitzes and Sobibors. Bring closer the great day of reckoning for the Jewish people for all the harm they did to mankind. Bring closer the day of the 'final solution' of the Jewish question!".

try is amusing to the Jewish organizations. Let us try to figure out whose money really supports the nationalistic publications[87].

The nationalist press is a very specific segment of the newspaper market with its peculiarities, problems, and complex interrelationships. First, all opposition publications (not just radical nationalist ones) are by definition politicized to the extreme – they are part of the non-commercial press. Both the nationalists and communists believe that they have lost the battle for the media and "their" newspapers actually do not report news, but only interpret it and promote their own views. But despite their small circulations and sometimes irregular periodicity (from once a week to once a month), the publication of nationalist and communist newspapers is frequently profitable business. Obviously, such publications cannot attract significant investments or many advertisers, but that does not mean that they are in the red.

The opposition press is characterized by a low cost of production. If we do not take into account the publications that inherited their premises and technology from the Soviet period ("thick", patriotic literary magazines, communist dailies, and partly Day / Tomorrow), then it is known that the initial investments into opposition publications are very small. Thus, Igor Dyakov began to publish the newspaper *Imperia* – Empire – with money from a Foundation for protecting investors' rights that had invited him to be a press liaison. The publication of the first 20 issues of the newspaper cost $6,000 and, unlike his other colleagues, Dyakov paid his authors their money. Eduard Limonov could begin the publication of the newspaper Limonka with the royalties for his book Executioner that he got from the Russian publishing house *Glagol* – Verb. Yet Limonka itself does not pay anything to its correspondents on the principle that they would "inflate" their materials otherwise. Ilya Lazarenko began to publish one of the first domestic national-socialist newspapers *Nash Marsh* – Our March – in 1992 (circulation – 10,000) with $1,000 received from American Nazi Gerhard Lauck

---

[87]   This section is based on information obtained during private contacts with members of the right-wing radical movement. Hence, there are no references to the sources for this section.

Aleksandr Aratov, the publisher and editor-in-chief of the Pagan anti-Semitic and anti-Christian newspaper Russian Truth, received an initial investment by misappropriating money from an Orenburg businessman (if we are to believe him) earmarked for a fugitive nazi from St. Petersburg. Aratov assured the businessman that he knew the whereabouts of the hiding "patriot". But the amount was so insignificant ($600) that Aratov was able to begin the publication of the newspaper only a year later, when he used personal connections (if we are to believe another ill-wisher) to get a small lump sum from a government agency.

The turnover of capital is very quick and many publications become self-sufficient after the first issue. Here is the standard model. Newspapers and magazines are originally published as small-circulation publications. They are deliberately overpriced, which results in a profit after selling the first issue. The profit is used to increase the circulation and the size of the publication. Five or ten issues later, the technology and periodicity are also improved, whereas the price is sometimes reduced. That is how the newspaper Storm Trooper's publication gradually unfolded. It increased its circulation from 3,000 to 20,000 in the first eight months, improved its periodicity from an issue in two months to an issue in two weeks, and its size from 4 pages to 8 – 12. That scenario is possible only if all copies are guaranteed to be sold, but that is not unusual in case of several thousand or even hundred copies. Usually, that scenario is followed for "conceptual" magazines – they are overpriced, the periodicity is not very significant, and the second issue is published only when the first one sells out. The journals *Nasledie Predkov* – Ancestral Heritage, *Ataka* – Attack, *Orientatsiya* – Orientation, *Athenaeum*, and *Nation* were published according to that scheme.

Typesetting, proofreading as well as the other technical jobs are performed by supporters either free, or for a symbolic payment. Thus, a lot of work on the same Limonka initially was done by a sympathetic designer who created a unique appearance of the newspaper, its logotype, emblem, etc. Then, Limonov "paid" his common-law wife, Liza Bleze, for typesetting. Aleksandr Dugin's magazine Elements is typeset by the editor-in-chief's wife, Natalia Melentyeva, and the magazine Nation is typeset free of charge by Viktoria

Vanyushkina who is the head of the department of translations and publications. In many cases, all technical operations are performed by the editor-in-chief himself. Aleksandr Aratov did the typesetting for the newspaper and magazine Russian Truth and national-socialist Konstantin Kasimovsky – for the newspaper Storm Trooper (furthermore, he accepted typesetting orders too).

Since such newspapers do not need much room, they occupy basements (e.g. Limonka), offices of institutes (e.g. National Gazette) or simply the editors' apartments (as do most similar newspapers). If a publication is sponsored by a party, then, naturally, the editorial offices are located on the party premises. With rare exceptions, the authors and correspondents do not demand payments. Accordingly, the only expense is the printing presses and paper. Often, nationalist publications are printed not in Moscow, but in Tver (Limonka in the first several years), Vladimir (Russia's Era, I am Russian, Limonka / Fundamental Line) in the Moscow region (Russian Order), where the printing presses are cheaper. One may deliver 10,000 copies of a newspaper from Tver to Moscow in a car, which is precisely how Limonka was delivered.

The next problem is distribution. Even though large companies distributing the press refuse to accept radical publications, except for Tomorrow and CPRF's press, as unprofitable or under the pressure of the government, the opposition newspapers overcome that obstacle easily. The availability of infrastructure belonging to the party publishing the newspaper or to ideologically similar organizations facilitates the distribution. Unlike private distributors, party members look at the selling of a newspaper not as an opportunity to make money, but as a necessary propagandist activity. As a rule, the profit made by ideological distributors is much smaller than that of the distribution companies. Sometimes, zealous supporters sell a newspaper at a loss or even free of charge and cover the losses with their own money. At some point, the initiation fee for a new NBP member was the obligation to distribute 50 copies of the newspaper. Often, left-wing organizations (e.g. Working

Russia, RCWP[E20]) require that their members distribute newspapers at a loss. Usually, the editors set a ceiling on the retail price that only slightly exceeds the wholesale price.

It may sound strange, but sending newspapers to other regions in small consignments (50 – 500 copies) is quite profitable. As they are not too time critical, most of the newspapers are sent to the regions by mail or by train. Sending 100 copies of a newspaper along with a train conductor costs 20 rubles at most but often it costs nothing. That assumes that there is a local organization in the region able to arrange meeting the train and distributing the newspaper further. Therefore, that is the way party publications are distributed – Limonka (the NBP), Russian Front (NPGR), I am Russian (PNP). Sometimes, if a newspaper is published irregularly but its circulation is large, such as RNU's newspaper Russian Order published once every several months with the official circulation of 500,000 copies, the typesetting is done centrally, but printing – locally, which reduces the expenses further. The Russian Truth went further by producing nearly regular regional issues in Kaluga and Ryazan.

Therefore, the cost of production of opposition newspapers is small. They exploit enthusiasm of the supporters and often the income from sold copies and from subscriptions covers their expenses. That does not preclude raising money among supporters and members of the organizations. Donations from readers, friends, and frequently from small and medium businessmen are an important part of the budget of the nationalist publishing houses. Practically every opposition newspaper constantly reminds its readers that it is published "under siege", and that only donations from supporters may rescue it. Usually, the names of the donors are published and there are probably quite a few of them. The St. Petersburg anti-Semitic newspaper Our Fatherland and the Moscow Black Hundred were able to survive "hard times" due to such donations. A total stranger on the street (near the Lenin museum, the communo-patriotic "Hide Park") gave $200 to Igor Dyakov mentioned above "for the

---

[E20]   RCWP is the English acronym for the Russian Communist Workers' Party – *Rossiyskaya kommunisticheskaya rabochaya partiya.*

newspaper". The largest donation in the publishing history of the "Empire" has been $1,000 given by a "nationalistically oriented" businessman. According to Limonov, he has received many donations from strangers after the weekly meetings with party members and readers in the NBP headquarters. Aratov received some "technical support" – a tape recorder, a modem, etc. – from sympathizers.

Direct donations from private companies are infrequent. One may recall only the enterprise "Hermes" of blessed memory and German Sterligov's exchange "Alisa". A more recent outbreak of a sponsor's altruism was a donation to Aleksandr Dugin for publishing the magazine Elements and the newspaper *Vtorzhenie* (Invasion) from the corporation "Russian Gold". There are more sponsors for opposition publications in the regions, usually among the "Red Directors". Petr Romanov, director of the huge chemical enterprise "Enisey" (currently vice-speaker of the State Duma from CPRF) sponsored the newspaper published by RNU's Krasnoyarsk branch, Russian Nation. He assumed the full funding of the newspaper, provided some editorial office space and made it possible to distribute it free of charge.

Hence, low budgets and small circulations of radical nationalistic and communist publications by no means preclude them from being commercially profitable projects.

Let us clarify what we have said so far. First, it would be unfair to claim that the publishers of such newspapers are unprincipled and cynical dealers. As a rule, they exemplify precisely that "altruistic enthusiasm" that they actively exploit in others. Second, it is not uncommon for them to experience either economic or legal pressure from the government – to some degree, practically all radical publications have had their share of it.

The economic influence is mainly pressure on the printing houses, as they are the only stage in the publication process carried out outside "their own" structures. Having received appropriate instructions, printing houses refused to accept orders from Limonka, Russia's Era, etc. The nationalist newspapers published in Moscow and the Moscow region used to be printed in Mytishchy and sometimes Timiryazev printing houses. In the last year, almost all Moscow publications have switched to a printing house in the Vladimir region.

The authorities resort to legal action reluctantly, under public pressure, but it has turned out to be the most efficient way of fighting extremist publications. However, the cases when nationalist newspapers have been shut down in the last several years may be counted on the fingers of two hands. Such rabid publications as Our Fatherland, Russian Truth and others quoted above come out without hindrance. Yet radical propaganda does not go unpunished for everyone. Let us list the publications shut down by court order.

The harbinger of the new policy was the shutting down of the openly nazi newspaper Storm Trooper in Moscow in 1998 (at the peak of its publication, the newspaper came out weekly; its official circulation was 20,000, but that period was rather brief and the circulation figure seems grossly exaggerated). Its editor-in-chief Konstantin Kasimovsky, who also got a suspended term for inciting inter-ethnic hatred, currently publishes the rather moderate (at least compared with the Storm Trooper) low-circulation newspaper Right Resistance.

RNU's newspaper Russian Order was shut down in early 1999 for a technical reason as part of the authorities' general attack on RNU. Its publication was resumed in 2001 – the newspaper was re-registered in Belarus. As of now, two issues of the renewed newspaper have come out; its circulation is 500,000 and both issues are still given away in the regions by Barkashovites.

The Vologod newspaper Slav was shut down in late 2001 on a technicality, too. In early 2002, the editor-in-chief registered a new newspaper titled Slavic Alarm Bell and he began its publication in May of the same year.

Another two papers – the Russian Register and Limonka – were shut down by court order in July of 2002. The magazine Russian Owner was banned in August of 2002.

It seems that the above mentioned crackdowns provide a reason to claim that the state has finally noticed the unbridled radical nationalist propaganda and has embarked on a consistent policy of shutting down radical publications. In our opinion, it is not the case yet, and a wave of court trials aimed at banning radical publications will not occur. Clearly, the quick ban on the three publications was caused only by the bureaucrats' need to demonstrate to society and the president that the fight with extremism was in full swing. However, only time will tell if the situation with radical nationalist publications will stay the same as it has been in the past 10 years or if something will change.

So far, tens of radical nationalist newspapers continue to sow xenophobia and hatred in the minds of their audience. Thank God that the size of that audience is very small.

2   Ideological Anti-Semitism and its Aspects

The majority of the anti-Semites in Russia cannot rationally justify or coherently describe their enmity towards the Jews. However, that majority are con-
sumers of anti-Semitic myths coming from a minority – from the people who
may coherently describe why they dislike the Jews. This ideological anti-
Semitism is the subject of this chapter.

Unlike various everyday manifestations of anti-Semitism based on prejudices
and irrational bigotry, ideological anti-Semitism is based on a certain view of
the world; it seems to derive from the individual's ideological outlook.

Let us discuss several myths of ideological anti-Semitism. To simplify this
problem, let us tentatively divide the entire system of anti-Semitic mythology
into "aspects", separate components or facets with their subject matters and
their features. Our main task is to find the intrinsic logic of these "aspects".
First, let us name the aspects of ideological anti-Semitism that we tentatively
identified to facilitate our analysis.

Most frequently, anti-Semitism is manifested in its *social* aspect. In that case,
the figure of a mythical Jew as an enemy is placed within the social environment. This motive is exploited using many different variations: the Jews are
not engaged in productive work, they are parasites on the body of a healthy
nation. The Jews are only capable of theft and financial machinations using
the most dishonest methods, not stopping at anything including lies and
crimes. The Jews climb up the social ladder and become corrupt journalists,
hypocritical politicians and dishonest businessmen. Having spread their tentacles throughout society, they begin to exploit the population ruthlessly. This
aspect of anti-Semitic ideology exists among the left-wing anti-capitalist
groups, but it is used often just for populist purposes by right-wing radicals,
too. The full version is the social aspect of anti-Semitism in its most developed form. It is much more common to find separate statements based on the
perception of the Jews as a socially alien, wicked and exploitative element
that will never relate to the host country as its own. This idea is expressed in

various specific statements: Jewish businessmen are dishonest, Jewish journalists are out to vilify everything that is sacred to the Russians, the Jews
"fought in Tashkent" during WWII, etc. Within the framework of that ideological complex, the Jew is viewed as a representative of a certain social corporation, not in light of his ethnic origin or religion.

The *conspiratorial* aspect of anti-Semitism is related to the idea of an international plot. The foundation of this aspect of anti-Semitism is the "Protocols of
the Elders of Zion" and the plentiful secondary literature. Sometimes, the
mythical enemy is labeled not as a Jew, but as a member of a euphemisti-
cally called force: "Zionists", "Zionist-Freemasons", "international behind-the-
scene forces", "the chosen people", etc. But the euphemisms should not confuse anyone – the gist of this way of thinking is to oppose a mythical monster
that cunningly and aggressively spins a web of international conspiracy. The
members of the conspiracy are Jews, although perhaps not all Jews, but only
the "initiated" ones. The idea of conspiracy is understandable – it is an attempt to explain the course of world history without grasping the intricate
socio-economic, cultural, geo-political and other global processes. It is simple: everything happens, because it serves someone's purpose. Since the
cause-and-effect relationship is unclear, it is obvious that the main events are
designed behind the scene of global history. Therefore, the whole world is an
arena, where invisible, mysterious, but nearly omnipotent forces act as a
clever puppeteer. Naturally, such a model may be taken seriously only by a
person whose consciousness is largely mythologized. But it is necessary to
notice that such pseudo-scientific notions that easily explain the course of
world history are typical for the disoriented post-soviet consciousness. After
the collapse of the Soviet Marxist macro-historical formational model, such
theories (from Gumilev's ethnogenesis to Fomenko's hypercriticism[E21]) became enormously popular among the reading public interested in history. The
role of conspirology for the contemporary Russian mentality may be under-

---

[E21]   A. Fomenko is a professor of mathematics at Moscow State University. He also
proposed a theory, based on numerical analysis of historical data, that drastically
revises the chronology of world history. According to his highly elaborate system,
for example, historical Jesus Christ lived a thousand, rather than two thousand,
years ago. Almost all credible historians reject his theory.

stood only within the general context of the mass historical consciousness of the Russians.

A separate aspect of the anti-Semitic ideology is *religious* in character. Often it is Judaism that engenders negative emotions, while the Jew as such is viewed as a negative figure, because he expresses the religious tradition or its stereotypes in a secular form. Judaism may be criticized from many angles. The most common anti-Judaic statements are based on the Christian dogma: the Jews crucified Christ, they drink blood of Christian babies and wait for their Messiah (who is equated to the Antichrist). The image of the Jew in the mass Christian consciousness is not just representative of one of the alternative religions. The image of the Jew in the Christian mind (especially as expressed in the traditional denominations – and RO Christian denomination is least prone to innovation) is largely demonized; the Jew is viewed as a consenting servant of the Devil's will and as God's enemy.

Anti-Semitic materials play an important role in the Orthodox-patriotic press. Furthermore, anti-Semitism for religiously oriented media is not a marginal theme - it is a conceptual one. It is natural for the RO commentators constantly to paint the Jewish issue with an intensely negative emotional color. This aspect of anti-Semitism is important for most of the ultra right-wingers, as their camp is traditionally religious. But if we talk about mass consciousness, then the picture is different. Since people with a traditional Christian view of the world are a minority among our contemporaries, the religious aspect of anti-Semitism in a conceptually and logically complete form is meaningful only for an insignificant part of the population, namely for the conservative part of the RO flock and for followers of the radical fundamentalist or pagan ideologies. Yet, since our culture even in its modern and secular form is still founded on precepts and values of the Christian outlook, the importance of the religious stereotypes should not be underestimated. Besides, traditional Christian prejudices in our country were superimposed on to atheistic propaganda castigating the fraudulent and inhumane religion of the Old Testament. Today, because of the traditional superstitions, both believers and non-believers, as well as people vaguely believing in "something", like most of the people in our country, may seriously ask "Is it true that the Jews use blood for baking matzo" or may describe the disgusting holidays celebrated by the Jews and their brutal god, such as the killing of the Egyptian first-borns or the slaughter of Persians.

The *racial* aspect of anti-Semitism in its purest form, complete with ideological justifications (i.e., the heterogeneity of mankind, multiple centers of man's origin and different evolutionary paths of primates, principal differences between human races, etc) occurs seldom. The post-Soviet consciousness quite justifiably associates orthodox racism with the Hitlerism that designated the Slavs as an inferior race. However, this aspect is applicable to anti-Semitism in its moderate, eclectic and logically incomplete form. The Jew is an adversary figure for the radically xenophobic Russian consciousness not due to his religion, profession or social status, but simply due to his origins. The most common anti-Semitic myths in mass consciousness (you cannot trust the Jews because of their intrinsic deceitfulness and depravity, the Jews are dirty, they have an inborn offensive odor and negative personal qualities) are elements taken out of the context of the racist methodology. In its mildest and ideologically complete form, that idea is expressed in the concept of incompatibility of different ethnic civilizations (the negative contribution of the Jews to Russian culture, the Jewish dilution of the cultural fund of the host nations, etc). According to L. Gumilev, for example, an ethnically and culturally heterogeneous civilization is not viable, destructive for all the mixing peoples and dangerous for the surrounding ones. With a clearly negative tone of voice, Gumilev called that "hybrid" entity a "chimera"[88].

Let us mention the last of the significant aspects – of "anti-Zionism". The *anti-Israeli* aspect of propaganda might stay within the acceptable bounds. Indeed, anyone may express his opinion and support one of the opposite sides

---

[88]   On Gumilev's concept of Khazarian Empire and its influence on the formation of contemporary Russian intellectual anti-Semitism, see Shnirelman V. *The Myth of the Khazars and Intellectual Anti-Semitism in Russia, 1970s-1990s*, pp. 44-59, Jerusalem: The Vidal Sassoon International Center for the Study of Anti-Semitism, The Hebrew University of Jerusalem, 2002. Rossman V. *Russian Intellectual Anti-Semitism in the Post-Communist Era*, pp. 72-101. Lincoln – London: The University of Nebraska Press, The Vidal Sassoon International Center for the Study of Anti-Semitism, The Hebrew University of Jerusalem, 2002.

in bitter international conflicts. However, the anti-Israeli commentators have a hard time keeping away from the temptation to switch from criticizing the Israeli policy towards the Palestinians in the occupied territories to discussing the intrinsic unrighteousness of Judaism and the viciousness and amorality of the Jews, largely due to the stereotypes of the late Soviet propaganda. Of course, it would be improper to follow some commentators and automatically label everyone who believes that it is his duty to support the Arabs rather than the Jews in the protracted conflict in the Middle East as anti-Semites. But it is also hard to overlook the covert or overt anti-Semitism that is often behind the author's anti-Israeli position on the one hand and the fact that anti-Zionism is an important, although not necessary, part of the anti-Semitic ideology. However, we are not going to discuss anti-Zionism for a number of reasons. It would be an exaggeration to qualify any criticism of Israel as anti-Semitism. This topic is so complex and delicate that it requires a separate careful study and deserves a separate discussion. But in those cases where there is a clearly expressed hatred towards the Jewish people behind anti-Israeli rhetoric, it becomes obvious after careful study that the Israeli-Palestinian conflict is just an excuse for expressing religious, racial and/or other types of hatred for the Jews.

Surely, the different aspects of anti-Semitism identified above are only tentative. In reality, they do not exist separately. They intertwine forming a complex pattern of the anti-Semitic mythology. But to figure out their internal logic, it seems justified to discuss each of the identified aspects separately. A detailed discussion of the various aspects of anti-Semitism will be illustrated by quotations from radical right-wing publications. This chapter covers anti-Semitism in its most candid and, at the same time, its most developed form, or as it is specifically used by the ideology of the Russian radical right-wingers.

2.1   The Social Aspect of Anti-Semitic Propaganda

The nationalistic anti-Semites have a peculiar approach to social problems. Although they - but not all of them - in general accept (with some reservations) the ideological system of permanent class warfare between the poor and the rich, the anti-Semites claim that the "oppression" as such is possible only in an ethnically heterogeneous society, where the members of a minority, depraved carriers of a spirit alien to the majority, occupy the dominant position. Neither oppression, nor opposing interests of various social groups are possible in a purely mono-ethnic state. The anti-Semites actively exploit the corporate (originally fascist) idea of solidarity among various layers of society in a mono-ethnic state viewed as a single body.

However, from the anti-Semitic point of view, the contemporary situation calls for the national liberation struggle of the Russian people. The Russian people are oppressed both ethnically and socially by big corporative structures. The top rulers are not just the financial oligarchs and the corrupt politicians controlled by them. All of them, regardless of their ethnicity are agents of the real, obviously foreign rulers of the world, anti-Russian agents of influence of the pro-Western forces.

The anti-Semite's social ideas are not limited to the primitive merging of ethnic and class enemies. Many nationalists believe that capitalism as such, as a model is not only unfair, it is foreign to the Slavic - or even broader, to the Indo-European, "Aryan" - mentality, it is unnatural. The myth about the "national mentality" and the consequent speculations are widely spread in the anti-Semitic community. Since the allegedly natural system for the Russian ethos is just, communal socialism, the "imposition" of capitalism cannot be carried out by people who are bone of bone and flesh of flesh with Russia. All active agents of capital belong to a different national mentality either by blood, or spirit (if their alien ethnicity cannot be proved in a specific case).

That opens a wide field for xenophobic and primarily anti-Semitic speculations. In the framework of this position, anti-Semitism, as different from other arguments, is justified by its proponents by attributing to the Jews the functions of the "quintessential bourgeois" (who is the embodiment of ugly, expropriated capital). A commonplace of anti-Semitic propaganda is the claim that the Jews are parasites who have never been involved in productive work. They have always fraudulently misappropriated the fruits of labor of their host nations. It logically follows from this statement that Judaism begot the capitalist relations alien to the "Aryan" peoples, as another weapon in the secret war for world domination. The seeds of capitalism appear to be in the Jewish psyche ("the Talmud is a trade code helping to make a profit at the expense of others"[89]; "Capitalism is a monstrous product of Jewry – a soulless Golem brought to life by a rabbi-kabbalist"[90]). The evil sides of capitalism, profiteering, inhumanity, etc. follow from characteristics of the Jewish mindset.

Social anti-Semitism in its pure form is a prerogative of the socialist movement that equates Jewry with capitalism. However, the radical right-wing ultra-nationalist elements easily borrowed that complex of the anti-Semitic mythology from the left wing as early as a hundred years ago and even advanced it. Following the traditions of historical fascism, Russian contemporary anti-Semites may claim that the communist ideology itself was artificially engendered by the Jews to undermine the goyim's national solidarity. "The communists are people accepting the dogmas of the imported satanic ideology created by Satanist Marx, a representative of the international cabal, and implemented in our land by a gang of dangerous international criminals led by Satan in human form, the bloody super-pogromist, agent of the world Zionism, lisper and syphilitic Ulyanov-Blank[E22][91]. Only an enemy of the state and the nation could come up with a theory, which splits a mono-ethnic and, more importantly for the Russian conservatives, mono-religious society into warring camps, a theory legitimizing violence in society. The Jews are viewed as the main carriers and spreaders of communism which is as destructive for the Russian people as Zionism, Satanism, and the New World Order, i.e. the ideologies designed to enslave nations, in the final analysis, by Jewry too. From

---

[89]   Yaryy V. Dialektika istorii. *Russkaya Pravda* (Ryazan' issue), No. 2 (2), 1996.

[90]   Dobroslav [Dobrovol'skiy A]. Prirodnye korni russkogo natsional'nogo sotsializma. *Russkaya Pravda* (special issue), No. 1 (3), 1996.

[E22]   Reference to Lenin. One of his four grandparents, Blank, was a Jew who converted to Christianity.

[91]   *Chernaya sotnya*, p. 15, Nos. 3-4, 1999.

the anti-Semites' point of view, any socialist rhetoric uttered by the Jews in reality is simply a cover for their actual plans to destroy the national system. The workers and peasants are victims of the conspirators as much as the clergy and nobility are. Naturally, according to that logic, the Jewish revolutionaries and "plutocrats" deep down realize their unity and common goals. Both real and imaginary facts of financial help of American bankers given to Russian revolutionaries are often provided as supporting arguments[92]. For example, the newspaper Black Hundred published a "secret instruction of the Petrograd branch of the International Union of Israelites" allegedly found in a pocket of a certain Red Commander Zunder killed in December of 1919. The "source" says: "We buy government bonds and thereby dominate on the world stock markets[E23]. Power is in our hands, but be careful! Do not trust deceptive, dark forces. Bronshtein (Trotsky), Apfelbaum, Rozenfeld, Shteinberg, all of them as well as many others are loyal sons of Israel"[93].

According to the traditional nationalist scheme, the people resemble a patriarchal family. Its head is a legitimate "Father-Czar" (Leader) who cares about his subjects. There is a class harmony in society where each group performs its functions, somewhat analogously to bodily parts. This primitive pastoral elegy, however, does not provide for the appearance of a group distinct from society. Naturally, the collapse of such a stable thriving society plays into the hands of only these aliens thrusting themselves into the society but, at the same time, keeping their own (secret) hierarchy. The more so, as these aliens (the Jews, of course) try to grab power, which anti-Semites do not doubt for a minute.

---

[92]   For example, the following quotation from Philadelphia Press of February 19, 1912, attributed to a certain banker Loeb is often used. "Raise money to send weapons to Russia, as well as leaders who would teach our youth to kill the oppressors like dogs". (From *Chernaya sotnya*, Nos. 8-9 (38-39), 1996).

[E23]   Curiously, the instruction does not make any financial sense. The new Soviet government refused to repay the debts incurred by the previous governments, thereby causing the collapse of the government bonds. Buying Russian government bonds was probably the worst investment at that time.

[93]   *Chernaya sotnya*, p. 15, Nos. 3-4, 1999.

Anti-Semites believe that they can find more confirmation of their theory in contemporary Russian life. Jews make up a large percentage of the so-called "oligarchs", prominent bankers and stock market brokers. That means that the Jews really control the state by manipulating the democratic institutions that are alien to the Russian consciousness. Using media holding companies, the "plutocrats" form public opinions in their own interests[94]. Often, the contemporary sources of mass information are directly associated with Jewry at least to the same degree as VChK[E24] was during the first years of the Soviet government[95]. For example, showing the movie "The last temptation of Christ" on the Russian television channel NTV is interpreted as intentional humiliation of the Russian Christians' by the Jews, "degrading and corrupting" Russian people who are less steadfast in their beliefs and provoking anti-Semitism.

We may sum up the social aspect of anti-Semitism described above with a quotation from the magazine Elements: "Socially, the image of a 'Jew' is equated with pawn-brokering, capital, cynical and corrupt journalists, with clannishness, with contempt for the goyim, with unjust wealth, with readiness to betray and sell out, or in short, with the System"[96].

---

[94]   On "Jewish media", see, for example: Rodionov" G. "Chetvertaya vlast'" i evrei. *Pamyat'*, № 1 (16), pp. 3-5, 1998.

[E24]   VChK (or simply ChK) is the Russian acronym for All-Russian Extraordinary Commission for struggle against counter-revolution, sabotage and speculation.

[95]   Endless publications and posters corroborate that idea. The following drawing is typical: a quintessential mythical hero with a sword raised in one hand stands in front of a huge TV set. A stream of filth flows out of the TV set, and monstrous creatures with distastefully exaggerated Semitic features lean out of the screen. The hero seizes the neck of one of the loathsome creatures with his free hand. There is a six-point star on the creature's neck, a curved swastika on the hero's buckle and a sharpened, almost diamond-shaped swastika on his shield. The caption says "Aborted fetuses of Zionism, tremble! The Russians are coming!" *Pamyat'*, No. 7 (22), p. 15, 1997. It is amusing that the Volgograd black-hundredist daily Bell printed the TV program to increase its popularity. But the program was accompanied by the slogan: "Russians! Turn your TV sets off!".

[96]   *Elementy*, No. 8, p. 71, 1998.

2.2 The Conspiratorial Aspect of Anti-Semitic Propaganda (the "Plot Theory")

The idea of a world Jewish conspiracy is the most common model of ideological anti-Semitism. However, this idea manifests itself differently in different ideologies. It is easy to notice that some of its manifestations are inconsistent, or mutually contradictory, with others. A Christian RO fundamentalist is sure that the Jews plot against Christianity. But neo-Pagans claim that Christianity itself is a product of a Jewish plot against other nations. (We should note that even though neo-Paganism as a willful denominational choice is pretty exotic and uncommon, some elements of the neo-Pagan mythology widely penetrate pop culture through various channels, such as fantasy books, popular historical and esoteric-religious books, etc.). Hence, conspiratorial anti-Semitism is not an ideology assuring popularity; it divides rather than unites anti-Semites.

The plot theory fascinates; objectively, it possesses a certain attractiveness, because it makes history more exciting, "live" and "three-dimensional". Many publications simply specialize in discovering the new and new aspects of the Jewish plot. The idea of a conspiracy by the "elders of Zion" plays the main role in anti-Semitic political ideology.

In the simplest and the most common version, all negative events occurring in the world and in our country are a result of the activity of subversive forces, presumably Jewish. The "elders of Zion" are behind all revolutions and wars that step-by-step lead to the absolute domination of the behind-the-scene masters. Since the publication of the Protocols of the Elders of Zion, this myth has undergone few changes. From the point of view of the followers of this ideology, everything that has happened in the 20th century supports the truthfulness of the Protocols.

According to the traditional anti-Semitic myth, the scheme of the Jewish conspiracy is as follows (with minor variations). A certain intrinsically wicked civilization, the pole of absolute evil has existed on Earth since the ancient times (or since the mythical times, for example, since Atlantis). According to some versions, the members of the civilization have always been Jews. According to others, the Jews were artificially created by a metaphysical Enemy in such a way that they possess the genetic qualities optimal for being agents of influence. During ancient, medieval and modern history, the Jews grabbed more and more power by using front men, economic channels and insidious plots and ruthlessly getting rid of their most principled and insightful enemies. By the beginning of modern times, "Russia remained the last vestige of the Aryan spirit", "it impeded the Levites' movement towards world domination, while England (and later – the USA) was the Levites' springboard and the Freemasons and Judeo-Christianity were their avant-garde". However, all attempts by the Levites to subdue the Russian people by applying the "soft scenario" used in Western Europe and in the USA ended up in failure. "The Russian people had a powerful and stable genotype, it was big and spread over a huge territory and it did not yield to corruption from inside, despite intrigues lasting for centuries". Then, the October revolution scenario was activated: through the efforts of the non-Russians who cleverly pulled Russia into the war and promoted an economic crisis. Power was grabbed by Jewish commissars. The genocide against the Russian people, which continues up to now, ensued. All political shocks since 1917 are fiction, superficial processes, power is in the hands of the Enemy's puppets who continue[97] the anti-national policies.

It is obvious for the RO Christian anti-Semites that the driving force of history is the Jewish hatred for the goyim's, especially Christian, world; the intention to subjugate that world to expedite their national and eschatological triumph – the coming of the Messiah who, as the Christian fundamentalists believe, is the Antichrist. In any case, the shadow of the Jewish plot is detected behind any significant historical event. All revolutions, wars, economic crises are results of the activities of the secret Jewish forces lustful for world domination.

The existence of the conspiracy is evidenced by numerous documents, the best known of which (but far from being the only one) is the Protocols of the

---

[97]   See, for example: Barkashov A. Razoblachennaya doktrina. *Russkiy poryadok*, Nos. 1-3 (32-34), 1996.

Elders of Zion[98]. This assessment is typical: "More than a hundred years ago, the Jews-Zionists developed the maximum program for seizure of power over the whole world. Those unique secret Jewish documents were obtained by Russian patriots and published under the title Protocols of the Elders of Zion[99]". The authenticity of the Protocols for anti-Semites is beyond question. That confidence is based not only, and not so much, on source study, or on philological or historical arguments (it would be unfair to require rational or even pseudo-scholarly justification of an ideological myth) but rather on "life itself"[100]. As the late Metropolitan Ioann of St. Petersburg and Ladoga wrote: "It is not important who compiled them [the Protocols], but the fact that the whole history of the 20th century agrees with the ambitions stated in that document with frightening accuracy"[101].

Anti-Semitic conspirology is pessimistic. It proclaims that by modern times, the tentacles of the Jewish conspiracy have already spread around the world causing social cataclysms useful to the Jews. The only remaining hope in the fight against the omnipotent conspirators is the apocalyptic scene of the triumph of faith and the coming of the Saviour after a hard period of the Antichrist rule that either has already started, or is about to start.

---

[98]   Our goal does not include refuting anti-Semitic myths, such as the authenticity of the Protocols. For detailed proof of their fraudulence, see Kon N. *Blagoslavlenie na genotsid. Mif o vsemirnom zagovore evreev i "Protokoly sionskikh mudretsov"*. Moscow: Progress, 1990. Dudakov S. *Istoriya odnogo mifa*. Moscow: Nauka, 1993. Burtsev V. *V pogone za provokatorami*. Moscow, 1991. The recent research of Ukrainian author Vadim Skuratovsky, who possibly identified the true author of the Protocols, is especially interesting, see Skuratovskiy V. *Problema avtorstva "Protokolov sionskikh mudretsov"*. Kiev: Dukh i Litera, 2001.

[99]   Volokhov V. "Vlasteliny" vremeni. *Nashe otechestvo*, No. 42, 1995.

[100] Although pseudo-scholarly attempts to justify anti-Semitism occur all the time, in reality they are not necessary in ideology (a person who does not believe in the Jewish conspiracy would not come to Memory) or in propaganda (the practice has shown that arguments based on emotions are more convincing than those based on fact and logic) of political organizations. Regarding attempts to prove the authenticity of the Protocols from a historical point of view, see, for example: Begunov Yu. *Taynye sily v istorii Rossii*, pp. 57-77, St. Petersburg: Izdatel'stvo im. A. S. Suvorina, 1995.

[101] Quoted from Filimonov S. "Protokoly sionskikh mudretsov" – real'nost' nashikh dney. *Kolokol"* (Volgograd), No. 89.

Unlike the RO Christian fundamentalists, some other anti-Semites claim that even Christianity, as a religion "invented by the zhids", is part of their conspiracy. According to that scheme, the Jewish domination had been established as early as the 10th century. Russia and Iceland, the last vestiges of the ancient Aryan spirituality in Europe, were baptized at that time. Aside from spreading Christianity, the Jews "planned to gain world power through cornering the financial and trade sectors, which they had achieved by the 10th century ensnaring the whole world with an invisible financial web"[102]. Since then, the forces of world Jewry have carried out the further and further enslavement of the peoples. All visible global changes, wars and revolutions are just different methods of that enslavement; fundamentally, they do not change the real status quo.

Just as the Christians do, the neo-Pagan racists view the current situation as difficult but not hopeless. They repeatedly express the hope that the Russian people still possesses a healthy vitality that will let it "free itself from the zhids' shackles, arrange its own rightful life, become an object of imitation for all peoples of the world <...>, leave no room for the zhids' parasitic existence"[103]. That constant danger for the world Jewish government causes the constant mimicry of the ruling class when the "zhids promise to meet the people's wishes, but in reality continue to solve their own, purely zhids' problems"[104]. That model explains both the shock of 1917 and the fall of the communist regime. It would seem that that outlook provides no reason for optimism; however, a solution was found in the following theory. According to this theory, the epoch of Jewish domination (the astrological era of Pisces) will end with the dawn of the astrological era of Aquarius. The zodiac sign Aquarius represents Russia, while Pisces – represents Judea. Therefore, according to the neo-Pagans, the two thousand years of planetary domination of the Jewish

---

[102] Kandyba V. *Rigveda: Religiya i ideologiya russkogo naroda*, p. 89. St. Petersburg: Maket, 1996.

[103] Nuzhen li Rossii Pinochet? *Rodnye prostory*, No. 4 (39), 1998.

[104] *Ibid.*

people will end in the beginning of the 21st century and the Russian era will dawn[105].

2.3   The Religious Aspect of Anti-Semitic Propaganda

As one may easily guess, religious anti-Semitism results from the faith professed by the nationalist ideologues. That is why there are different approaches to the "Jewish issue" according to different ideological denominational schemes. Hence, it is justified to study the main radical right-wing ideologies and the role of religious anti-Semitism in them in sequence.

Contemporary religious (Christian Orthodox) anti-Semitism has basically been borrowed from the Russian Black Hundred of the early 20th century. The main anti-Semitic myths of the RO fundamentalism are the theses about the God-killing people, the blood libel and claims of a metaphysical contradiction between Christianity and Judaism and the Satanic essence of the latter. The Jews, whose precept was to spread the word about God to other peoples, adopted the secondary idea about being the chosen people as the main one and did not fulfill their precept. That's why God's blessing was taken away from them and God's son came into the world. The Jews failed to recognize Jesus as the Messiah since, being drunk with the idea of being a chosen people, they expected someone who would elevate them above other peoples rather than someone coming to save all peoples. Since then, the Jews continue to persist in their delusion. As they missed the true Messiah (although they obviously recognized him and that's why they crucified him), the

---

[105]   It seems that the model, whereby the transition from one astrological epoch to another will be accompanied by a global realignment of the forces on the world arena, which will result in the birth of a new type of spirituality and in the strengthening of Russia, was first formulated in the works of a founder of the New Wave movement, Alice Bailey (see Shnirel'man V. Vtoroe prishestvie ariyskogo mifa. *Vostok*, No. 1, pp. 96-99, 1998). Bailey's books have been translated into Russian (see, first of all: Bailey E. *Sud'ba natsii*. Moscow, 1994). However, that idea has been present in the Western occult-nationalistic circles in some form since the beginning of the 20th century (cf., for example, Aleister Crowley's theory of "Aeon of Osiris" and "Aeon of Horus"). So far as we know, the first domestic ideologue who picked up that idea was writer, journalist and mythologist V. Shcherbakov.

one they are waiting for now is no one else but the Antichrist. The devil's willing warriors, the Jews embody the evil in this world, being visible demons.

Unlike the Jewish people, the Russian people is truly a God-bearing people, the good pole of the earthly world. The Jewish people "is guided by other principles in its national life". Because of the conscious efforts of the Jewish people "helped by philosophy destroying religious fundamentalism", many peoples in the world (including the Russian people under the Soviet rule) came to atheism and materialism that are "just a step away from the conscious and ritual worship to the absolute evil – the devil"[106]. As a rule within religious anti-Semitism, that metaphysical side of the Jewish issue comes before any other side: economic, cultural, etc. That follows from general logic of the thinking of the RO Christian anti-Semites. "Our contention with the Jews is over God's vows, not over who will grab the fattest chunk or who will take the warmest place under the sun in this world"[107].

Following the logic of Christian anti-Semitism, the Jews are willing theomachists hating Christianity, especially the RO branch, as it is the purest one, both in form and in content, as they understand its truthfulness. The Jews did not accept Christ, although prophets predicted his coming. In that sense, the Jewish prophets are precursors of Christianity rather than Talmudist Judaism. Judaism after Christ is illegitimate, it holds on only due to hatred for Christianity. Practically all "old right-wingers" are convinced that the Messiah who the Jews wait for must be the opposite of the goyim's Christ, i.e. the Jews wait for the Antichrist. Hence, in the grand scheme of things, Judaism equals Satanism.

Since Judaism is viewed as a religion "from Satan", it must be depraved, ruthless and amoral. For example, it is always claimed that the religious commandments demand that the Jews lie, steal and kill non-Jews. The repeatedly refuted charges of ritual killings still make their appearances in anti-Semitic

---

[106]   Barkashov A. Metafizika russkogo natsionalizma. *Russkiy poryadok*, No. 3, December 24, 1992.

[107]   Bychkov R. Kakoy anti-Semitism nam nuzhen? *Shturmovik*, No. 13 (25), August 16-31, 1996.

propaganda up to now. However, let us notice that, while the link "Judaism – anti-Christian religion", "Judaism – amoral religion" is simple, the reverse link is ambiguous. It is possible to describe Judaism as misanthropic from the atheistic viewpoint (which is done by the left-wing patriotic press) or from the neo-Pagan one (which assumes the depravity of the Christian viewpoint too). Such models are relatively new compared to the traditional anti-Semitic scheme. The model of a non-Christian, or even anti-Christian, denunciation of Judaism was characteristic for both the hitlerite ideology and Soviet anti-Semitism.

Unlike the followers of the above-mentioned position, the neo-Pagans, who are very active in their anti-Semitic propaganda, believe that Christianity and Judaism are similar and harmful religions. In general, monotheism is humiliating for man, it promotes a slave psychology, it takes the joys of life away from people and teaches them to mistreat nature. According to neo-Pagan notions, "Aryans", especially Slavs and other Indo-European peoples, had a highly developed state system supported by their native religion and high moral norms in the pre-Christian period. But the Jews, who by definition plan to achieve world domination, put an end to the Golden Era. "The zhids realized that they cannot prevail over other peoples and subdue them by force. Then, the Sanhedrin[E25] decided to prevail upon and subdue non-zhid peoples not with weapons in a battlefield but with cunning and deception, shrouding their brains with lies. <...> That's how the Christian religion, that still is a burden on the neck of the trusting Russian people, came up"[108]. The baptism of Russia, according to "Vedic" studies[E26], was dramatized by the previous event – a defeat of the Judaized Khazar Kaganat[E27] by the Pagan Russian warriors. According to the most common neo-Pagan model, "Prince Vladimir was Svetoslav's illegitimate [precisely! – V. L.] son from his Jewish concubine Malka.

[E25] The council of seventy one Jewish sages performing both legislative and judicial functions in Judea during the Roman period.

[108] Evseev D. Ded Ostromysl pristupil k razmyshleniyam. *Rodnye prostory*, No. 4 (31), p. 3.

[E26] Studies of the Vedas, the ancient Hindu scriptures.

[E27] State that existed between the 7th and 10th centuries between the lower Volga and the Dnieper. Judaism was the state's official religion.

He had no legitimate right to the throne, but he came to the throne through fratricide"[109].

Hence, from the point of view of Pagans, Christianity is a religion artificially created by Jews who introduced it to non-Jewish peoples by using cunning and lies. However, while neo-Pagan ideologues may treat Christianity leniently (the justification being that the peoples have revamped the harmful teachings), such treatment of Judaism is impossible. Within the framework of that logic, Judaism becomes "monotheism squared"; all negative traits of world religions are hypertrophied in it, since it is the original source of the depraved attitude towards the world: "The religion of the zhids', due to the fact that they could not work, did not want to work and did not work, became the quintessence and the idea of the exploitative society. Having left the other monotheistic religions far behind, zhidoism defined the shape of the world community by the 20th century, <...> excelled in developing all the evils of the predatory capitalist society by promoting infinite growth of the people's material demands at the expense of their spiritual development"[110]. For the neo-Pagans, Judaism is the prime ideology of misanthropy, a totalitarian ideology not tolerating different positions (Paganism is deliberately tolerant); all sins of Christianity follow exactly from the Jewish heritage. But having invented Christianity ("whose gist was the idea of submissiveness of the subdued peoples, acceptance of the authorities and savage reprisal to the rebels and dissidents"[111]) for the "goyim", the Jews themselves are faithful to their nationalistic even ethnocentric religion.

---

[109]   Quotation from Dobroslav. Op.Cit. So far as we know, the interpretation of the baptism of Russia as an act of revenge by half-Jew Vladimir for the defeat of the Khazars was first presented in the book Emel'yanov V, *Desionizatsiya* (Paris), 1979.

[110]   Sokolov E., Fedosov V., Boykov A., Tishchenko A., Protasov B. Zdravomyslie. *Rodnye prostory*, No. 2 (26), 1995.

[111]   Kandyba V. *Op. cit.*, p. 66.

2.4   The Racial Aspect of Anti-Semitic Propaganda

In its hitlerite (i.e. primarily anti-Semitic) form, racism is not particularly popular in contemporary Russia. Only radical anti-Semitic publications claim that the Jew is an enemy of mankind due to the very fact that he was born a Jew. In other words, for them a non-modifiable factor – blood – is the foundation of anti-Semitism. One may change one's religion (a baptized Jew will look suspicious, but no more than that) or occupation (from the bank operations to farming); but one cannot do anything about one's origin. The guilt for the "Jewish crimes" is, by definition, borne by the entire people rather than the cruel Hasidic sect or the secret rulers. The racial approach is precisely what separates anti-Semitism of the new and newest time, including the nazi anti-Semitism, from the traditional medieval Christian religious approach. Only the former, with its ruthless and relentless agenda made the Holocaust possible.

Indeed, this aspect of anti-Semitism has the most developed ideological justification within the framework of Orthodox Hitlerism. Its logic is approximately as follows. History is a global confrontation of the Nordic "Hyperborean race", the Aryan race of anthropologically and spiritually gorgeous people and the Southern Gondvanic race of the "untermenschen", among whom the Jews are the ugliest and most amoral. And the Jews are not just inferior to the Aryans, they are their willful and mean racial enemy. According to that ideology, the Jews look upon intentional mixing with the "superior race" as an important means of confrontation.

The Jews themselves, according to the most common concept, are a mix between the Nordic Aryan people who came to Egypt from the north and the Blacks. Presumably, the Whites and non-Whites are totally different species. It is further claimed, with references to Darwinism, that the "interbreeding of different species results in curs, inferior beings violating natural laws"[112]. There are even more exotic viewpoints. Thus, a book claims that the followers of Moses were "artificially and intentionally bred for enslaving mankind[113]".

---

[112]   Pomesi itdalennykh vidov. *Rodnye prostory*, p. 21, No. 2 (29), 1996.

[113]   The official doctrine of the Party of Spiritual Vedic Socialism, the quotation is from Shnirel'man V. Ariystvo ot krishnaitov? *Diagnoz*, No. 2, November, 1997.

According to another recently published book, the Jews are descendants of the "bald marsh apes"[114].

Therefore, all the depravity of the Jews expressed later in Judaism and in other teachings spawned by Judaism is rooted in the very origin of the Jews. Nobody can correct the genetic code, hence the racial approach to the "Jewish issue" is the most ruthless one. Biological anti-Semitism professes to take a scientific approach. Headings and titles of the publications promoting it look like "The Department of Social Genetics and Eugenics of the Russian University"[115], "A Compilation of Genetics Textbooks"[116], etc. Yet, they are characterized by simply pathological forms. Thus, one of the publications describes the outward features of Jews on five pages for "real Russian readers for use in special circumstances"[117]. Among these features: "3. Eyes. 3.1. Bulging eyes are a main feature of most of the Jews. <...> There is a hypothesis explaining the origin of bulging eyes. The men preserved their eyes in the fights with wild animals more often, if the eyes were deeply set. Parasites, however, risked neither their lives, nor their eyes and multiplied faster spreading the bulging eyes' gene". Therefore, we see a tightly interrelated ideological image: the Jews are physically ugly as a result of the inter-racial mixing; the Jews are morally ugly; the Jews are inventors of the most depraved and amoral doctrines; the Jews are parasites not involved in productive work; the Jews are cunning and wicked criminals, money-lenders, cheaters; the Jews are secret rulers of the world.

That ideology in its pure form occurs in the contemporary Russian ideological space only among extremely marginal racist groups. More often, the instances of racially biological anti-Semitism are rarely justified by rational arguments. Racially based anti-Semitism is the most chauvinistic of the anti-Semitic ideas, but as a rule, it appears as secondary and insignificant, as for instance: "besides, the Jews are not good looking". Nevertheless, declaration of anthropological aversion to the Jews is common, especially in conversa-

---

114   Popov V. *Obez'yany Putina*. Moscow, 2002.
115   *Russkaya Pravda* (magazine) p. 32, No. 1 (7), 1998.
116   *Rodnye prostory*, p. 21, No. 2 (29), 1996.
117   *Russkaya Pravda* (magazine) p. 32-37, No. 1 (7), 1998.

tions. One can hear phrases like "ugly like a zhid", "inarticulate as a Jew" in the street and on public transportation, but the people using such expressions, as a rule, are unaware of the intricacies of the racist theories; they simply are following oft-repeated xenophobic stereotypes in the mass consciousness.

Even after such a brief discussion of the main elements of the anti-Semitic ideology, it seems superfluous to refute them – that eclectic set of superstitions and phobias seems too absurd, inconsistent and farfetched. And indeed, this is obvious to the overwhelming majority of the people in Russia. Experience of the latest Russian political history shows that the people are pretty reluctant to accept this crude and unhealthy propaganda. The politicians who exploit anti-Semitic myths in their ideology and propaganda get a negligible percentage of the voters. However, ideological anti-Semitism is dangerous because it nourishes impetuous xenophobia, being like a stone falling into the water of mass consciousness that generates spreading circles.

III   Religion

1   Anti-Semitism, the Russian Orthodox Church (ROC) and the State in Contemporary Russia

This chapter discusses the role of anti-Semitism in the contemporary Russian Orthodox Church (ROC). The very statement that the modern ROC includes a large degree of anti-Semitism is a commonplace of all studies touching on this area. Even a priest writes about "sad participation of the Church in anti-Semitic propaganda and in spreading the anti-Semitic myth"[118]. There is no doubt that the "Church's anti-Semitism is an important element of post-Soviet anti-Semitism"[119] in general. Such statements are practically a truism, but taken by themselves, they cannot satisfy a researcher. Without claim of covering this matter exhaustively, this essay will touch on three issues.

First, the causes of such widely spread anti-Semitism in the ROC and more broadly – in the religious communities of contemporary Russia – are interesting. Second, it seems important to take a closer look at the situation inside the ROC, since the Church's diversity is obvious, which is very important for us. And the last issue with which this work deals is more practical: what may be expected from the current situation. Although this work is theoretical, it is impossible to completely avoid the real aspect of the problem, when the theme is as vehement and stirring as anti-Semitism, and we will briefly touch on that issue as well.

---

[118]   Borisov A., priest. *O natsionalizme v Russkoy pravoslavnoy tserkvi. Nuzhen li Gitler Rossii?*, p. 194. Moscow: Independent publishing house "Pik", 1996.

[119]   Messmer M. *Anti-Semitism in Post-Communist Russia*, p. 10. Cape Town: Kaplan Centre for Jewish Studies and Research, 1998.

1.1   Religious consciousness and intolerance

Traditional religiosity, by definition, is characterized by intolerance for the representatives of other religions[120]. It is natural for the religious consciousness to claim a monopoly on the truth[121]. As Aleksandr Verkhovsky, a scholar of fundamentalism and religious radicalism, rightfully notes, "confidence in the exclusiveness of one's faith, its superiority over others are an integral part of almost any religious system"[122]. The fundamental problem of the religious view of the world is that it does not condone ambiguous or middle-of-the-road solutions, especially where monotheistic religions are concerned. If a follower of a religion believes that his religion is true and, therefore, guarantees his salvation, then practically it follows that all other religions are somehow not quite as sound for him, they are the result of mistakes, delusions or distortions of the Truth[123]. The assumption of the "equivalency", "equal salvation" of different faiths contradicts the traditional religious consciousness and is possible only in the context of the modern secular society. "The true faith, true

---

[120]   Compare with Romanian-French philosopher Emil Cioran: "A faith that recognizes another and does not view itself as the only bearer of truth is doomed... That is the scary truth that is supported by the entire experience of the Judeo-Christian world: monotheism entails intolerance, whether we want it or not". (Choran E. *Zhozef de Mestr: Ocherk reaktsionnoy mysli*; *idem. Posle kontsa istorii*, pp. 312-313, St. Petersburg: Simposium, 2002).

[121]   However, we should note that attempts to revise that traditional point form a trend in inter-religious relations now. For example the Roman Catholic Church and some branches of Judaism have made cautious statements about their readiness to recognize the possibility of salvation for followers of other denominations. At the level of mass consciousness, that is expressed in a trite thesis: "It is unimportant what to believe in or how to pray; God is the same anyway". But for a number of reasons, some of which are discussed below, that trend has not become common in the Eastern Christian world. Hence, it will be left out in this chapter.

[122]   Verkhovskiy A. Religioznaya ksenofobiya. In Verkhovskiy A., Mikhaylovskaya E., Pribylovskiy V. *Natsionalizm i ksenofobiya v rossiyskom obshchestve*, p. 168. Moscow: Panorama, 1998.

[123]   In light of the above, the following idea brought up by Helen Fry seems justified. According to her idea, it is Soteriology, the doctrine of salvation and the Savior, rather than Christology and other concepts dividing Christian and Jewish theologians, "engendered anti-Judaism in Christian theology". See Fray Kh. *Na puti k khristianskoy teologii iudaizma. Khristiansko-iudeyskiy dialog. Khresomatiya*, p. 41. Moscow: Bibleysko-bogoslovskiy institut sv. Apostola Andreya, 1998. (further referred to as *Khristiansko-iudeyskiy dialog*).

not in the sense of the chosen religion but in the sense of man's actual, willful spiritual work in the service of God, in his self-sacrifice in the hope of deserving eternal life, always assumes the correctness of its way and the readiness to defend it. Perhaps, that readiness is that stumbling block that divides the faithful" from the unfaithful[124]. That is, the traditional religious consciousness is intolerant. However, this mental and conceptual enmity is not always manifested in specific aggressive actions against the "opponents".

Obviously, religious intolerance is not a static constant. The degree of intolerance varies depending on the dogmas of denomination, the specifics of time, culture, etc. Different religious doctrines include different perceptions by adherents of different creeds and form complex hierarchical systems from indifference or even some empathy to aggressive enmity. However, with some simplification we may state that intolerance in religious consciousness is a general rule. This preliminary statement is not redundant or a truism, because while there is a rather common opinion, whereby all religions (or all so-called "traditional religions") teach love, good neighborliness and tolerance, that opinion is far from reality, at least with respect to traditional types of religious consciousness[125]. Tolerance is not an absolute equally applicable in the context of any culture and civilization. Intolerance within religious consciousness is a normal and natural phenomenon, but it conflicts with the values of the modern and post-modern western civilization presently laying claim to world domination[126].

---

[124] Ostrovskaya Z. Orientatsiya – Islam, ili Nazad v budushchee [interview with Dzhamal G]. *Chelovek*, No. 3, 1999.

[125] The type of religious consciousness that very staunchly holds on to the values and authorities established once and for all, unquestionably rejects any innovations both in the ideological sphere and in everyday life, believes that it is necessary to follow the rituals, is referred to as traditional religiousness in literature. For a definition of "traditional believers", see Kaariaynen K., Furman D. *Religioznost' v Rossii v 90-e gody. Starye tserkvi, novye veruyushchie*, pp. 23-24. Moscow: Letniy sad, 2000. However, it would be more useful for defining the traditional religious consciousness to use less formal qualities related to the mentality and world outlook, rather than the statistics of how strictly the rituals are followed. In general, the methodological opposition of the traditional and contemporary consciousness is fruitful for solving problems related to social, religious and inter-ethnic conflicts.

[126] In this context, an idea of Metropolitan Kirill (Gundyaev), Chairman of the Department of External Church Relations of the Moscow Patriarchate, is interesting. Ac-

The main religions in the territory of the Russian Federation are Christianity in the RO form and Sunni Islam. In these religions, the ideas that may be called anti-Semitic (anti-Judaic) are rather natural and central which has been clearly shown in history. Anti-Semitic trends in contemporary Russian Islam will be discussed in the next chapter.

Clearly, one should realize that the usage of the word "anti-Semitism" with respect to the religious viewpoint is not quite correct[127]. Strictly speaking, "anti-Semitism" is a secular ideology formed in the latter half of the 19th century, and it is hardly appropriate to equate traditional religious intolerance with a xenophobic political doctrine. However, we shall use the term "anti-Semitism" here in a broad sense for the sake of simplicity; it will refer to any intolerance towards the Jews, including religious intolerance[128].

---

cording to his idea, there is no conflict between traditional religions; all problems are caused by a conflict between religious and secular world outlooks. See: Mitropolit Smolenskiy i Kaliningradskiy Kirill (Gundyaev). Problema sootnosheniya mezhdu traditsionnymi i liberal'nymi tsennostyami v vybore lichnosti i obshchestva. *Nezavisimaya gazeta*, February 16, 2000.

[127]   There may be several opinions about the relation between anti-Semitism and anti-Judaism and the degree of danger of the latter in its pure form. For example, according to Yury Tabak, "the religious notion of a follower of Judaism and the ethnic notion of a Jew were closely intertwined in the ancient world and in the middle ages. Therefore, while it is important to differentiate historical circumstances determining the Christian attitude towards the Jews, it is easy to figure out that speaking of Jews as "dirty and disgusting" even in the "anti-Judaic" sense contained the racist, anti-Semitic seed that has bloomed centuries later. (See: Tabak Yu. Otnoshenie Russkoy Pravoslavnoy Tserkvi k evreyam, p. 495. *Dia-Logos*, No. 2, 1998-1999).

[128]   For more details on terminological problems related to the word "anti-Semitism", see Likhachev V. *Istoriya antisemitizma: nenavist' skvoz' veka*, pp. 1-5, Moscow: Evreyskiy mir, 2000. Likhachev V. *Antisemitizm kak chast' ideologii rossiyskikh pravoradikalov*, p. 4. Moscow: Panorama, 1999. Zolotarevich V. Likbez. Ob upotreblenii terminov "antisemitizm", "yudofobiya" i "zhid". *Mezhdunarodnaya evreyskaya gazeta*, No. 46 (245), December, 1998.

1.2   Orthodox Christianity and Anti-Semitism

Due to its claim to be the legitimate heir of the same tradition (the Old Testament), Christianity has a number of radical grudges against Judaism. According to common opinion, Christianity (or more broadly, the Christian-Muslim civilization) is responsible for the emergence of anti-Semitism as a unique phenomenon[129]. That is not so, of course – and it will suffice to recall anti-Judaic writings of the pre-Christian Hellenic authors[130].

This chapter covers the present situation of anti-Semitism in RO Christianity only. Christianity in Russia is not just a numerically dominating faith due to the number of its followers. RO Christianity is de facto the semi-state religion despite the separation of state and church proclaimed by the Constitution of the Russian Federation[131].

The Eastern Christian Church's doctrines and general thinking are marked by conservatism, strict adherence to the positions set in the past, and reluctance for innovations, especially ones related to the foundations of the faith. A revision of the official RO doctrine concerning the Jews similar to the revision carried out by the Catholic Church and most of the Protestant Churches is hampered largely by those characteristics of the ROC's mindset. Let us recall that after the Holocaust, Western denominations accepted the responsibility of

---

[129]   For example, Mikhail Chlenov writes that anti-Semitism is a "specific cultural code inherent to the Muslim and Christian civilizations that at some point arose from Judaism and as a counteraction to Judaism" (Chlenov M. *Antisemitizm v politike Rossii. Nuzhen li Gitler Rossii?*, pp. 145-146).

[130]   For details, see: Lazare B. *Anti-Semitism: Its History and Causes*, pp. 19-28. Lincoln and London: University of Nebraska Press, 1995; Chanes J. *A Dark Side of History: Anti-Semitism through the Ages*, pp. 17-28. New York: Anti-Defamation League, 2000; Ruether R. *Faith and Fratricide: The Theological Roots of Anti-Semitism*, pp. 23-40, Minneapolis: Seabury Press, 1974.

[131]   The Constitution of the Russian Federation, article 14. The "Semi-state status" of ROC in contemporary Russia may be debated. Perhaps, a more accurate form of that thesis is as follows: "The state recognizes the primacy of ROC on a symbolic level and the latter allows the state to use it for shaping a positive image of the government. For details, see Verkhovskiy A. Bespokoynoe sosedstvo: Russkaya Pravoslavnaya Tserkov' i putinskoe gosudarstvo. In: Verkhovskiy A., Mikhaylovskaya E., Pribylovskiy V. *Rossiya Putina. Pristrastnyy vzglyad*, pp. 79-135. Moscow: Panorama, 2003.

Christianity for anti-Semitism and repudiated their main traditional charge against the Jews, God-killing. A similar revision has not been carried out by the ROC and it is unlikely to be carried out soon for a number of reasons. All traditional medieval charges against the Jews presented by the Church Fathers in rather harsh ways are still in effect and unquestionable within the ROC up to now. They are periodically repeated in the ROC's publications[132].

Among the reasons hindering the revision of the "Jewish problem" within the ROC, we can identify two major ones. First, the revision is hindered by objective factors. Revision of the Church's doctrines is in principle impossible within the framework of the RO logic. The difference between the mindset of Western and Eastern Christianity, especially when innovations are concerned, is colossal, although it is not always recognized. As far as the Western Catholic tradition is concerned, theological creativity by each generation is normative and legitimate, since a Pope's authority is equal to that of the Writings of the Church Fathers (the ROC has no analogous institution that is legitimate and authoritative enough to question aspects of the Writings). The Protestants treat the Writings themselves with much less piety. The following is normative for Western Christianity: "Each new generation of Christians has to re-evaluate theological concepts in order not to allow elements of anti-Judaism to return"[133]. The same approach is impossible in the Eastern Church – since the basic concepts may not be revised. The task of each generation is to follow the tradition as accurately as possible; any innovation is viewed as a departure from the purity of Orthodoxy.

The other reason is rather subjective. The ROC in Russia has directly depended on the authorities and on the political situation for too long to forge a new tradition of active theological creativity. There was a brief upsurge in theological and pastoral activity related to courageous and innovative proposals in the teachings and organization of the Church. The culmination of

---

[132]   Besides, anti-Judaic motives are strong in the RO liturgy, unlike the catholic and protestant ones after the Second Vatican Council. See Dyubua I. *Pravoslavnaya tochka zreniya. Khristiansko-evreyskiy dialog*, pp. 47-50.

[133]   Fray Kh. *Pered litsom budushchego. Khristiansko-evreyskiy dialog*, p. 330.

that upsurge was the tragically interrupted Local Council held in 1917 – 1918 that did not really have any full-fledged follow-up. The ROC in the Soviet Union was destroyed in the 1920s – 1930s and when it was restored in the 1940s – 1980s, the behavior of its hierarchy towards the government reached a level of servility that was unheard-of, even compared to the pre-revolutionary situation[134]. In a sense, the situation has not changed much since the fall of communist rule. First, most of the ROC hierarchy received their positions back in the Soviet time with all the resulting biographical and psychological consequences. Second, the state has continued its control over the Church to a large extent and the latter supports the authorities (we will discuss that later). The ideological clash among various factions within the Church should not be viewed outside of the wider context of socio-political life in post-Soviet Russia.

Organizationally, the main (but not the only, yet often positioning itself as such) Christian structure in the country is the ROC of the Moscow Patriarch (ROC MP). Before we discuss the role of anti-Semitism in the ROC, let us take a close look at its internal structure. That will allow us to understand the complex and sometimes contradictory process in the ROC better. The Moscow Patriarchy is not as homogenous as it would like to be seen, and there are opposing developments and antagonistic forces within it.

There are three main ideological currents inside the ROC MP, let us tentatively call them "church liberals", "orthodox fundamentalists", and "the bureaucratic clerical center". The roots of these currents may be traced back to the 1960s – 1970s. It was natural then for intellectual frondeurs to come to churches to demonstrate their opposition to the existing regime, among other things. While Orthodox Christianity might not have been a completely free zone, it was at least a zone where opposition tolerated by the state was permitted. That brought all types of dissidents to the Church; to baptize oneself and attend services meant to show one's non-conformity. That is why the political position (or rather opposition) bringing them to Church was the primary

---

[134]   Those who are interested in the latest history of the Russian Church may be referred to the following comprehensive work: Pospelovskiy D. *Russkaya Pravoslavnaya Tserkov' v XX veke*. Moscow: Respublika, 1995.

factor for many intellectuals joining the ROC then. They remained "western-ers" or "rooted-in-soil Slavophiles", "liberals" or "nationalists" and developed their own understanding of faith based on certain views of the world. "The Church liberals" were and remain, figuratively speaking, reflections of the lib-eral world outlook in the RO mirror. That explains their weakness, or even marginality in the Church environment. The situation with Orthodox funda-mentalists is somewhat different. Fundamentalists are supported, on the one hand, by rich traditions of Russian nationalism that has been closely linked to Orthodox Christianity since its origins, and by the tradition of Church patriot-ism (or perhaps nationalism, if not "chauvinism") and ultra-conservatism on the other hand. Hence, they are more "natural" in Church than the liberals and enjoy a more solid support by all levels of the RO believers.

The discord within the ROC MP had not been major and had not been made public up until around 1988[135]. The opponents were allies in the fight with the common enemy, the communist system. The dissidents' solidarity, as a rule, prevailed over ideological differences. There was no evidence of the alien-ation begun later between the politicized lay activists and the ROC clergy: at the earlier both were deprived of civil rights and were in a half-strangulated state, consequently both were interested in mutual support[136].

The situation changed after the fall of the Soviet regime. The "liberals" and the "fundamentalists" lost their common enemy and naturally switched to very sharp polemics and the "Jewish issue" became one of the main ones in their confrontation. The clergy, on the other hand, is still controlled by the authori-ties, but having received substantial rights and privileges, it was no longer in-terested in support from the marginal left or right wings. On the contrary, the political activity of laymen of both wings worries the conservative episcopate for one simple reason – a revision of any elements of the existing church doc-trines threatens the legitimacy of the church hierarchy.

---

[135]   We may take 1988 as the starting point in the modern stage of ROC history. That was the thousandth anniversary of the baptism of Russia and marked the "exonera-tion" of religion in the USSR.

[136]   There is a different theory that is not very convincing but still it has the right to exist. According to that theory, the ROC was so infiltrated with KGB agents and informers that the Church clergy willingly worked as provocateurs for baiting dissidents.

Having described the general context in which the ROC currents arose and presently exist, let is discuss them separately paying especial attention to the meaning of the "Jewish issue" for each group.

1.3   "Church Liberals": Post-Holocaust Theology on Orthodox Soil

The "Church liberals" (and archpriest Aleksandr Borisov quoted in the begin-ning of this chapter certainly belongs to that group) are most inclined to inno-vations and revisions of the doctrines that are clearly obsolete in their opinion. They severely criticize the church clerics' passive and conservative position and insist on a full-fledged, creative re-examination of various controversial layers of the religion and its practice, taking into account the experience of western Christianity. That covers a rather wide circle of issues painful for the ROC, beginning with some immediate issues, like the severe assessment of the collaboration of the church clerics with the communist regime, and ending with conceptual ones, like calendar and language reforms. The "Jewish issue" is not left without attention either. Regarding the latter, we may mention a col-lection of papers titled "The Russian Idea and the Jews"[137] published in 1994. Two timely articles in that collection written by its editor, Zoya Krakhmalnik-ova, and by a scholar of Christian theology, Sergey Lyozov, show two ap-proaches to revision of attitudes towards the Jews traditionally accepted by the ROC. The two approaches are different but each is Judeophilic in its own way.

S. Lyozov states that Christianity is largely responsible for anti-Semitism in modern times and therefore – for the Holocaust. Accordingly, he solves his personal existential problem – how one can be a Christian but not an accom-plice to the mass murder of Jews[138]. He follows the Protestant paradigm of

---

[137]   *Russkaya ideya i evrei. Rokovoy spor. Khristianstvo. Antisemitizm. Natsionalizm.* Edited by Krakhmal'nikova Z. Moscow: Nauka, Vostochnaya literatura, 1994. (fur-ther referred to as *Russkaya ideya i evrei*).

[138]   That the "Jewish theme" has a personal, almost intimate meaning for him, Lyozov admitted frankly enough elsewhere: "It is clear from the text that the Jewish issue

post-Holocaust theology and describes three stages of solving the problem: 1) "accepting the moral and political responsibility of the Churches for the Holocaust"; 2) looking upon "Church centuries-old anti-Judaism" as a "source of modern racist anti-Semitism"; and 3) re-evaluation of deep foundations of the Christian faith ("the meaningful center of the Christian doctrine should look differently after Auschwitz")[139]. In general, Lyozov tries to adapt the approach of Western theologians, mostly Protestant ones, to Russia.

For Krakhmalnikova, a similar existential problem does not exist. From her point of view, True Christianity is inconsistent with anti-Semitism and it is necessary to refute the attempts of some unscrupulous priests to deviate from that teaching. Krakhmalnikova writes: "If today or tomorrow, a false bishop of the ROC (appointed on KGB's recommendation and working as KGB's secret agent) or his students or followers claim that the Jews destroyed Russia and call for violence against them, may we call that Orthodoxy? That is misanthropy and a diabolic slander of Christianity"[140].

Attempts to cultivate ideas borrowed from post-Holocaust theology in the Russian environment have failed (S. Lyozov himself gave up on them soon[141]). That set of ideas has turned out to be alien and unwanted in Russia because of totally different theological traditions and the nature of the intellectual context of the post-Soviet religious revival. The second approach formu-

---

[139]   appeared to me (only to disappear later) as I was trying to solve my own problems, problems of my faith, my Christian identity (Lyozov S. *Ot avtora.* Lyozov S. *Popytka ponimaniya*, p. 6. Moscow – St. Petersburg: Universitetskaya kniga, 1999).

Lyozov S. Natsional'naya ideya i christianstvo. In *Russkaya ideya i evrei*, pp. 101-103.

[140]   Krakhmal'nikova Z. Zachem eshche raz ubivat' boga? On vse ravno voskresnet. In *Russkaya ideya i evrei*, p. 188. Krakhmalnikova's ideas are not unique, they have been used both in the RO context, and even more clearly – in Western Christianity. Thus, Protestant theologian Franklin Little writes: "Anti-Semitism for Christianity is not simply a common disgusting form of racial bias. Anti-Semitism is sacrilege which is much more serious!". And further: "The Christians should take up arms against their own anti-Semitism for the sake of the truth" (Little F. Usvoili li khristiane uroki Shoah? In *Khristiansko-evreyskiy dialog*, p. 46).

[141]   S. Lyozov, verbal communication, 1998. In the course of his research of history of early Christianity, S. Lyozov haas come up with a paradoxical conclusion that Christianity did not originate from Judaism.

lated by Krakhmalnikova is much more common among the Church liberals. (We have to note, however, that she herself is a member of the "Karlovatsky[142] Church", rather than the ROC MP, which allows her not to be shy about criticizing the latter)[143].

The Church liberals' appeals to the "non-orthodox" RO theology of the early 20th century or to the innovative decisions of the unfinished Local Council of 1917 – 1918 are invalid, because the reformist movement in the ROC will long be associated with "innovationists"[144], which immediately discredit any reform in the eyes of a wide section of the believers (that is why in the intra-church debates, the liberals are often referred to as neo- innovationists). Inside the Church, the liberal wing is a minority. It is conspicuous enough due to its collaboration with non-religious structures (those involved in human rights or liberal politics) and close interaction with media. At present, that group is primarily associated with "kochetkovites", a community that has strained relations with the Church hierarchy.

---

[142]   The "Karlovatsky Church" is a branch of ROC abroad. It was named after the city Sremski Karlovtsi in Serbia where its First Council was held in 1924.

[143]   Although polemicizing with the positions and opinions mentioned here is outside the scope of this book, we ought to comment on the common misconception, whereby true Christianity has nothing to do with anti-Semitism. We share the opinion of Yury Tabak, a researcher of Judeo-Christian relations: "The ROC doctrine has been supported, both formally and substantially, by the medieval church consciousness. Hence, even the statements by the most rabid anti-Semites among the Orthodox Christians justifying their monstrous anti-Jewish invectives by the Church doctrine seem quite logical. Indeed, if for example, John Zlatoust, one of the most respected Church Fathers, called Jews "filthy and disgusting" and a synagogue – "a refuge for demons", then why should an Orthodox Christian believing in the sanctity of the Writings of the Church Fathers think otherwise? <...> In that sense, the positions of those contemporary authors, who angrily hold up to shame anti-Semites and deny their belonging to "true" Christianity, seem strange". (Tabak Yu. Otnoshenie Russkoy Pravoslavnoy Tserkvi k evreyam ..., p. 495).

[144]   Innovationism is a movement in Orthodox Christianity inspired and supported by the Bolsheviks aimed at splitting the Church. It used revolutionary rhetoric in its propaganda and tried to "revolutionize the Church's teaching and practice. Because of its obvious links with the "godless authorities", the movement was held in low respect by the believers and it could not fulfill its task. Later, the innovationist clerics were persecuted and the authorities reached a compromise with the mainstream Church.

1.4 "Zealots of the Orthodox Devotion": Fighters against "Jesus-Haters"

The fundamentalist and rightist elements are much more numerous within the ROC[145]. They harshly criticize the Church hierarchy too, although not for its "stagnation" and "obscurantism", but on the contrary, for its "modernism". The Patriarch and many clerics are criticized for a conciliatory approach, a betrayal of the inflexible militant Orthodoxy for the sake of short-term political interests. The RO fundamentalists reject all attempts to modify the Church doctrine from the "left", including the part related to the Jews, as a betrayal of the Faith.

Originally, the "zealots of the RO devotion" were involved only in the dispute over suggested reforms of Church liturgy and rituals (translating the liturgy into the Russian language, switching to the New Julian calendar, etc.), but gradually they developed a comprehensive ideological and religious system of responses to modern challenges. The RO fundamentalism has been shaped as a full-fledged ideology comparable with similar movements in Protestantism, Islam, Judaism and Hinduism[146].

While Ioann (Snychov), Metropolitan of St. Petersburg and Ladoga, known for his conservative views, was alive (he died in the fall of 1995), he was a generally recognized authority for all right-wing radicals within the ROC[147]. There

---

[145] Regarding fundamentalism in ROC, see: Verkhovskiy A. *Op. cit.*, p. 66; Kostyuk K. Pravoslavnyy fundamentalism. *Politicheskie issledovaniya*, No. 5, 2000; Filatov S. Novoe rozhdenie staroy idei: provoslavie kak natsional'nyy simvol. *Politicheskie issledovaniya*, No. 3, 1999; Kas'yanova K. *Religioznyy fundamentalizm.* Kas'yanova K. *O russkom natsional'nom kharaktere.* Moscow: 1994; Ulyakhin V. Fundamentalizm v pravoslavii: teoriya i praktika. In Levin Z. Ed. *Fundamentalizm*, pp. 127-165. Moscow: Institut vostokovedeniya RAN, "Kraft", 2003.

[146] For general literature on fundamentalism, see: Levin Z. *Op. cit.*; Marty M., Appleby S., eds. *Fundamentalists and the State.* Vo. 1, *Fundamentalisms and Society.* Vol. 2. Chicago and London: Chicago University Press, 1993; Cole St. *The History of Fundamentalism.* Westport, 1971; Cohen N. *The Fundamentalist Phenomenon.* Grand Rapids, 1990; Caplan L. *Studies in Religious Fundamentalism.* Albany, 1987; Kochanek H., ed. *Die verdraengte Freiheit.* Freiburg, 1991.

[147] However, there is an opinion that Metropolitan Ioann himself was not an adherent of the "Black Hundred" Orthodox Christianity. For example, one may quote this state-

has not been anyone among those in the highest layer of the ROC episcopate since his death who could replace that charismatic patron of the fundamentalists. Although fundamentalists have no support from the highest-level
Church clerics, they enjoy the support of the Church laymen and numerous
nationalist-radical and anti-Semitic organizations[148].

Actually, the fundamentalists do not put forward any new ideas. They are just
conservatives rather than "conservative revolutionaries", although there are
exceptions. In the sphere of anti-Semitism, they do not even try to adapt classical Christian anti-Judaism to modern conditions. Their activity is to stress
those parts of the Bible and other religious literature that are ignored or simply violated by the ROC hierarchy. The group of such problems is pretty wide
– beginning with routine violation of the rule banning the sale of all items on a
Church's property or banning a priest's charging money for occasional religious rites, and ending with the Moscow Patriarchy's ecumenical activities
that are equivocal from the point of view of RO intolerance towards followers
of other religions and "heretics". The traditional attitude towards the Jews belongs to the same group. One may be surprised, perhaps, by the pathological
persistence that the "zealots of RO devotion" use to address the "Jewish is-

---

ment: "Although his admirers called His Excellency the "leader of the RO patriotic
movement", he was not a leader of any movement, just a man whose kindness and
weakness was used by many. People around him used his name to sign all new
essays. " (Fedorov V. Chto meshaet khristianskomu edinstvu v Rossii? *Dia-Logos*,
p. 137, No. 3, 2000-2001). As a rebuttal, one may state that there is no noteworthy
information leaving doubts over Metropolitan Ioann's authorship of his main works
viewed as essential by the fundamentalists.

[148]   The fact of a tight linkage between religious and political groups is quite interesting.
One may state that, on the one hand, a vigorous liberal Christian-Democratic political movement has not been formed in Russia yet, and all RO organizations actively
participating in politics adhere to nationalist positions of various degree of radicalism. On the other hand, of all ideological currents of the contemporary political
spectrum, the right-wing radicals objectively have more common points with religious organizations than any other group. With some simplification, we may state
that right-wing radicalism is a result of applying religious values in the political
sphere. This theme was discussed elsewhere by us in more details. See: Likhachev
V. *Religioznyy faktor v ideologii i deyatel'nosti sovremennykh rossiyskikh pravoradikal'nykh politicheskikh partiy i dvizheniy*, pp. 205-210. Moscow: Izdatel'skiy tsentr
RGGY, 2001. Likhachev V. Rol' religii v ideologii i deyatel'nosti sovremennykh rossiyskikh pravoradikalov. *Dia-Logos*, pp. 139-156, No. 3, 2000-2001.

sue". But there is nothing inherently strange here. As other researchers have noted, the image of the enemy is very important in the eschatological drama painted by the fundamentalists in their defense against modern challenges[149].

The main anti-Judaic myths found in RO fundamentalism are claims about the sinful and amoral character of Judaism, the thesis about the God killing people, "blood libel", the premise of metaphysical confrontation of Christianity and Judaism and the satanic essence of the latter. In a nutshell, here is the view of Judaism within the framework of Christian radicalism. The Jews, who received the covenant to spread the word of God to other peoples, accepted the secondary idea about being a chosen people as the primary one, and did not fulfill their part of the covenant. That is why the Lord's blessing was taken away from them and God's son came into this world. The Jews did not recognize the Messiah in Jesus, because being intoxicated with the idea of their chosenness, they expected someone who would elevate them above other peoples instead of someone coming to save all mankind. Since then, the Jews have insisted on their misconception, while the chosenness was transferred to the Christian community, the New Israel. The logical conclusion of that theory is to equate the Messiah expected by the Jews with the Christian Antichrist[150]. Judaism is viewed as a collective "eternal Jew" who has fallen into disgrace with the Almighty because of his own sins and crimes. Hence, Judaism is the pole of metaphysical evil, theomachism, and therefore Satanism; not only are the Jews the enemies of mankind, they are also God's willful enemies. "The word 'zhid' refers to a man who personally hates Christ"[151], writes the ROC priest Father Alexey Kagirin. "One may disengage oneself from contemporary Judaism and imagine a Jew who knows nothing about Christ – such a Jew is not a zhid"[152], he continues. That idea is the logical consequence of the traditional Christian thesis about the Jews as the God-

---

[149]   Marty M., Appleby R. Introduction: A Sacred Cosmos, Scandalous Code, Defiant Society. In *Fundamentalisms and Society*, p. 3.

[150]   That scheme is reflected in numerous publications. See, for example: Vorob'evskiy Yu. *Put' k apokalipsisu: stuk v Zolotye Vrata*, pp. 314-315. Moscow: 1998.

[151]   Kagirin A., priest. Nenavidyashchie siona. *Russkiy vestnik*, No. 7, 1999.

[152]   *Ibid.*

killing people, which for fundamentalists is self-evident and not subject to any revision[153].

Since the Jews awaiting the Antichrist-Messiah may be, in some sense, called Satanists, Christianity should fight them as Christ's enemies. From the fundamentalists' viewpoint, "Orthodox Christianity is the only faith that not only has nothing to do with Judaism, it squarely opposes the zhids"[154]. Consequently, the idea that Christ haters channel their emotion mainly against Orthodoxy as the purest and most consistent Christian denomination seems natural within the framework of that logic. That idea was expressed by the fundamentalists' incontestable religious authority, the above mentioned Mitropolitan Ioann. "All the hatred of the God-killing people has appropriately and inevitably concentrated on the God-bearing people"[155], he writes in his main and most popular essay "The Autocracy of the Spirit". If one accepts that thesis, one can easily grasp the motives of the Jews who tirelessly spin a web of conspiracy against Russia. "None of such [religious – V. L.] conflicts is comparable, in terms of brutality or results, with the religious war that has been stubbornly and continuously waged by Judaism against the Church of Christ for two thousand years. The spiritual values of both sides are opposite and irreconcilable"[156], states Ioann elsewhere.

A natural continuation of that thought for RO fundamentalists is to posit that Jews and Christians secretly following Judaism have penetrated the ROC hierarchy. The notion of the "fifth column" within the ROC is very common both

---

[153]   See, for example, Beseda A. Shtil'marka so svyashchennikom Alekseem Astaf'evym. *Chernaya sotnya*, pp. 12-13, Nos. 8-9 (38-39), 1996. The interlocutors put forward a thesis whereby perhaps the guilt for Christ's crucifixion lies not on the entire Jewish people but only on the "Pharisees and Sadducees" or even on the Romans. However, in the course of the dialog, both theses are refuted. Father Alexey referring to the canonical sources proves the guilt of the entire Jewish people.

[154]   Ostaev A., priest. Otpoved' neoyazychnikam. *Chernaya sotnya*, p. 5, No. 2 (32), 1996.

[155]   The quotation is from the Information and Research Center Panorama's database "Labyrinth".

[156]   The article was published several times. Our quotation is from: Ioann, mitropolit Sankt-Peterburgskiy i Ladozhskiy. Tvortsy kataklizmov na Russkoy zemle. *Chernaya sotnya*, p. 22, Nos. 3-4 (69-70), 1999.

among quite conservative people in the ROC, including clerics, and, to a greater degree, among the believers leaning towards "alternative Orthodox Christianity". Cautious and inconsistent ecumenical and liberal trends within the ROC in the last several years have been painful for RO Christians. Naturally, the guilty are Jews who allegedly convert to RO Christianity en masse with the (perhaps subconscious) desire to change it and, therefore, distort it. Of course, that reproach is directed against the "Church liberals", rather than against the entire Church hierarchy. "Changing the liturgy, translating Church Slavonic language into the modern street language, dropping the names of 'unacceptable' saints or even 'uncomfortable' parts of the faith, all of that is easy for them", writes Vladimir Osipov, the leader of the fundamentalist Union for Christian Revival in a document with the characteristic title "Church under Siege"[157]. True, Osipov seems to believe (and he supports his thesis by the example of Father Aleksandr Men[E28]) that the danger of the RO priests who used to be Jews but later converted to Christianity[E29] is not in their destructive intention, but in their mindset, "in their organic rejection of all historical, i.e. canonical Orthodox Christianity that they stigmatize as ultra-reactionary"[158].

A similar statement is contained in a classic work of modern RO anti-Semitism – the book "How They Make Us Anti-Semites"[159] by Deacon Andrey Kuraev. According to Kuraev, the Jews, by virtue of the national character of their religion, even after baptism, do not look for salvation by joining the church. Rather, they attempt to 'salvage' the church itself from 'heresy' (in their opinion) from the left or the right. Kuraev's position deserves attention for another reason as well – it may be looked upon as the semi-official position of the ROC. True, the author himself writes: "This book has not been officially blessed. That means that only I, rather than the ROC, am responsible

---

[157]　Osipov V. Tserkov' v osade. *Natsional'naya gazeta*, special issue No. 4, 1997. The document was hugely popular and it was re-published several times.

[E28]　Born a Jew and baptized by his mother as an infant, A. Men became a popular RO priest. He was murdered in 1990.

[E29]　The original simply says "Jewish priests", but the Translator had to use the awkward expression "the RO priests who used to be Jews but later converted to Christianity" to convey its meaning to the Western reader.

[158]　*Ibid.*

[159]　Kuraev A., deacon. *Kak delayut antisemitom*, pp. 79-83. Moscow: Odigitriya, 1998.

for its contents"[160]. However, A. Kuraev is a prominent figure; he is practically the only person in the Church expressing its position on the burning issues of the day. He regularly appears on TV and actively publishes his comments on various problems. Within the Church, he is practically regarded, possibly for lack of a better candidate, as a figure of official authority. So far as we know, there has never been a single rebuke or doubt of the correctness of his works, whereas there have been rebukes of other fundamentalist leaders. Kuraev seems to be the spokesman for the "moderate right-wingers" in the ROC[161].

According to another, more radical viewpoint, Jewish penetration of the clergy is part of their global agenda – to grab world power; it is "designed according to the scheme drawn by the great rabbis" to pursue the "goals defined by the talmudic laws". That is the viewpoint of Anatoly Makeev, "catacomb-nik"[162], the leader of the Fraternal Order of Saint Iosif Volotsky.

Every attempt by the ROC hierarchy to establish friendly contact with the Jews encounters extremely anxious and painful reactions in reactionary Orthodox circles. The most prominent among these was the famous speech by the Patriarch of Moscow and All Russia Alexy II in New York at a meeting with rabbis in 1991 ("Our prophets are your prophets...") that almost led to a split in the ROC. The response to that speech was very loud. The Patriarch was called a "heretic", his critics stressed his "non-Russian" background and last name, etc. There was even a movement of "non-mentioners", i.e. some priests excluded the mention of the Patriarch of Moscow and All Russia from

---

[160]   *Ibid.* p. 23

[161]   If one wishes to, one can find elements not of religious (Christian) but of racial anti-Semitism in V. Osipov's and A. Kuraev's positions, as they look upon baptized Jews as still Jews and talk about "national mentality", etc. However, in our opinion, Osipov and Kuraev still talk about stereotypes of upbringing, etc. rather than the "national character" in the racist sense of the term. On the contrary, UOB and UOG leader A. Simonovich, for example, clearly deviates from Orthodox Christianity into a racist heresy (see Simonovich A. Utverditsya li v Rossii "russkaya eres'". *Oprichnina*, No. 9, December, 2001). In light of our comments above, it is not surprising (although it is not widely promulgated), that Simonovich belongs to the Catacomb Church, rather than ROC MP.

[162]   Makeev A. Evreyskiy vopros v Tserkvi. *Tsarskiy oprichnik"*, No. 3, 1998.

the liturgy, thereby demonstratively avoiding his "ecumenical" line[163]. However, having understood that the "non-mentioning" created conditions for a schism, most of the parishes discontinued that practice soon (the menace of schism is a factor seriously restraining the intra-Church right-wing opposition). Yet, it is obvious that the Patriarch's statements that followed declaring his tolerance and favorable attitude towards Judaism and other religions in general have become more cautious and less provocative.

Still, the most consistent opponents of Alexy II have switched to alternative RO jurisdictions – the Russian Orthodox Church Abroad (ROCA)[164] and the Russian True Orthodox (Catacomb) Church (TOC)[165]. That allows the most active and consistent RO radicals not to identify with the "Sergian" Church ROC MP and to criticize it in the most radical way[166]. That is why many leaders of right-wing radical groups are members of the TOC, ROCA or Old Believers.

The desire of the ROC head to demonstrate his friendly attitude towards Judaism is looked upon by fundamentalists, even those who belong to the ROC, as an attempt to "transform Orthodox Christianity into Judaism with a Christian 'postscript'"[167]. They perceive the idea of reconciliation of Christianity and Judaism as an attempt at compromise, which is fundamentally impossible in the area of religion: "Either – or. Either you are with Holy Orthodox Christianity, or with Christ-hating Talmudism"[168].

---

[163]   For details, see Senderov V. Russkaya Pravoslavnaya Tserkov' i ee otnoshenie k antisemitizmu. *Dia-Logos*, No. 1, 1997, especially pp. 125-126.

[164]   The Russian Orthodox Church Abroad has parishes in Russia too since 1990.

[165]   To be exact, there is no single Catacomb Church in Russia now. There exist about six different groups, under similar or sometimes even identical names, not recognizing each other.

[166]   Aside from various branches of TOC and ROCA, there is also the Russian Orthodox Autonomous Church (ROAC) headed by ex-bishop Valentin Rusantsev who was defrocked by a ROCA Council and excommunicated by a ROC Council. ROAC can be traced to the "Catacombs", it was within the jurisdiction of ROCA for a while, and it has been independent since 1996. ROAC criticizes ROC MP from moderately fundamentalist and anti-communist position.

[167]   Dubrovin N. Ravvinu eto ponravilos'. *Zemshchina*, p. 14, No. 101, 1995. The name of the section in which the article was published – apostasy – is characteristic.

[168]   Osipov V. *Op. cit.*

The classic charge that Jews commit ritual murders appears in the right-wing radical semi-religious press. That charge sanctified by the tradition blends well with the logic of RO anti-Judaism. Sometimes, only certain Jewish sects (usually the Hasidim) but not Judaism as a whole are charged with ritual murders. "I want to calm down the ordinary Jews who view the murder of a child as the worst sin, just as any other person does. But there are sects of Judaism performing satanic rituals using the blood of Christian babies", writes the paper "Black Hundred"[169], the highest "authority" in the area of ritual murders. Many articles by RO monarchists claim that the murder of Nicolas II was ritual too[170]. From the point of view of the right-wing lay radicals, the policy of state atheism after the fall of monarchy was actually imposed by the interests of "theomachist anti-Russian forces" (i.e. the Jews), in their intention to subvert Orthodox Christianity. Destroying churches and killing priests during the Soviet government were allegedly prescribed by Jewish holy books and they were carried out exactly according to the prescriptions[171].

---

[169] *Chernaya sotnya*, No. 11 (18), 1994.

[170] That statement appears very often, almost everywhere in RO patriotic propaganda. See, for example: Sud" naroda ili ritual'noe ubiystvo? *Pamyat'*, p. 7, No. 2, January, 1991. This subject overstepped the boundary of the marginal right-wing radical fundamentalist press. The official Church commission on Nicholas II's canonization had to answer several questions including this one: Was the murder of the Emperor and his family a ritual one?

[171] See, for example: *Chernaya sotnya*, p. 1, Nos. 8-9 (38-39), 1996.

1.5   The ROC Episcopate: Moderate Conservatism

Yet despite its popularity among relatively wide circles of believers, RO fundamentalism still remains the right-wing opposition to the ROC hierarchy. The latter may be accurately characterized as the center of the bureaucratic administration. Both the left and right wings of the ROC are under strong pressure from the conservative center that includes most of the Episcopate and clergy[172]. Being interested in neither reforms, nor strict observance of traditions, the Episcopate simply prefers to ignore painful issues, such as the Jewish issue[173].

In order to emphasize their moderation and civility, the ROC bureaucrats and their head make periodic statements that are very friendly or at least neutral to "traditional" religions, including Judaism[174]. Such statements always generate new waves of indignation on the part of the Church fundamentalists. However, such gestures on the part of the Church administration serve, in some sense, to demonstrate its loyalty to the state authorities and, hence, they are necessary despite many believers' displeasure.

---

[172]   The case of "kochetkovites" is usually used as an example of pressure that ROC clerics put on the liberal opposition. The cases of suppression of fundamentalists are less known but they include removing deviant priests from their parishes (for example, Father Nikon (Belavenets), the leader of the movement "For the Faith and Motherland", lost his position after an unsuccessful attempt to run for the State Duma in 1999) and banning publications in the Church press (the case of Metropolitan Ioann). For details, see: Beseda Konstantina Dushenova s glavnym redaktorom zhurnala "Revnitel' pravoslavnogo blagochestiya" igumenom Aleksiem (Prosvirinym). *Rus' pravoslavnaya*, No. 9, September, 2001.

[173]   A major example of a topical issue that split ROC and exposed contradictions between the RO fundamentalists and the administrative center is the issue of using Taxpayer's Identification Number. The same issue clearly shows the dependence of the ROC administration on the state and the conformity of the clerics.

[174]   That fact, as well as analogous statements by the leaders of other religions, seems to refute the thesis put forward above whereby religious consciousness is intolerant by nature. To resolve this contradiction, it is appropriate to quote Muslim religious and political activist Geydar Dzhemal: "The priests of all religions find a common language, because they support each other. <...> A person who has faith is God's soldier, he does not belong to himself, he may not indulge in doubts... Naturally, a soldier does not have to fight. But the spiritual aspect should be present in his life every day. (Ostrovskaya Z. *Op. cit.*)

However, the above does not mean that the ROC administration is fundamentally tolerant towards Judaism. The Church is an institution that, by definition, is conservative, keeping intact many prejudices rejected by more flexible "information structures"[175]. If we keep using political science terminology, the ROC center has noticeably shifted to the right on the world view scale. No one in the church hierarchy has taken responsibility to disavow anti-Judaic concepts and they remain a valid, though not actively used, part of the Church ideology. In addition to others, the decrees of the old Ecumenical Councils banning personal contacts with Jews, having meals with Jews, etc., remain. However, as is true in many other cases, neither the letter, nor the spirit of the decrees is observed by the ROC clerics themselves.

We may illustrate the position of the Church "center" in part by A. Kuraev's case described above. As an example to clarify the ROC position more clearly, let us mention the polemic that occurred between two RO publications – a fundamentalist newspaper and the Patriarchate's official organ. It started with Konstantin Gordeev's article in a paper published by the Metropolitan Ioann Memorial Society[176]. The article commented on the photo of Patriarch of Moscow and All Russia Alexy II holding a cross containing a six-point star within its ornament. The author who signed as Layman Gordeev expressed his bewilderment regarding the defilement of the Holy Cross by the "theomachist symbol of the Christ-haters".

The article was sharply refuted in the pages of the Moscow Patriarchate's official organ[177]. Much of the emotion of the response to the "bewilderment" of the layman boiled down to the following. A six-point star has been traditionally used in the RO symbolism and it does not carry any anti-Christian connotation, unlike the "hexagram formed by two overlapping triangles" that has "the special name of Magen David. The latter is the symbol of the Zionist move-

---

[175]   The expression "conservative information structure" was applied to the ROC by political journalist Gleb Pavlovsky. See, Soldatov A. Ot RPTsZ k RPATs: istoki al'ternativnogo Pravoslaviya v sovremennoy Rossii. *Russkiy zhurnal* (Internet edition), September 10, 2001, http://www.russ.ru/ist_sovr/200110094_sold.html.

[176]   Gordeev K. Magendovid vmesto kresta? *Rus' pravoslavnaya*, No. 1, January, 2000.

[177]   Polishchuk E. Ob odnom "nedoumenii". *Moskovskiy tserkovnyy vestnik*, Nos. 3-4, 2000.

ment" and "it indeed superficially resembles a six-point star. That's why many countries have avoided the use of the six-point star after the birth of the State of Israel and replaced it with five- or eight-point stars".

That reply did not satisfy fundamentalists. The next issue of Orthodox Russia contained a new article on the same subject[178]. Its author, Andrey Smirnov, supports the "bewilderment" of the first article, accusing its opponent of "spiritual blindness". Smirnov states that the *Vestnik* (Herald) has a serious problem, namely "the indistinguishability of zhido-masonic and RO symbolism". In the author's opinion,

The six-point star is "Satan's star" (these words are printed in boldface in the text), it is the "zhido-masonic seal of the Antichrist". The author draws a pessimistic conclusion: "The penetration of Satan's zhido-masonic symbolism into RO culture is not funny".

Characteristically, all participants in that discussion have no doubts about the inadmissibility of mixing Judaic and Christian religious symbols or about the harm that such a mix can do to RO culture. The only point of contention is the issue of what exactly should be viewed as a Judaic symbol. Besides, if the official Herald is restrained in its rhetoric, the petulant Orthodox Russia may allow itself the bold reference to "Satan's zhido-masonic" symbolism.

The description above is sufficient to draw some preliminary conclusions. Orthodox Christianity takes the most conservative position among all the Christian branches. It is in no rush to react to the new trends coming from the West, including the trend to revise the traditional Christian view of Judaism. It may be stated that despite certain liberal and pro-Semitic currents in the ROC, by and large, the Church continues to hold the medieval position that, with a certain degree of exaggeration, may be characterized as Christian anti-Semitism. Besides, there are strong ultra-reactionary elements both within and without the ROC that pay especially close attention to the "Jewish issue".

---

[178] Smirnov A. Demagogiya i oskorbleniya vmesto argumentov. *Rus' pravoslavnaya*, No. 5, May, 2000.

1.6   State and Church: Present and Future

This section mainly discusses conceptual issues. However, because of the complexity and pungency of the problems, it seems appropriate and even necessary to address a question belonging rather to political science. Looking at the big picture of the post-Soviet period, it is easy to notice that the Church is a reputable institution, millions of Russians turn to religion, and the State actively flirts with the Church. Then, it would be appropriate to ask the following question. Could the traditional religious intolerance towards the Jews spill over to a broad section of the population? Or in the extreme case, could the authorities utilize religious intolerance as part of the "spiritual revival" and the new state ideology?

Of course, the stormy post-Soviet reality makes unequivocal predictions difficult. Nevertheless, it seems that we can reply to the question in the negative. Let us try to justify our point of view.

First, the phenomenon of the contemporary Russian religious revival is interesting, because it is a very superficial process, it does not affect the basic foundation of the world outlook of the masses. Yet Christian anti-Judaism is conceptually a pretty complex scheme that may be understood and accepted only within the general context of the religious viewpoint. As a rule, most of the Russians who recently turned to Christianity are not inclined to engage in the more traditional side of the religion or to reach for theological wisdom. They are satisfied with the ritual aspect of the religion and with a vague "spirituality" unrelated to strict religious dogmas[179].

---

[179]   See: Kaariaynen K., Furman D. *Op. cit.*, pp. 7-48. The authors provide unambiguous results of public opinion polls and draw these conclusions: "The directions of the superficial and deep currents in the Russian mass consciousness are different. The religious revival occurs "on the surface". "Deep down", there is no religious revival. On the contrary, a small marginal group of people who at least somehow may be classified as "real" Orthodox believers gradually disappears. There is no reason to expect a real growth of Orthodoxy in the future. (Ibid, p.41). And then, "The future (and the present to a huge extent) of the Russian viewpoints, Russian attitudes toward the main questions of life is a future in which most of the people, practically all people, seem to believe a little bit in something, but then again, not really. Their

That speculative conclusion is supported by the results of public opinion polls. It might seem that, since the Church enjoys the trust of 94% of the Russians and anti-Semitic stereotypes are strong within the Church, society should demonstrate a high level of anti-Semitism. Yet the results of public opinion polls show the opposite – Judaism elicits a positive, rather than a negative, attitude from the respondents (the sum of both the positive and negative attitudes is positive). Even various Protestant denominations, not to mention the Hari Krishnas or the Moonies, elicit more negative attitudes from the contemporary Russians (the sum of attitudes for the Lutherans, Baptists, Methodists or Pentecostalists is negative)[180]. According to other polls, 72% of the Russians believe that nothing prevents the Jews and Christians from living in peace and harmony and without conflicts, whereas only 10% of the respondents believe that that is not so (it is unclear which part of the "pessimists" believe that living without conflicts is indeed impossible for conceptual or historical reasons and which part simply stated what they see as that sad fact)[181].

Second, conceptually, the cooperation between State and Church is as superficial as the Russian religious revival is in general. The State uses the "RO consensus"[182] in society and ask the Church for support when that is appropriate, e.g. during election campaigns. The ROC, in turn, enjoys many special economic opportunities but it does not claim to be the nation's spiritual leader. Aleksandr Verkhovsky, a researcher in the area of the State-Church relations in contemporary Russia, writes: "The State does abandon attempts to use Orthodoxy and the Church to get ideological support, but the State has no intention of bringing the Church closer to the government or of giving it a special

---

world outlook will by fuzzy. Most of the people will simply live without seriously thinking about philosophical issues". (Ibid, pp.43-44).

[180] Kaariaynen K., Furman D. *Op. cit.*, p. 12.
[181] Gudkov L. *Antisemitizm v postsovetskoy Rossi*, p. 90.
[182] The expression is borrowed from: Kaariaynen K., Furman D. *Op. cit.* The authors use it to indicate a high degree of the population's trust of, and respect for, the Church as a spiritual and historical authority without being really religious.

role within the government. And that is not surprising"[183]. And then, after the Presidential election of 2000, "everyone in the Kremlin has forgotten about the Church's ideological support"[184]. Verkhovsky's opinion is also supported by pretty sharp words from Maksim Meyer, a former high-level bureaucrat in the President's Administration who handled religion-related issues as part of his duties: "Our Administration believes that the ROC Administration is dishonest and we do not trust it"[185].

If one looks superficially at the Orthodox phraseology, and that is how the authorities look at it, anti-Judaism remains hidden. To perceive it, one needs to be immersed deeply and seriously into the religious world outlook. Besides, there is another factor. Within the framework of the PR project "New Russian State Ideology", Orthodoxy is viewed as the foundation for positive self-identification and is positioned as a creative, positively oriented outlook. By contrast, the spin masters offer Russians the more obvious negative image of an enemy who heightens the danger of terrorism and another Caucasian war. Political expert Vladimir Pribylovsky names another reason that prevents the Kremlin from using anti-Semitism to consolidate the nation. "Anti-Semitism cannot become a significant trait of a state ideology, because anti-Semitism is unfashionable, say, in Switzerland and Switzerland is exactly where our bosses like to spend their vacations. <...> The opinions of Switzerland and America are paramount. They will not allow us to use anti-Semitism. Yet, they have allowed us to use Chechenophobia, Caucasus-phobia and generally Black-phobia[E30]. And it has become a substantial part of our ideology"[186].

---

[183]   Verkhovskiy A. Religioznyy factor v prezidentskoy kampanii i posle nee. In Verkhovskiy A., Mikhaylovskaya E., Pribylovskiy V. *Natsional-patrioty, Tserkov' i Putin*, p. 82.

[184]   *Ibid.*, p. 83.

[185]   Feygan Dzh. Neozhidannye otkroveniya... (interview with Meyer M.). *NG-Religii*, September 26, 2001. However, due to a strong political resonance caused by the interview, a number of bureaucrats stated that Meyer had no right to make official declarations on behalf of the President's Administration, and he expressed only his personal opinion. Soon after the interview, Meyer was dismissed from the Administration. It is possible that the interview and the resulting scandal were the reason for his dismissal. Yet, it is our impression (and perhaps it is wrong) that he simply expressed the thoughts of others in the Kremlin.

[E30]   *Chernye* (Blacks) is a slur used by Russians to degrade several ethnic groups that live in the southern part of the former Soviet Union.

Under such conditions, anti-Semitism, especially religious anti-Semitism, is not functional at all; it is doomed to marginal existence on the fringes of the main social and ideological processes in contemporary Russia. However, that does not diminish the fact that anti-Judaism and anti-Semitism are an intrinsic and inseparable part of the RO outlook and that fact is unlikely to change in the near future. Yet, one should not forget that these problems are important only for a hopelessly marginal segment of society. As a matter of fact, we have to agree with the researcher who said: "The real problem is that the ROC itself, as well as any other religious organization, is marginal in contemporary Russian society. Hence, any social activity under the Church banner dooms its participants to social and political marginality in today's Russia"[187].

---

[186]   Pribylovskiy V. Zaklyuchitel'nye soobrazheniya. In Verkhovskiy A., Mikhaylovskaya E., Pribylovskiy V. *Natsional-patrioty, Tserkov' i Putin*, p. 113.

[187]   Pavlov I. RPTs v kontekste politicheskoy transformatsii Rossii. *Dia-Logos*, p. 71, No. 3, 2000-2001.

2   Russian Muslims and Anti-Semitism

2.1   Muslims in Contemporary Russia

Let us briefly describe the Russian Muslims before further discussion of anti-Semitism in the Russian Muslim community (RMC).

The question about the number of Muslims in the contemporary RF has no simple answer. Islam is the traditional religion of many ethnic groups living in Russia: Tatars, Bashkirs, Chechens, Avars, Kabardins, Ingushes, Karachays, Adygheans, etc.

All such groups are defined by the term "ethnic Muslims" and together their total number provides the largest estimate of the RMC. Obviously, that approach is incorrect. Secularization and the sometimes forceful separation from religion in the 20th century have substantially weakened the role of Islam in society. Hence, it is inappropriate to count all "ethnic Muslims" as believers, just as it is inappropriate to count all Russians and Ukrainians as Orthodox Christians. Yet, that approach is partly justified – if Islam is not really a religion for all of them, its stereotypes undoubtedly affect their culture and world outlook, which is reflected in their religious and ethnic phobias.

The upper estimate of the number of Muslims in Russia is 15 – 20 million people, though a more realistic estimate is 4 – 9 million[188]. The RF Ministry of Justice and its regional branches had registered 2734 local RMC's by January 1, 1998, and approximately the same number functioned without registration. According to Muslim leaders' estimates, more than 5,000 communities are operating in the country.

There is no single organization uniting all Russian Muslims. Unlike Christianity, which claims that salvation outside the Church is impossible, Muslim Mosques and their structure do not function in this role. There is no vertical

---

[188]   See, for example: Tul'skiy M. Islam v neislamskom mire. *Nezavisimaya gazeta*, September 29, 2001.

authority or fixed clerical bureaucracy legitimized by the direct transfer of Grace in Islam. According to Muslim theologians, a Mosque is a meeting place for prayer and worship without an altar, curtain or a priest as intermediary between the believers and the Almighty. There is no concept of spiritual guidance or ministering in traditional Islam. An Imam who leads the prayers is there like the rest of the people before God. He stands in front of the congregation to let the others synchronize their movements by looking at him; he simply sets the standard for such movements, which are important for the Muslim praying rituals[E31].

Four Central Muslim Spiritual Boards (MSB) or Muftiats existed in the Soviet times: MSB of the Transcaucasus headquartered in Baku, MSB of Central Asia and Kazakhstan headquartered in Tashkent, MSB of the North Caucasus in Makhachkala and MSB of the European part of the USSR and Siberia, MSBES, in Ufa. The heads of the MSBs are Mufties. The regional and local administrative functions are performed by Muhtasib Offices headed by Muhtasibs and controlled by Muftiats. At present, independent MSB's exist in all the newly independent Muslim states of the former Soviet Union and in most of the autonomous republics and regions of the Russian Federation.

After the disintegration of the USSR, the main Muslim centers and the largest Muslim communities were located in Azerbaijan and Central Asia. MSB of the North Caucasus quickly ceased to exist, as each of the autonomous republics created its own independent MSB. Hence, the MSBES has assumed the main role in post-Soviet Russia. Mufty Talgat Tadzhuddin has been its head since 1980. In 1992, the MSBES was transformed into the Central Muslim Spiritual Board (CMSB) and it became the only organization of that kind on the Federal level. One would think that nothing threatens Tadzhuddin's status

---

[E31]   The Editor disagrees here with the Author's characterization above. In the Editor's opinion, the Muslim clerics influence society as much as, if not more than, their Christian counterparts do. The degree of that influence varies from country to country and from region to region. Generally, Muslim clerics deliver sermons that are televised in some countries. In the United States, Imams perform other duties for the community, such as ministering to the Armed Forces and prison inmates. In many countries, they actively influence or even control other spheres of life including education.

as the sole representative of the RMC. He was even awarded the lifetime title of Grand Mufty.

Yet, the stormy post-Soviet reality quickly made corrections. Independent MSBs in Tatarstan, Bashkortostan, and then in other autonomous republics sprang up on the wave of the "sovereignty parade" and with the support of the regional secular authorities. By now, a total of 43 MSBs supervise the religious life of the followers of Islam in Russia. At the initiative of Kazan Mufty Gabdulla Galiulla, the dissenters (not only from the above mentioned autonomous republics, but from other regions as well) united under the auspices of the Supreme Coordinating Council of the Muslim Spiritual Boards of Russia (SCC MSBR). A few years later, SCC MSBR partly disintegrated and became less influential, while the role of CMSBs main competitor was assumed by the Council of the Mufties of Russia (CMR).

The CMR backbone is the Muslim Spiritual Board for the European Part of Russia (MSBER) headquartered in Moscow. MSBER's head and CMR's elected leader, (not a lifetime appointment) is Mufty Ravil Gainutdin who skillfully plays complex games with the media. The refined and diplomatic Moscow Mufty has managed to charm journalists and, as a result of his successful PR, Grand Mufty Tadzhuddin living in Ufa had been labeled as the "Soviet Mufty". The CMR's co-chairman is Sheikh Naafigulla Ashirov.

It is difficult to compare the degrees of real influence of alternative spiritual boards on the Russian Muslims. The Mufties themselves tend to exaggerate the support they receive from the rank-and-file believers, whereas the local communities are often reluctant to get involved in these quarrels and are in no hurry to choose sides. The newspaper "Independent Gazette – Religions" has come up with these data: some 2,100 local communities are within the jurisdiction of the CMSB, which is practically identical with the CMSB's own estimate, and 3,000 belong to the CMR[189].

---

[189]   For details on the structure of the Russian Muslims, see, for example: Likhachev V. Raskolotaya umma. *Liga natsiy*, May 5, 2000.

However, one should keep in mind that, while the CMSB is a centralized organization with a rigid hierarchical structure, the CMR is a much more amorphous union. It includes independent MSBs whose heads become co-chairmen of the Council of the Mufties. The CMSB has received an offer to join the CMR under the same conditions, but the offer obviously was not answered. The CMR is rather a consultative entity – it includes people who are far from being like-minded. Perhaps, the only real trait they have in common is their resentment of the authoritarian style of Tadzhuddin's leadership. Besides, many people are repelled by the "ecumenical" position of the Ufa Grand Mufty. For example, one of the reasons for their indignation was his instruction to decorate a new Mosque in Nabereznye Chelny with a stained-glass window including images of a crescent, a cross and a six-point star. Such a brave decision caused unrest among radicals and simple conservatives; the window was first covered with a curtain with quotations from the Koran, and then it was simply broken.

Both Tadzhuddin and Gainutdin claim to be the RMC representatives to the secular government and abroad. That is why the two Grand Mufties try to maintain the image of respectable and tolerant religious leaders who do not allow any xenophobia or statements that may be interpreted as manifestations of medieval obscurantism. Tadzhuddin actually represents "Islamic ecumenism", as was clear from the above-mentioned stained-glass window example in Nabereznye Chelny. Even though Gainutdin is a "traditionalist" rather than a "liberal", and has repeatedly been accused of having links with foreign and domestic Wahhabists, he has made numerous statements in support of religious tolerance and has condemned all forms of anti-Semitism[190].

In addition to the CMR and the CMSB, another structure claiming more than just regional support is the Coordinating Center of the Muslims of the North Caucasus. Its leadership changed on April 17, 2003, when Ismail-Hadji Berdiev replaced Magomed Albogachiev. It seems that the three structures are equivalent in the eyes of the authorities.

---

[190]   See, for example: Kutakov A. Po kom zvonit kolokol? *Vestnik "Da"*, No. 4, 1998.

The continuing activities of the SCC MSBR that still claims nation-wide scope, those of Abdul-Vahed Niyazov (Islamic Cultural Center), Geidar Dzhemal (Islamic Committee), etc. further complicate the motley mosaic of MSBs. It is the alternative, unofficial Islamic public figures unrelated to the MSB hierarchy but active on the political arena who are the most active anti-Semitic leaders in the Muslim community.

To some degree, Russia follows the pattern existing in other countries with large Muslim communities. Officially, tolerant leaders loyal to the authorities unite Muslim organizations and structures. However, there is a powerful layer of "parallel", unofficial Islam and its followers who hold radical fundamentalist positions including the anti-Semitism so characteristic of them. An example can be found in the anti-Semitic positions of Louis Farrakhan, leader of the Nation of Islam, one of the largest Muslim organizations in America[191].

Anti-Semitism is definitely an eclectic phenomenon. It blends superstitions existing in mass consciousness, religious and political ideologies, cynical use of an image of the enemy and antagonism based on real conflict of interests. But allowing some simplification, one could identify two main directions within the anti-Semitic ideology of modern Russian Muslims: religious, dogmatic anti-Judaism proper and anti-Zionism (the ideology and activity directed against Zionism and the state of Israel and its policies) supported by feelings of pan-Islamic solidarity. Solidarity and a feeling of commonality are characteristic of Islam more than they are of other major religions: ideally, all Muslims feel they belong to the global Muslim community. Naturally, that idea may conflict with nationalism of the Muslim people[192]. However, from the point of view of anti-Semitism, there is no conflict: nationalist emotions require an outburst of xenophobic emotions. Historically, the Jews have been a target for such outbursts, and they are the natural enemy in traditional Islam.

---

[191]   A collection of materials on anti-Semitism in the ideology of L. Farrakhan and the Nation of Islam is presented on the Anti-Defamation League's web site: www.adl.org

[192]   See for example: Levin Z. *Islam i natsionalizm v stranakh zarubezhnogo Vostoka. Ideynyy aspect.* Moscow: Nauka, 1988.

A typical example of such ideological symbiosis based on the "common enemy" is seen in Chechnya in the mid 1990s. First, Dzhokhar Dudaev tried to
lay the foundation for a secular ethnic Chechen state with the support of ethnic intellectuals. However, a difficult military situation forced him to appeal to
Islamic ideas to mobilize supporters and foreign aid. "Russia forced us to em-
bark on Islam, even though we were not well prepared for accepting Islamic
values"[193]. Movladi Udugov known for his anti-Semitic views handled the PR
job for the Chechen separatists. As a result of the separatists' temporary victory in 1996 – 1999, Chechnya became a region of victorious anti-Semitism,
which is a good illustration of the ability of anti-Semitism to exist without any
Jews, because in that case, the anti-Semitism was based on mythology
rather than on a real conflict with an enemy. Journalists surprisingly reported
that while "Chechens had a sufficiently friendly attitude towards the Jews before the war, today the situation is different"[194]. When the Chechen militants
give interviews to journalists, they claim "Chechens became victims of a world
Zionist plot" and that the "Jews kill Muslims by using the stupid Russians for
their own end". Georgian public figure Georgy Zaalishvili who was a POW in
Chechnya for a year reminisces: "For some reason, the fundamentalists
mostly hated the Jews rather than the Russians. They provided me with literature that basically was the same as what Memory and other similar groups
disseminate in Moscow. The zhido-masonic conspiracy was one of the favor-
ite subjects of conversations"[195]. It was taken for granted that, having captured power in the Christian world, world Zionism fights the only force in the
world arena that has not been subdued yet – the Muslim community. Chechnya is one of the fronts in that total global war between Zionism and Islam.
The Chechen radicals take part in the same conflict as the Palestinian and
Lebanese radicals do. The outcome of the war depends on the fight on all
fronts. Clearly, that propaganda was primarily meant to attract support from
various radical Muslim funds. But it was also successful in consolidating the
Chechens themselves.

---

[193]   Terms of War and Peace. *Time*, p. 19, March, 1996.
[194]   Rotar' I. *Pylayushchie oblomki imperii. Zametki voennogo korrespondenta*, p. 52.
        Moscow: Novoe literaturnoe obozrenie, 2001.
[195]   *Nezavisimaya gazeta*, February 28, 2001.

The perpetrators of the invasion of Islamists into Dagestan in the summer of 1999 heralded the invasion as a continuation of the fight not against the Russians, but rather against "world Zionism" and it was announced that the ultimate goal of the war was the "liberation of Jerusalem"[196].

Therefore, the Chechen example makes it obvious that the explosive mixture of dogmatic Muslim anti-Semitism with an anti-Semitism based on a mythical conspiracy theory may become the foundation for an aggressive ideology that, under conditions of a real conflict, may become relatively popular and may directly lead to bloodshed.

2.2   Dogmatic Anti-Judaism: Ideology of Muslim Fundamentalists

Just as Christianity does, Islam holds certain clearly expressed dogmatic grudges against Judaism based on its own genesis and doctrine. Anti-Judaism is a fundamental part of Muslim dogma; it is manifest in religious documents nearly from the very beginning of Muhammad's sermon. The analogy with Christianity is clear, although Christianity-versus-Judaism tension is somewhat more bitter due to obvious elements on both doctrines, especially in the areas of Soteriology[E32] and Christology[197]. Earlier, we referred

---

[196]   See those as well as other statements by rank-and-file militants and their leaders, M. Udugov and Sh. Basev, described by journalist Igor' Rotar': Rotar' I. Pod zelenym znamenem islama. Islamskie radikaly v Rossii i SNG. *Nauchnye doklady i diskussii. Temy dlya dvadtsat' pervogo veka.* Vol. 12, p. 40. Moscow: AYRO-XX, 2001.

[E32]   Soteriology and Christology are areas of theology concerned with salvation and the study of Christ, respectively.

[197]   According to an alternative point of view, anti-Semitism was not common in the Muslim world up until the 20th century. Muslim anti-Semitism was formed only as a result of the political conflict in the Middle East. For example, Bernard Lewis, the author of the must-read book "Semites and Anti-Semites" writes: "For a long time, there were only 'normal' superstitions about the neighboring people with a different religion, cultural traditions and ethnic origin. But the conflict with Israel and its population in the 20th century took the form of anti-Semitism, a destructive attitude that crossed the boundary of superstitions and perceived the Jews as the world evil" (Lewis B. *Semites and Anti-Semites. An Inquiry into Conflict and Prejudice.* New

to the existing opinion that the Christian-Muslim civilization is responsible for anti-Semitism as a unique phenomenon[198], and we mentioned that such an opinion does not seem justified (is it reasonable to speak of the Christian and Muslim worlds as a single entity?[199]), but further discussion of that issue is definitely outside the scope of this book.

Anti-Jewish passages in the Koran are numerous and sometimes pretty aggressive. For example, according to the sacred book of Islam, those of the Jews "who did not come to believe are in Gehenna fire forever. They are the worst creatures"[200] (it is necessary to note, however, that one can find quotations with exactly the opposite meaning[201]). There is no doubt that Muhammad and other leaders of early Islam were sure that people familiar with the Bible would more readily accept Muslim teachings than Pagans would. And when that did not happen – neither the Christians, nor the Jews were in a hurry to recognize Muhammad as the latest prophet (the Jews even less than the Christians) – the Muslim preachers attacked them fiercely. However, historically the Christians and Jews in Muslim countries were in a privileged position compared to the Pagans. The Pagans were viewed as "infidels" and Islamic law allowed violence against them, whereas the followers of the Revealed Religions originated from Abraham were considered 'zimmi' or the People of the Book and they, at least theoretically, were protected by the au-

---

York, London: W. W. Norton & Co., 1999). In our opinion, the political conflict of the 20th century was not the only reason for the rise of anti-Semitism, although the conflict surely resulted in a sharp increase of anti-Semitism existing earlier. Of course, the Jews in Muslim countries before the 20th century were not as demonized as they were in the Medieval Christian Europe. However, the Muslims' attitude towards the Jews was never limited by a set of 'normal' superstitions. For details, see: Goyteyn Sh. *Evrei i araby*. Moscow-Jerusalem: Gesharim – Mosty kul'tury, 2001/5761.

[198]   Chlenov M. *Op. cit.*

[199]   In another paper, Mikhail Chlenov himself clearly separates the Muslim and Christian civilizations: Chlenov M. Evreystvo v sisteme tsivilizatsiy. *Diaspory*, No. 1, 1999.

[200]   *Koran*, 98:6 (Sura "Yasnoe znamenie"). Quoted from *Koran* (translated by Krachkovskiy I.), p. 493. Moscow: Raritet,.

[201]   For example: "Surely those who believe, and those who are Jews, and the Christians, and the Sabians, whoever believes in Allah and the Last day and does good, they shall have their reward from their Lord, and there is no fear for them, nor shall they grieve". Koran 2:62.

thorities[202]. That ambiguity towards the People of the Book has remained in Islam until now.

During the middle ages, religious intolerance and fanaticism were present equally in practically all religions that were lucky enough to become state religions for reasonably long periods of time. But times have changed and denominational mentalities have changed too. Attempts to reach mutual understanding among the various religions and inter-denominational dialogues have become the norm in the modern world. Fundamentalism was born as a response to attempts to modernize religions. It is a movement back to the mythical past, to "unpolluted sources" of the faith. Being a universal phenomenon (all religions have to deal with the same reality today), fundamentalism exists in Abrahamist religions and in Hinduism and Buddhism. Yet because of several denominational characteristics, fundamentalism has gained the strongest position and become a substantial political force in Islam.

Islamic fundamentalism is aggressive, just as any fundamentalism is. Conceptually, that aggression manifests itself in the idea Jihadism, whereby Jihad is a natural state of every believer. A person who refuses to take a fair part in Jihad may not be called a Muslim, as Jihad is one of the pillars of faith, on the same level as, if not higher than, a pilgrimage to Mecca or praying five times a day. Jihad is interpreted in a very narrow sense as a holy war with the infidels (in traditional Islam, that interpretation is called the "Lesser Jihad" whereas the "Greater Jihad" is one's struggle with one's own soul)[203].

The primitive understanding of the essence of Islam as a holy war with the infidels is ideal for mobilizing the adherents in cases of military conflicts between Muslim and non-Muslim states or local groups. In Islam, abstract theology and political activities are bridged easily and both the sincere believers

---

[202]   On anti-Semitism in traditional Islam, see: Likhachev V. *Istoriya antisemitizma,* pp. 16-18; Chanes J. *A Dark Side of History: Anti-Semitism Through the Ages,* pp. 89-103. New York: Anti-Defamation League, 2000.

[203]   See: Khanif S. *Chto dolzhen znat' kazhdyy ob islame i musul'manakh,* p. 233, Kiev: Molod', 1998. Generally, the term jihad means "diligence (efforts) in faith", rather than a "Holy war". See: Rodionov M. *Islam klassicheskiy,* p. 235. St. Petersburg: Peterburgskoe vostokovedenie, 2001.

and cynical politicians readily appeal to religion in antagonistic situations. The ideas of Muslim fundamentalism (Wahhabism, Salafism, Jihadism) have been exploited in many parts of the globe in political, social and ethnic conflicts since the late 1970s. When torn by hundreds of internal problems, the Soviet regime collapsed and interrupted history resumed on one sixth of our planet's land, our fellow Russians suddenly encountered Muslim fundamentalism among other previously unknown facts of life. It has found a fertile ground in Russia.

The conflict with the Christian world makes Muslims revise their relatively tolerant concept of 'zimmi'. The Muslim fundamentalists hold the opinion that the Christians and the Jews are infidels and a Holy war should be waged against them. As a justification for their radicalism, Islamists, especially Wahhabists, say that the Christians and the Jews have deviated from strict monotheism: "May Allah's curse fall upon the Jews and the Christians who have turned the graves of their prophets into temples!"[204]; they "belong to the worst of all creatures before Allah"[205]. Interestingly, some of the ideological materials trying to prove the deviation of Judaism and Christianity from strict monotheism, specifically single out and castigate Judaism. One of the possible explanations for the specific anti-Judaic bitterness is based on myths allegedly describing the early history of Islam. We will discuss that issue further below but let us note the following quotation here. "The study of Jewish history led Muslims to conclude that it is impossible to place great expectations on those whose history contains such events. If you become familiar with the cruelty of those repulsive people, you may be disillusioned and heart-broken. During many centuries, that people has become repugnant and spoiled. They mock the vital verses of the Koran. They have corrupted the true religion and they have changed it at will"[206].

---

[204]   Tamimi M. *Kniga edinobozhiya*, p. 119. Moscow: Badr, 1999.

[205]   *Programmy po izucheniyu shariatskikh nauk*, p. 62. Moscow: Ibragim Al' Ibragim, 1999.

[206]   Maududi S. *Tolkovanie Velichestvennogo Korana*. Sury: al' Fatikha I al' Bakara, p. 95.

Notes made by a student in a Muslim fundamentalist class and subsequently found by a researcher state that "belief in such destructive doctrines as Judaism, Communism and Jewish Judaic Masonry" is the "gravest sin"[207]. The juxtaposition of Judaism with Communism and Masonry is explained further. According to the student and his teacher, "Judaism is behind all enemies of Allah and behind every destructive doctrine undermining moral and spiritual values. World Judaism embeds staunch, cunning and knowledgeable thinkers in Masonic lodges, who are not only up to date with the current world, but are also well adjusted to the specific conditions of every nation, people and country"[208]. That excerpt from a Wahhabist's notes is an expanded and slightly modified version of the thesis that "Judaism is behind each and every destructive doctrine undermining moral and spiritual values" from the popular book (sort of a fundamentalist "catechesis") by Mohammad ibn Jamil Zinu[209]. Furthermore, according to a flyer distributed in the Karachaevo-Cherkessia Republic, the "Jews have greatly succeeded in employing their skills to destroy other peoples using women's seduction and allure[210].

Obviously, for contemporary Muslim fundamentalists, unlike medieval Muslims, anti-Judaism is not just part of consistent and uncompromising following their own faith. Rather, it is part of a political ideology that has been almost mythologized with a conspiratorial flavor that may be called anti-Semitic in every sense of that word. Contemporary Islamic fundamentalism is a political rather than a religious movement and anti-Semitism adds an important part of

---

[207]   Yarlykapov A. Kredo vakhkhabita. *Dia-Logos*, p. 232, No. 3, 2000-2001. Akhmet Yarlykanov found and published excerpts from the notes of a student at a religious school in the Kadar zone in several scholarly publications (with his comments). Yarlykapov found the notes during his research in Daghestan Republic in the summer of 1999. The name of the notes' author was on the notes' cover page, but it was withheld by Yarlykapov probably for ethical reasons.

[208]   *Ibid.*, p. 243.

[209]   Zinu M. *Islamskaya akida – verouchenie, ubezhdenie, vozzrenie*, p. 68. Moscow: Badr, 1998.

[210]   Zachem nuzhen khidzhab (leaflet). Quoted from Kratov E. K voprosu ob ideologii sovremennogo religiozno-politicheskogo ekstremizma. In *Terrorizm i politicheskiy ekstremizm: vyzovy i poiski adekvatnykh otvetov*, p. 142. Moscow: Institut voennogo i politicheskogo analiza, 2002.

it by promoting mobilization and consolidation of its adherents in facing a common, though mythological, enemy. Though the enemy is described in religious terms, it is always recognized as a political reality.

As a political ideology, Islamic fundamentalism declares war on modern western democratic values as "Jewish": "the essence of a democratic society consists of letting the Jews lust, lie and cheat"[211]. Another author writes: "Anyone who tears the Muslim community away from their religion and the Koran must be a Jewish agent intentionally or unintentionally, regardless of their origin"[212].

Anti-Semitic Islam highlights their fight with the Jews who are seen as the conduits for modernism and democracy, which, in the Islamists' opinion, are contradictory to the human values in the Koran. This fight has also achieved the status of opposition to a metaphysical "Absolute Evil". A popular and authoritative Islamic theologian writes: "Allah commanded the Muslims to fight Satan's friends anywhere they may be found. And among all his friends, perhaps Satan's best friends now are Jews"[213].

When Muslim radicals, based on their understanding of the problem, look into the past of Islam, they find confirmation of their views. Thus, one of the most popular Islamic web sites "Independent Islamic Information Channel Islam.ru" published an article by Mohammed al-Asi "Truth and lies about Muslims and Zionists from the times of the Prophet – peace be upon him – to the present".

---

[211]   The statements are from the North Caucasian Wahhabist newspaper 'Kaf'. The quotes are taken from Muzaev T. *Etnicheskiy separatizm v Rossii*, p. 54. Moscow: Panorama, 1999.

[212]   Seyid Kutb. *Nasha bor'ba s evreyami*, p. 2. The pamphlet was disseminated as a self-published brochure in the circles close to the Islamic Revival Party in the early 1990s. Probably, it is based on the English translation of the book *Our Struggle With the Jews* by S. Qutb, Cairo, 1970, published under the same cover with the *Protocols of the Elders of Zion.*

[213]   That statement was made by Sheikh Abd al-Halim Mahmud, the Grand Sheikh of the most influential Muslim theological University al-Azhar in Cairo in his book al-Jihad wa al-Nasir (Holy War and Victory), quotation is from Nettler R. *A Muslim Fundamentalist's View of the Jews*, p. 21. Vidal Sassoon International Center for the Study of Anti-Semitism, The Hebrew University of Jerusalem. Pergamon Press, 1994. Many spiritual leaders of Russian Muslims, including T. Tadzhuddin, have studied at al-Azhar University.

The author quotes several traditional stories from Prophet Muhammad's biography in which Jews appear. They recognize the Lord's Messenger in the founder of Islam and sometimes they are suspected of scheming against him[214]. From those legends, the author draws this conclusion: "… When the Prophet – peace and blessings be upon him – predicted by the Bible appeared and it became clear that he was not Jewish, then they became downright worried. Soon, they came up with a plot against the Lord's Messenger – peace and blessings be upon him – justified by his encroachment on the Jews' religious and ethnic privileges. It is no exaggeration to say that a people whose history knows details and treacherous murders of prophets and apostles, whose sermons were not in the interests of Israel, could come up with the idea of liquidating Muhammad for the same reason".

It is interesting that the author of the text easily believes (or pretends to believe) medieval anti-Judaic legends and uses them to justify subsequent violence against the Jews in Mecca. The author bridges the events of that time with the present, which shows how dogmatic Muslim anti-Judaism turns into paranoid political anti-Semitism: "In the atmosphere of modern politics, when the state of Israel exists and where they clearly realize the threat that Islam poses for the Zionist elite's global domination, it is obvious that the public sentiments are similar to those existing at the time of the Prophet, peace and blessings be upon him. The contemporary political descendants of Banu Nadir, Banu Qaynuqa and Banu Qurayza (Semitic tribes who lived in the Saudi peninsula and followed Judaism – V. L.) try to find allies among the world financial and industrial oligarchy. The latter, despite their opportunity to get to know and accept the Prophet, peace and blessings be upon him, continue to pursue their selfish ends and impose values alien to most of the people on them".

---

[214]   For a translated collection of episodes of his biography, see *Khrestomatiya po islamu*. Moscow: Nauka, 1994. In one of the episodes, Christian monk Bahira tells Abu Talib, Muhammad's uncle who raised the boy: "Keep him away from the Jews. For, by Allah, if they see him and know about him what I know, they will try to injure him, because something very great will happen to this nephew of yours". (Ibn Khashim. Zhizneopisanie gospodina nashego Mukhammada, poslannika Allakha. In *Khrestomatiya po islamu*, p. 15).

An anonymous preacher whose audiocassettes are disseminated in the North Caucasus uses the same stories and attributes a very drastic, traditionally unknown (as far as we know) conclusion to the Prophet himself: "The Jews… They always lie… When Muhammad made agreements with them, they always broke them. Muhammad came to a decision and told Muslims and all his followers: he who sees a Jew should kill him"[215].

2.3   Anti-Zionism: Ideology Amenable to Masses

Dogmatic and conspiratorial anti-Semitism in the ideology of Muslim radicals is tightly linked with their aggressive criticism of the state of Israel. Anti-Zionism among the Muslims takes different shapes – from expressions of solidarity with the "struggling Palestinian people" to support for fanatical terrorists. But only radicals like M. Udugov make statements expressing their readiness to send volunteers to participate in the war in the Holy Land against the "infidels and Zionists", while the support of the "legitimate right of the Palestinian people to create an independent state with Jerusalem as its capital" is a commonplace for all Russian Muslim leaders. That is the danger of anti-Zionism.

Full-fledged dogmatic anti-Judaism may be part of the ideology only for Muslim fundamentalists. It implies an ardent attitude towards the foundations of the faith. That would lead the rather unique Russian Islam – one that has actively interacted with both Christianity and Pagan traditions in Russia for centuries – to a bitter conflict with the traditionally accepted forms of Islam in our country. Besides, fundamentalism assumes a relentless struggle not just with Judaism, but also with Christianity and, even to a greater degree, with the secular democratic state model. The inevitable conflict with the authorities and with the Muslim clerics interested in stability drives the radicals underground, which of course is fraught with extremism and terrorist activities, but that dooms the fundamentalists to the margins. Yet, anti-Zionism may be

---

[215]   Druzhba i neprichastnost' v islame. Audiocassette. Quoted from Kratov E. *Op. cit.*, p. 143.

quite acceptable to a wide segment of practicing Muslims because of their solidarity with the Palestinians and to the political establishment of contemporary Russia because of the traditions of Soviet propaganda.

Anti-Zionism was part of the official ideology and propaganda of the Soviet regime. Hence, the Muslim leaders and Russian communists easily find a common language. Taking into account anti-Semitism immanently present in the Communist Party of the Russian Federation and some of its main characters, that trend has gained in scope. The newspaper Soviet Russia has published pro-Palestinian materials in almost every issue since the beginning of the present Intifada. Some of the materials contain unrestrained criticism of Israel, which turned into openly anti-Semitic rhetoric.

As strange as it would seem, even RO fundamentalist publications, such as Russian Herald, Radonezh and Russian Home, cover the conflict in the Holy Land exclusively from the Palestinian position[216], while representatives of the Palestinian Autonomy constantly stress their positive contacts with the ROC. Although the RO patriotic press uses the fact that some Palestinians are Christians as a trump card, the presentation of the material clearly demonstrate a common platform based on anti-Semitism. Thus, the RO press concentrates its attention on the actions of the Israeli Army or Jewish radicals against Christian buildings in the Holy Land, whereas the actions of the Muslim radicals – that happen at least as frequently – are outside the scope of interest of the Russian press.

The thesis that anti-Semitism is a common base for Muslim radicals and Russian nationalist patriots, especially due to the traditions and the pro-Soviet, national Bolshevik orientation, may be illustrated by the example of the Movement in Support of the Army (MSA) participating in the State Duma elections in 1999. The leaders of the Movement, Albert Makashov and Viktor Ilyukhin, overtly positioned that election block as the one opposing the "Zionists". The Federal list of the Movement included one of the leaders of the

---

[216]   See, for example: *Radonezh*, No. 2 (120), 2002; *Russkiy dom*, No. 12, December, 2001.

Russian Muslim fundamentalists, Geydar Dzhemal, who is often involved in radical anti-Semitic propaganda.

Of course, the example above concerns marginal players on the political scene. MSA captured less than 0.58% of the vote, while G. Dzhemal does not represent any countrywide Muslim organization. Other facts of collaboration of Russian and Islamic radicals are just as marginal. For example, the site of Dmitry Vasilyev's National Patriotic Front Memory has a page "Radio Islam" and editor-in-chief of that "radio" Ahmed Rami is associated with Evgeny Shchekatikhin, the publisher of St. Petersburg's radical anti-Semitic newspaper "Our Fatherland". Yet, a full-fledged bloc of Russian nationalists and Islamic fundamentalists has not occurred and it is hardly possible – anti-Semitism and, perhaps, anti-Westernism are the only things they have in coomon, whereas their differences include many major issues, such as the Chechen question.

A somewhat more serious phenomenon is the growing anti-Semitic trend among a broad segment of Russian Muslims. Anti-Zionism is quite apprehensible and acceptable to the Russian Muslims, and one may use it as a cover to sneak in full-fledged anti-Semitic ideas of world conspiracy.

The terrorist attack on the USA on September 11, 2001, and the subsequent reaction of the Western societies gave impetus to aggravation of that trend. The Russian Muslims believe that the "West has declared war on Islam". Hence, they look for, and find, super-mythical Zionists behind the mythical aggressive West.

Thus, one of the most popular domestic Muslim web sites, Islam.ru, carried an editorial "Terrorist acts in the USA: who stands to gain?" The authors of the editorial are absolutely sure that "no Muslim could commit that action for religious reasons" and the "noisy campaign of blaming Islam and Muslims in the media" is part of the plan whose author is either Israel, or the "international financial mafia". "How can Israel gain from the terrorist acts?", ask the authors. Here is their answer: "In every way. The Muslim countries that do not recognize the Israeli occupation get weaker. Islam itself that teaches true monotheism cleansed from the Pagan-Judean Nazism gets discredited. Israel succeeds in stirring up Christian public opinion against the Muslims, in playing the two largest world religions against one another, so that the Christians, led on the leash by Israel, become its heavy weapons. Israel gets the right to commit acts of terror against the Palestinian population on the occupied territories with impunity under the pretext of the fight against terrorism. Israel gets an opportunity to suppress the Palestinians, and consolidate and legitimize the de facto annexation of the stolen property".

True, the authors of the editorial do not necessarily blame Israel; rather they offer an alternative version putting the responsibility for the plot that led to the terrorist acts on the "international financial mafia that sides with the euro and tries to destroy the dollar". Yet, that mafia also has clearly detectable ethnic characteristics, as they are talking about "European oligarchic capital (Rothschild and Co., Israel)".

Let us stress that such ideas are promoted not on a site like kavkaz.org controlled by the radicals, but rather on a solid (and the most popular, too) Russian Muslim Internet resource.

The editors returned to the idea of conspiracy that caused the terrorist acts and the "war against the Muslims" in the article "Judean Myth as a Means for Fighting Terrorism" published on the same site. The article offers a theory, whereby the USA itself, while pursuing its geopolitical goals, spawned international terrorism that, like the Golem, has gotten out of control and eventually become dangerous for its creator. However, here the Jewish theme is not limited to the mention of the legend about the Golem either. According to the authors, the creation of the Islamic "arc of instability from the Balkans to Sumatra" "led to a conflict between the Muslims and the Christians or between two out of the three Abrahamist religions, which objectively plays into the hands only of the Orthodox Jews". Judging from the subsequent discussion on the site forum, that interpretation of the world events was in accord with that of the Russian Muslims.

In summary, anti-Semitism has a strong position among the Russian Muslims. As dogmatic anti-Judaism, it is a traditional part of Islam; as anti-Zionism, it claims a high degree of popularity in the contemporary Russian political and cultural context. Intertwining and complementing one another, the two anti-Semitic doctrines form an elaborate and peculiar ideological maze leading to paranoid theories of the "world Jewish conspiracy".

3   Right-Wing Radicals between God and Nation

A link between nationalistic and religious components in the ideology of the contemporary Russian right-wing radicals is undisputed. National self-identification, the essence of the ultra-right is closely related to religious self-identification. But that is not the only point.

The Russian right-wing radical's view of the world per se is a religious view. That statement, of course, implies a broad (perhaps an excessively broad) notion of religiosity. Perhaps, it would be more appropriate to reformulate that statement as follows: of all the modern political currents, right-wing radicalism has more typological characteristics that are similar to religious values, authorities and mentality in general. Naturally, that results in a close intertwining of nationalistic and religious motives in the ideologies of the movements belonging to the right end of the political spectrum. By and large, any study of the views of right-wing radical groups should discuss their religious component to some degree.

There have been attempts to study some aspects of the issue of "right-wing political radicalism and religion" in the literature. Most of the attention has been devoted to two themes: Russian neo-paganism (let us mention the works by Viktor Shnirelman[217], Vladimir Pribylovsky[218] and Evgeny Moroz[219])

---

[217]   See, for example: Shnirel'man V. Neoayzychestvo. Neoayzychestvo v Rossii. *Diagnoz*, No. 1, p. 16, April 1997. Shnirel'man V. Izobretenie proshlogo. *Novoe vremya*, No. 32, p. 44, 1996. Shnirel'man V. Mif o sverkhcheloveke vozrozhdaetsya v Rossii. *Novoe vremya*, No. 13, pp. 37-38, 1997. Shnirel'man V. Russkoe neoyazychestvo i antisemitizm. *Evreyska istoriya ta kul'tura v Ukraini*, pp. 122-125, Kiev, 1997. Shnirel'man V. Neoyazychestvo i natsionalizm. *Issledovaniya po prikladnoy i neotlozhnoy etnologii*, No. 114, Moscow: Institut etnologii I antropologii Rossiyskoy akademii nauk, 1998. Shnirel'man V. Russkoe neoyazychestvo: poiski identichnosti ili neonatsizm? *Stranitsy Bibleysko-bogoslovskogo instituta sv. Apostola Andreya*, v. 4, No. 1, pp. 124-135, 1999. Shnirel'man V. Neoyazychestvo na prostorakh Evrazii. *Dia-Logos*, No. 2, pp. 201-205, 1998-1999. Shnirel'man V. Perun, Svarog i drugie. *Neoyazychestvo na prostorakh Evrazii*, pp. 10-39. Moscow: Bibleysko-bogoslovskiy institut sv. Apostola Andreya, 2001. Victor A. Shnirelman. *Russian Neo-pagan Myths and Anti-Semitism* (=Analysis of Current Trends in anti-Semitism, No. 13). Jerusalem: The Vidal Sasoon International Center for the Study of Anti-Semitism, 1998.

and relations between the ROC and ultra-right groups[220] (RO fundamentalists within the ROC MP generated especial interest; also, there have been a lot of effort to prove that the Nazis' Christian rhetoric is superficial and insincere[221]). We shall try to avoid repetitions of these issues as much as possible; rather we shall concentrate on issues that have not received much attention.

Domestic right-wing radicals are mostly followers of Orthodoxy. It should be noted that that affiliation is by far not always denominational, religious. Often, the national version of Christianity is meant to be a cultural guide. "A patriot must be Orthodox" is a stereotype of traditional nationalism that is intentionally exploited for purely selfish reasons. One may actually notice the trend: the more radical an organization is, the more it is influenced by the experience of European fascism rather than by traditional Russian state patriotism and the weaker its links to the ROC MP (although Orthodoxy may still be declared) and vice versa. All nationalist groups tracing their traditions to the pre-

---

[218]   See, for example: Pribylovskiy V. Novye yazychniki – lyudi i gruppy. *Russkaya mysl'*, No. 4220, April 30 – May 6, 1998. Pribylovskiy V. Russkie yazychniki. *Ekspress-Khronika*, February 21 and March 7, 1998. Pribylovskiy V. Russkoe neoyazychestvo – kvazireligiya natsionalizma i ksenofobii. *Dia-Logos*, No. 2, pp. 137-160, 1998-1999. Pribylovskiy V. Neoyazycheskoe krylo v russkom natsionalizme. *Religiya i SMI*, October 31, 2002. (http://www.religare.ru/article.php?num=490). See also Verkhovskiy A., Mikhaylovskaya E., Pribylovskiy V. *Politicheskaya ksenofobiya: radikal'nye gruppy, predstavleniya liderov, rol' Tserkvi*, pp. 123-134. Moscow: Panorama, 1999.

[219]   See, for example, Moroz E. Vedizm i fashizm. *Bar'er*, No. 3, pp. 4-8, 1993. Moroz E. Vedizm. Yazycheskaya versiya russkoy idei. St. Petersburg, manuscript, 1992. Moroz E. Yazychniki v Sankt-Peterburge. *Neoyazychestvo na prostorakh Evrazii*, pp. 39-56. Moscow: Bibleysko-bogoslovskiy institut sv. Apostola Andreya, 2001.

[220]   See, for example, Nuzhen li Gitler Rossii? *Bulleten' fonda "Antifashist"*, No. 6, pp. 184-239. Polosin V. Natsional-patrioty i Russkaya Pravoslavnaya Tserkov'. *Dia-Logos*, No. I, pp. 114-122, 1997. Ilyushenko V. Russkiy fashizm i religiya. *Dia-Logos*, No. II, pp. 160-172, 1998-1999. Verkhovskiy A. Ksenofobiya i religiya v Rossii. *Dia-Logos*, No. II, pp. 97-137, 1998-1999. Verkhovskiy A. Tserkov' v politike, politika v tserkvi. *Politicheskaya ksenofobiya*, pp. 60-123, and especially pp. 101-113.

[221]   Here is a commonly held opinion: "Fascism is the most dangerous form of Paganism demanding bloody sacrifices. One might say that fascism is a rebellion of subterranean elements against the divine order" (Ilyushenko V. Dve modeli khristianstva I russkiy fashizm. Nuzhen li Gitler Rossii? p.197). That opinion decisively separating Christianity and "fascism" seems unconvincing and idealized to us.

Soviet times recognize the church hierarchy or the spiritual authority of the heads of the church, even if they criticize certain traits of the ROC MP. On the contrary, more radical organizations may have a very critical attitude towards the "official" church[222]. A substantial number of nationalistic radicals, if not a majority, tend to dissociate themselves from the "state" organized church.

Mistrust of the ROC MP is especially common among Christian nationalist socialists. The thesis that the ROC has "betrayed Orthodoxy" is wide spread among them. Thus, K. Kasimovsky, a leader of the Nazi group RNU-KK[223] that uses the slogan "Purity of faith and purity of blood", unleashed a diatribe against clerics and the Patriarch: "When the Patriarch of Moscow and All Russia tells the zhids 'Shalom to you brothers, we believe in the same God and we have common prophets and Gods'[224], he deserves to be defrocked and even excommunicated"[225]. Compare that with the position of Black Hundred leader Aleksandr Shtilmark which is more typical for traditional Orthodox nationalists: "Like people, like priest. To scold the Patriarch is super-blasphemy <...> If we shape up, there will be a different Patriarch"[226]. Kasimovsky is a ROCA parishioner. A picture in which a ROCA bishop blessed RNU-KK comrades illustrated the front page of the first issue of the newspaper Storm Trooper which he edits. Most of the members of the Fraternal Order of Saint Iosif Volotsky that publishes the newspaper Czar's Guardsman and is affiliated with RNU-KK also belong to parishes under the jurisdiction of

---

[222]   Partly, that is related to a general ambiguity the radicals feel towards the Russian statehood: on the one hand, it is fervent patriotism turning into chauvinism; on the other hand, it is a clearly expressed unwillingness to identify with the contemporary political "regime".

[223]   Known as the movement "Russian Actions" since 2000.

[224]   That is a corrupted quote from the above-mentioned speech given by Alexy II in New York at a meeting with rabbis ("Your prophets are our prophets").

[225]   Onegina S. Natsional'naya revolyutsiya Kasimovskogo (interview with K. Kasimovskiy). *Russkaya mysl'*, November 20-26, 1997. Here is a continuation of the interview:
> -What is your attitude towards the official Orthodox Church?
> -Bastard priests, that is our attitude towards the official Orthodox Church.
> -Why?
> -Because they betrayed the faith.

[226]   Chernaya sotnya: vchera, segodnya, zavtra (an interview with A. Shtil'mark). *Shturm*, p. 23, No. 2, 1996.

the ROCA or the TOC. And a former leader and founder of RNU-KK, Alexy Vdovin, was brought up in the TOC.

RNU leader Aleksandr Barkashov was also a parishioner of a TOC branch called the Church of the Apocalypse a.k.a. "Interregional Spiritual Board of the TOC". As RNU activities expanded, the links with the TOC gradually faded. Barkashovites, especially in the regions, try to establish friendly cooperation with ROC bishops and clerics. But in its initial stages, the largest domestic nationalist radical organization was closely connected to some groups within TOC. For example, Barkashov's personal spiritual mentor for a while was Konstantin Vasilyev, self-appointed "Archbishop Lazar, the Lamb of Revelation", the leader of one of the TOC splinter groups, an adventurer and an extremely unstable person. In 1990, he blessed the ephemeral "Russian Orthodox Guards Corps" which is based on RNU and he even ordained Barkashov as a sub-deacon. However, by 1996, Lazar had pulled out of RNU and withdrawn his blessing because of inactivity of the corps"[227]. In 1990 – 1992, many groups of the Barkashovites officially registered as fraternities and TOC communities, such as The Archistrategos[E33] Michael Community in Mytishchy, etc. They also used versions of the famous poster "Russia awaits your freedom"[228] which shows a young man in a black shirt armed with a sword and a shield. An eight-point star and the inscription "Truly Orthodox Church" are clearly added to the shield.

Later, as RNU expanded its activities, it became harder for it to be confined to small sectarian communities[229]. The regional leaders used every opportunity

---

[227]   Agnets Otkroveniya Vladyka Lazar' (K. Vasil'ev). A fax of October 14, 1996, sent to A. Barkashov. (A xerox copy in the author's archive.)

[E33]   Orthodox liturgy confers the title Archistrategos (Supreme Commander in Greek) to Archangel Michael, which is an allusion to Apocalypse 12:7 – "And there was a great battle in heaven, Michael and his angels fought with the dragon." Ironically, the Bible and Kabbalistic traditions portray Michael as "the advocate of the Jewish people."

[228]   The poster is shown in Likhachev V., Pribylovsky V. *Russkoe Natsional'noe Edinstvo*, p. 40. Moscow: Panorama, 1997. The original version of the poster is used as an illustration.

[229]   Now, after the RNU split, it is hard to talk about the RNU orientation in general, including its religious orientation. RNU-II (the Group of the Lalochkins) is oriented to-

to establish friendly contacts with the bishops and individual clerics by offer-
ing cooperation in the publication sphere, help in restoration and protection of
churches, and by conducting popular activities. In exchange, they asked the
priests for help in their educational and ideological activities, and if they succeeded, they proclaimed that loudly for propaganda purposes. Still, they kept
a distance from the ROC hierarchy[230]. The official party newspaper Russian
Order published a "Question for the ROC"[231]. The question was: "Did not you
forget, Holy Fathers, what faith you serve and what people – what faith and
ethnicity – crucified God's Son, Jesus Christ?" And then: "For it is time for you
to decide who you are with, because you represent the Holy Church rather
than a cheap whore. And if you do not make a choice, we will make it for you
- render to everyone according to his deeds. RNU hereby officially warns the
Moscow Patriarchy of the inadmissibility of compromises and betrayal with
respect to both the Russian people and the Orthodox faith". The article was
unsigned which, in view of its style, gives it the status of an official statement.
It is no coincidence that the standard propaganda text appearing in many
leaflets proclaims that "RNU members are guided in their lives by the old
forms of Orthodoxy that existed in the early Middle Ages and served our an-
cestors as the spiritual foundation when they created and strengthened the
Russian state"[232]. One may only guess if the ROC MP fits that definition.

The founder of RNU and its leader during the 1990s clearly does not belong
to any parish under any jurisdiction of the ROC[233]. Furthermore, according to
his religious mentality, he is closer to being a racist mystic, rather than an Orthodox Christian in the canonical sense[234] even though he tries to appear as

---

wards ROC MP. D. Demushkin's Slavonic Union (RNU Moscow regional organization) is oriented towards a branch of the "catacomb church", etc.

[230]   The official position of the ROC towards RNU is strongly negative. The official organ
of the Patriarchy has published an article titled "Orthodox cross or swastika?" specifically to clarify that issue.

[231]   Russkiy poryadok, p. 11, Nos. 9-1 (12-3), December, 1993, January, 1994.

[232]   Chto Takoe RNE, p. 12. Moscow: 1996.

[233]   Thus, answering a correspondent's question "When did you receive communion last
time?", Barkashov irritably shouted: "I've never received and will never receive anything from a member of this Jewish cabal, Moscow Patriarchy!" (A verbal communication of A. Semenov).

[234]   For a critical review of Barkashov's views and the RNU religious ideology in general

such[235]. There has been some information about the RNU leader's "better than favorable" disposition towards Buddhism. Specifically, according to the press, Barkashov along with Chairman of the Union of Russian Buddhists Igor Antonov, who is also a Memory alumnus, undertook a pilgrimage to the Ivolginsky Datsan[E34] in Buryatia[236].

Instances of cooperation between some representatives of the ROCA with RNU have been reported, too[237]. Occasionally, friendly contacts between Nazis and Old Believers[E35] have been established[238]. In general, right-wing radicals often appeal to the latter as members of the national, original, unspoiled Orthodoxy. Thus, NRPR leader Nikolay Lysenko, the only radical nationalist in the State Duma in 1993 – 1995, talked about converting to the Old Believers' faith[239] (however, already in 2003 he actively preached about converting to Islam). As it transpired during a round-table discussion devoted to Old Belief at the newspaper "Tomorrow", a large number of politicians belonging to

---

showing that they are not based on Orthodoxy, see, for example, Shatrov A. Karayushchiy namestnik Boga. *NG – Religii*, April 15, 1998.

[235] Thus, Barkashov undoubtedly has observed fasts, visited monasteries, etc.

[E34] The ROC adopted a number of liturgical reforms in the 17th century. The Old Believers rejected the reforms and formed their own denomination that soon broke into several groups.

[236] A communication from A. Semenov. See also: Sukhoverov V. Legendy i mify zheleznogo Shurika. *Moskovskiy komsomolets*, February 12, 1999. An interest in Buddhism occurs occasionally among Russian radical nationalists. Thus, the Press Secretary of the racist Freedom Party (its leader is Yu. Belyaev), Lev Nechipurenko, for a while was the head (with questionable justifications though) of the Buddhist community Datsan Gunzechoyney on Primorsky Prospect, St. Petersburg.

[237] For example, known anti-sect activist Oleg Stenyaev who was ordained in the ROCA (he later transferred to the ROC MP) gave theological classes for RNU members.

[E35] The ROC adopted a number of liturgical reforms in the 17th century. The Old Believers rejected the reforms and formed their own denomination that soon broke into several groups.

[238] Here is an example. The Archbishop of Perm Afanasy (a person with moderate views) insisted on depoliticizing the diocese. As a result of his liberalism (thus, he ordained a Jew as a priest), the large fundamentalist Orthodox fraternity named after Stephen of Great Perm en masse joined RNU and converted to Old Belief. See: Shchipkov A. *Vo chto verit Rossiya?* St. Petersburg: Izdatel'stvo Russkogo Khristianskogo gumanitarnogo instituta, p. 54, 1998.

[239] Osipov V. Nikolay Lysenko na svobode (interview with N. Lysenko). *Desnitsa*, No. 5, 1997.

the radical national patriotic opposition (Aleksandr Prokhanov, Mikhail Filin) empathized with the followers of the "Fiery Archpriest"[E36], even though they did not identify with the movement. Aleksandr Dugin, an ideologue of the post-Soviet National Bolshevism, and a group of his followers from all over Russia went the furthest in their support of Old Belief: going from proclaiming its historical rightness to actually joining the denomination.

Beginning in 1996, Dugin began to speak and write in books and periodicals in support of the schismatics' doctrinal and historical correctness[240]. His arguments boil down to the following. "Generally, we should finally conclude that Orthodoxy is what is related to Old Belief, or what at least tends towards it. The Nikonian spirit is an aberration, a compromise, a not very interesting, moralistic and artificial phenomenon, or worse"[241].

At that time or slightly later, he became a parishioner of an *Edinoverie*[E37] temple in Mikhaylovsky settlement, Ramensky district of the Moscow region. The ideologue's conversion to Old Belief was followed by similar conversions by a few members of the NBP in Moscow[242], St. Petersburg and Kazan.

The attempt by nationalist intellectuals to embrace a specific denomination as "traditional" and containing the "profound doctrinal truth" is a very interesting phenomenon. This is an example of mythological thinking generally typical for the ultra-rightists. According to the traditional myth that is accepted one way

---

E36   Reference to Russian Archpriest Avvakum who led the opposition to the reforms in the ROC in the 17th century. He was burned at the stake by the Russian government.

240   See, for example: Dugin A. *"Yako ne ispolnisya chislo zverinnoe" (smysl russkogo raskola) – Konets sveta*, pp. 50-64. Moscow: Arktogeya, 1998. Dugin A. Kadrovye. *Limonka*, No. 80, 1997. Dugin A. "Storozh! Skol'ko nochi?". *Limonka*, No. 82, 1998, etc.

241   A statement made in the Internet group "Old Belief" on March 12, 1999.

E37   *Edinoverie* is a movement within Old Belief.

242   See *Limonka*, No. 86, March, 1998. However, for most of them, Old Belief is just a cultural position affecting their views of the world and followed at the level of some symbolic gestures (refusing to wear a necktie, growing a beard, etc). Only few of them became truly religious members of the faith. They included Aleksandr Sotnichenko, the leader of the St. Petersburg branch of the society Arctogea headed by Dugin and Pavel Zarifullin, the leader of the Kazan branch of the same society.

or another by almost all right-wing radicals, history may roughly be divided into these periods: the Golden Age, the Catastrophe and a Modern Decline that calls for a Revolutionary Revival[243]. Dugin and his followers' version equates the tragic catastrophe with the Nikonian reforms – they use eschato-logical numerology usual in Old Belief to come up with the Antichrist's date 1666. "The deviation from the true Orthodoxy during the schism, then the fall of the Nikonian church during the revolution and today's downfall of secular Russian culture strangled by Western liberalization – all of that are steps in a certain direction. The same phenomenon has been behind all catastro-phes"[244].

Curiously, Dugin's followers and similar "ideological" Old Believers continue to find a warm reception in the Church (or Churches, to be precise, as they join different brands of Old Believers). Thus, Dugin was an invited speaker at the Council of the Russian *drevlepravoslavnaya*[E38] (Ancient Orthodox) Church on October 20, 1998. Partly, it is due to the fact that among the "first generation" Old Believers (who are not numerous but active[245]), most joined Old Belief during the general religious revival of the 1980s for the same rea-sons as the nationalists did in the late 1990s.

But of course, most of the nationalists belong to the ROC MP, or to its fundamentalist, right wing, to be exact. However, the spectrum of the right-wingers' religious beliefs is not limited to the standard and sectarian Ortho-doxy.

A lot has been written about neo-Paganism as a political and religious move-ment and we will try to avoid repetition. We may only add that the Pagans ex-

---

243   See Sheehan T. Myth and Violence: the Fascism of Julius Evola and Alain de Be-noit. *Social Research*, pp. 61-62, No. 1, 1981. I became familiar with this idea (and this reference) through a reference in Shnirelman V. *Russian Neo-pagan Myth...*

244   A round table discussion at the newspaper *Zavtra*. Its full text was published on the Internet.

E38   Ancient Orthodox Church is a movement within Old Belief.

245   It is well known that newcomers to the ROC, or first-generation Christians, are the most zealous ones in the social and religious areas. Father A. Men's followers are a good example.

ploit the "traditionalist" historical model described above and claim a general degradation and the consequent necessity for revolutionary rejuvenation. Pagan nationalists tend to look upon their religious affiliation as a way of viewing the world rather than just as membership in a particular denomination expressed in a specific set of rituals, and they do that to a larger extent than do the Orthodox patriots. Hence, we will be primarily interested in the historical, philosophical and other "ideological" theories of the neo-Pagans rather than in the ritual side of their religion. It is interesting how the Vedists and their followers view contemporary society and its prospects for national revival.

In a nutshell, the mythology of the aficionados of Slavic antiquities is as follows. The "Catastrophe" for the neo-Pagans was surely Christianization, which put an end to the glorious and mighty ancient Russian (Aryan) statehood. The sway of its foes (aliens, Jews) was established as early as the 10th century (hence, the Russian Golden Age really happened in time immemorial). Since then, the anti-national forces (or world Jewry, to be precise) have enslaved peoples further and further. All seeming global changes, wars and revolutions only modify the methods of enslavement, but they do not really alter the reality[E39].

There are very few followers of the pre-Christian viewpoint in a strict sense of the term, who belong to communes[249], participate in appropriate services, etc. Yet many neo-Pagans identify themselves as such. Having in mind their view of the world, they believe they have to reject Orthodoxy, as "its main part boils down to an idea of submission of conquered nations, tolerance for the ruling

---

[E39]   The Editor deleted the paragraph that immediately follows this one in the original, because it largely repeats a paragraph elsewhere in this book. In the original, the two similar paragraphs are on pp. 127 and 179. This deletion causes the discontinuity of the reference numbers.

[249]   For a brief survey of neo-Pagan societies, see: Pribylovskiy B. *Russkoe neoyazychestvo...* On a large group centered in Omsk and not described there (the old Russian Ingliist Church and Old Believers – Ingliists), see: Likhachev V. Omsk drevnee egipetskikh piramid. Potomu chto on – Asgard. *Russkaya mysl'*, No. 4281, August 5-11, 1999; Yashin V. "Tserkov' pravoslavnykh staroverov-inglingov" kak primer neoyazycheskogo kul'ta. In *Neoyazychestvo na prostorakh Evrazii*. Moscow: Bibleysko-bogoslovskiy institut sv. Apostola Andreya, 2001, pp. 56-68.

government, and brutal punishment of the rebels and dissidents"[250]. Rather, they want to return to national roots, to a pre-Christian religion. It is easy to notice that the specific choice of a denomination is secondary to their nationalistic desire to cleanse the culture off alien features.

The neo-Pagan view of the world occupies a peculiar position in terms of influence. As a whole, the neo-Pagan view is accepted only by a small minority even among the radical nationalists, but it spawned certain myths that are commonly accepted within the ultra-right camp. Furthermore, they are widely circulated in mass culture.

Even the radical nationalists who claim their allegiance to Orthodoxy readily use neo-Pagan theories to explain Russian pre-history, as well as in their speculations concerning the oldest Russian civilization that allegedly occupied huge territories in Europe and Asia (and even Africa sometimes). Pretty often, the ultra-right wing picks up the myth about global racial confrontation or picks up Slavo-Aryan myths spawned in the neo-Pagan environment. Sometimes, the nationalists explain their borrowing of neo-Pagan ideas quite pragmatically. "We need a heroic myth and, undoubtedly, only an Aryan myth may become one"[251] admitted Aleksandr Eliseev, one of the ideologues of the left-wing national socialists. Another neo-Pagan idea about upcoming liberation from Jewish enslavement as a result of the change of the astrological epochs ("the era of Aquarius is the Russian era"[252]) is common too.

Another way of disseminating some neo-Pagan ideas is through the mass culture (fiction literature, vulgarized occultism). The ideas of global confrontation, of ancient Russian civilization, images of Jewish-looking rational villains and Slavic fighters of the world's evil, etc.[253] began to penetrate science fic-

---

[250]   Kandyba B. *Op. cit.*, p. 66.
[251]   Eliseev A. Natsional-revolyutsionnaya ideologiya i stil'. Talk at the conference *Gosudarstvo i natsional'naya ideologiya*, Moscow, 1997.
[252]   See, for example: Ariyskiy novyy god. *Russkiy poryadok*, March, 1993.
[253]   See Kaganskaya M. Annotirovannyy obzor nauchnoy fantastiki 70-kh–80-kh godov. *Byulleten' tsentra po issledovaniyu dokumentatsii vostochnoevropeyskogo evreystva.* (Unfortunately, I had only a Xerox copy of that article without a title page and I could not find the issue number or the year of publication). See also: Kaganskaya

tion novels at the end of the Soviet period. But the real boom in neo-Paganism in literature began with the invasion of the fantasy genre[254] in the domestic book market. Many Russian authors[255] base their works on these same neo-Pagan myths (pre-history, the Aryan myth, etc)[256]. Their publications easily find their way to the mass reader, because even people with no nazi leanings get tired of the foreign literature in this genre and they welcome "Slavic fantasies".

Although the most common theories in the occult-esoteric community are not purely Vedic ones, they still are closely related to Russian neo-Pagan myths. Such common theories include the racial theory of E. P. Blavatskaya, a founder of theosophy, and those of her followers (its extreme form is Ariosophie[E40]), ancient Slavs and Germans' runic magic[257], astrological speculations[258]. "Science and Religion", a formerly reputable journal preaches from the perspective of semi-nationalist occultism. Numerous other publications devoted to mysticism and puzzles of ancient civilizations take similar positions. And the almanac "Myths and Magic of Indo-Europeans" prints purely occult and neo-Pagan materials with an overtly nationalist bent.

M. Mif dvadtsat' pervogo veka, ili Rossiya vo mgle. *Strana i mir*, No. 11, 1986; No. 1, 2, 1987. Kaganskaya lists books by Shcherbakov V., Nazarov V., Zhukova L., Serba A., Medvedev Yu. and others. These authors tend to glorify the Slavic heritage and sometimes resort to overt or covert anti-Semitic myths.

[254] Certain Western founders of that style, such as Robert E. Howard and H. P. Lovecraft, were attracted to Nazism and that attraction was laid as a foundation of the genre.

[255] The most popular among them are the authors of endless serials, like Nik Perumov, Galina Romanova, Yury Nikitin, Sergey Alkseev and many others.

[256] See: Shnirel'man V. Gde lezhat istoki "Mirovogo zla"? Neonatsizm v rossiyskoy massovoy literature. *Diagnoz*, pp. 14-15, May 1999.

[E40] Ariosophie (occult wisdom concerning the Aryans) is one of several quasi-religious theories exploited by the Nazi regime in Germany. This term was coined by von Liebenfels who theorized, among other things, that Aryan peoples, unlike the "lower" races, are descendants of interstellar deities.

[257] The main popularizer of that doctrine is Anton Platov who is one of the most active leaders of neo-Paganism, the editor-in-chief of the almanac *Myths and Magic of Indo-Europeans* and a contributor to the journal *Legacy of the Forefathers*.

[258] The main popularizer of astrology in the late Soviet and post-Soviet times is Pavel Globa. Some of his writings border on racist emotions. See Shnirel'man V. *Vtoroe prishestvie ...*

The general spectrum of occult and Pagan movements that exploit nationalist rhetoric one way or another and have contacts with right-wing radical groups is extremely diverse. Besides Vedic groups proper, there are political-religious sects that exploit mixed paradigms enriching the standard myths based on the "Veles Book[E41]" with doctrines taken from both traditional religions and modern sectarian teachings. Thus, the Party of Spiritual Vedic Socialism[259] absorbed elements of Krishnaism and the Moscow Tantra Sangha[260] absorbed elements of Tantrism[E42]. Yet another curious group promoting the occult and racism is the Navi Church.

The Navi Church is an obviously quasi-religious organization[261]. Its doctrine is pretty unique within the domestic ideological landscape and is defined by the sect's leader Ilya Lazarenko as "Pagan gnosticism"[262] or as Ariosophie[263].

[E41]   The Veles Book is a pre-Christian Slavic chronicle allegedly written by Pagan Magi in the 9th century or earlier. It was found in the 20th century and the original was subsequently lost. Its authenticity has been debated by historians.

[259]   Pribylovskiy V. *Russkoe neoyazychestvo – kvazireligiya* ..., pp. 155-156.

[260]   Sect leader Swami Sadashivacharya is a regular participant of nationalistic activities. "A feature of Tantra Sangha is <...> the continuation of the esoteric Hindu-Tantric cult as it exists in India now and an attempt to revive the ancient Rudraist (that's the name of a reconstructed Slavic religion; Vedic Rudra is an independent God and also one of the names of Vishnu; he is equated with Slavic Rod) version of Vedism as a live and dynamic modern spiritual movement", Sadashivacharya writes. And then, "A spontaneous formation of neo-Pagan groups and syncretic communities combining neo-Paganism with elements of Hindu Tantrism may succeed. <...> Since both the Slavic cult of Rod and Rozhanits and the Tantric cult of Shiva and Shakti date back to a deep archetype in the Indo-Europeans' mystic and ethnic consciousness, then bringing them together is a vital necessity for a revival of Russia". (*Nasledie predkov*, p. 12, No. 5, 1998).

[E42]   Tantrism is an ancient teaching that appeared in India. It is still practiced there within both Hinduism and Buddhism.

[261]   Witnesses claim I. Lazarenko came up with the idea of creating a religious organization when he realized his incompetence as a political leader. The "doctrine" was concocted after leafing through a mythology reference book.

[262]   Bobrova I. Ispoved' natsista. *Moskovskiy komsomolets*, January 24, 1998.

[263]   "Instructions for the comrade" is a document fulfilling the role of the Navi Church's Manifesto. We copied it from the Internet. Ariosophie is a mystic-racial doctrine spawned in Germany in the late 19th – early 20th centuries. See: Goodrick-Clark N. *The Occult Roots of Nazism*. New York: New York University Press, 1992. The book was published by the St. Petersburg publisher "Eurasia", which is clear only from their logo, with no mention of the year or the place of publication. See pages 139-196.

Even though it indeed remotely resembles gnosticism, the teaching of the Church is rather based on the views of Miguel Serrano[264]. In a nutshell, it boils down to the following[265].

"Nav" proper is an ideal spiritual world, an immaterial world of the "light-skinned Aryan gods". By the very fact of creating the material world (Yav), the insidious Demiurg bound the gods to the frame of the "concentration universe", with chains of "perpetual return". The White race equates to the Aryans, the light-skinned gods in the material universe. The Black and Yellow races are a product of the evil creation of a Demiurg in its purest form. These races have no "God's genuine spark", no "soul". To help the White people to cast off their material chains, the Aryan gods materialize as heroes-avatars in the earthly world (both the idea and the term are borrowed from Hinduism). One of the avatars was Odin-Wotan-Veles[E43] (the equivalence is the fruit of Lazarenko's mythological creativity) who gave the Aryans the secret knowledge of the runes and the esoteric teaching – Ariosophie. Another avatar was Hitler (that is Serrano's idea in a pure form). A practical way out of the present global degradation is to revive Ariosophie and to practice the rituals of calling on the "Aryan gods" and to struggle for racial purity, since only the pure White race has a chance to break out of the chains of matter, as its motherland is an immaterial world, Nav. Navi Church practices mystical rituals and services developed for achieving such purposes.

We should notice the novel interpretation of the Vedic terms Nav and Yav, as compared to their traditional neo-Pagan interpretation, as well as the special role of racism as a spiritual principle. (For the classical neo-Pagans, Yav is the material world, while Nav is the immaterial world, the life hereafter, the

---

[264] M. Serrano is a Chilean public figure, diplomat and a journalist. He is known for enriching the racist political ideology with pretty elaborated Gnostic metaphysics. He called his ideology "occult Hitlerism". In Russian, see: Serrano M. *Voskreshenie geroya*. Moscow: Russkoe slovo, 1994; *idem. Nashe mirovozzrenie*. Moscow: Nasledie predkov, 2002.

[265] The Navi Church's ideology is described on the basis of its main documents - "Instructions for the comrade" and "Navi Book" (both were published as booklets with no identifying information, such as the year, etc. They are posted on the Internet, too).

[E43] Odin is the highest god in Norse mythology; Wotan is the German version of the same god; Veles is one of the major Slavic gods.

shadowy side of existence. By itself, Nav is not demonic, but its appearance in Yav is harmful. Prav is the highest, ideal, spiritual world of the gods[266]. However, it is a big stretch to call that scheme primordially Slavic, as scientists do not know such details about pre-Christian philosophy. The triad Yav-Nov-Prav was probably introduced by Yury Mirolyubov[267]).

The Navi Church's membership is identical to that of the overtly nazi party "National Front", thereby exemplifying a political-religious synthesis based on the neo-Pagan paradigm.

Curiously, Moscow Satanists, especially the "Satanic Order Black Dragon", actively cooperate with Lazarenko and his Church. Their main points in common are nazism, anti-Christianity and a proclivity for exotic rituals and teachings. Mikhail Naumenko, an active member of both the Church and the Order, was arrested on September 4, 1999, on suspicion of conspiracy to bomb Moscow synagogues in May of the same year[268]. The Church is connected with the most extremist and clandestine Russian Satanist organization "South Cross" (the Moscow Satanic Church)[270] via the Church's ideologue Ruslan Vorontsov (he is the author of Navi Book and the second ranking member of

---

[266]   See, for example: Bus Kresen'. *Russkie vedy*. Moscow: Kitezhgrad, pp. 345-349, 1992.

[267]   Yu. Mirolyubov is the first "researcher" and popularizer of the Veles Book. On the triad Yav-Nav-Prav, see: . Mirolyubov Yu. *Russkaya mifologiya – Sakral'noe Rusi*, pp. 22. Moscow: Assotsiatsiya Dukhovnogo Edineniya "Zolotoy Vek", 1996, vol. 2. See also Skurlatov V. Krug vremeni. Doklady laboratorii "Inversor". *Tekhnika – molodezhi*, pp. 40-44, No. 8, 1977.

[268]   See a description in: Likhachev V. Tyazhkie budni terroristicheskoy bor'by. *Russkaya mysl'*, No. 4291, November 4-10, 1999. During a search, the police found explosives and firearms in Naumenko's possession.

[270]   See *Novye religioznye organizatsii Rossii destructivnogo i okkul'tnogo kharaktera. Spravochnik*, Belgorod: 1997. (Chapter: "Destructivnye religioznye organizatsii sataninskoy napravlennosti "). However, all data about the Satanists are notoriously scanty, unreliable and / or biased. Despite the wealth of information, the reference book mentioned here cannot be used as a valuable source, as it was published by the ROC Missionary Department and it pursues a clear-cut polemical goal. Besides, the reference book does not mention the names of either the informers, or the sectarians as a matter of principle. Thus, a leader of "South Cross" is referred to as Ruslan V. It is interesting that the Navi Church is mentioned exclusively as a recruitment arm of the "Cross".

the Church after Ilya Lazarenko[269]). Vorontsov is a charismatic and authoritarian leader of "Cross". There are many rumors concerning that group and its sources of funding, such as that it gets its resources from drug dealing, underground trade in body parts, and even from contract murders. In any case, the organization is doing quite well. The Satanists try to indoctrinate two youth movements – heavy metal music fans and skinheads – who represent the neo-nazi subculture.

National Satanism is relatively widely spread, but not as a specific religious doctrine, but rather as a "religious" component of the right-wing view of the world. The most famous and active promoter of that ideology is a popular radio commentator Georgy Osipov who is organizationally close to the NBP. For instance, he expounds in his broadcasts and newspaper articles that "Nazism strives for perfection, while Satanism strives to live according to the natural laws... It is not Satanism when old farts sacrifice the young and the strong to prolong their own miserable existence, as the banks in the United Stench of America do. The true National Satanism today is when the young and healthy individuals – no, they do not sacrifice anyone, because they do not care – they simply wipe off all that is rotting, dying, unessential, needless, all that stands in the way..."[271]. We should add that personally Osipov has a certain charm and appeal which facilitated the wide spread of such ideas both among the nationalist radicals (which let journalists assess the NBP ideology as "Old-Belief-flavored Satanism"[272]) and even beyond that community.

Concluding this Chapter, let us make several observations concerning the political and religious aspects of the ideology and activities of the right-wing radical groups. We believe that when the ultra-rightists choose a specific religious denomination, they are guided by a view of the world that has already been shaped and they look for the most "traditional" religion that can be used as a foundation for their new national viewpoint. If such a religion cannot be

---

[269]   The collaboration with Satanists did not prevent I. Lazarenko from running for a state Duma seat in 1999 under the umbrella of the movement "For Faith and Motherland!" headed by ROC celibate priest Nikon Belavinets.

[271]   Radio program "Transil'vaniya bespokoit". *Radio 101*, November 27, 1997.

[272]   Shatrov A. Natsboly: iz satanizma v staroobryadchestvo. *Tat'yanin den'*, p. 10, No. 24, September, 1998.

found, it is "reconstructed" from their notions (as is the case with the "primor-dial" pre-Christian religions) or, as a last resort, it is just invented (as is the case with Navi Church). The latter alternative leads to a unique political and religious sect.

The same observation also explains the proclivity of the most creative and "searching" radical nationalists to change their religious positions often, mov-ing towards more traditional and nationalistic ones[273]. Interestingly enough, aside from a few cases where practical advantages were involved, once the individuals have chosen their religion, they believe in it sincerely and deeply.

Besides, even the leaders and the organization that take no clear-cut reli-gious position still actively exploit religious rhetoric, both Christian ("America is the Antichrist", "God is with us", etc) and Pagan (either the Slavic type, or an imitation of the paradigm of German Nazism[274]). Sometimes they simply resort to mystic and occult stories and reasoning[275].

We have already written that the value system of the right-wing radicals in principle is close to the religious viewpoint. Furthermore, we believe that the nazi groups in many ways fit the notion of a "New Religious Movement"[276].

---

[273]   According to some information, before A. Dugin became an Old Believer, he had converted to Islam under the influence of Geydar Dzhemal. Dugin hoped to find a basis for "a rebellion against the modern world" in Islam. There are quite a few cases of conversion from Christianity to Paganism. Thus, I. Lazarenko kept Ortho-dox views in 1992 – 1994, and furthermore, insisted on making Orthodoxy the state religion of Russia. Alexey Shiropaev, a prominent leader of the right-wing move-ment and a prolific journalist, has undergone a similar evolution. The religious bounces of NRPR leader N. Lysenko have been mentioned above. Leader of the minuscule Movement of the Solidarists Artur Yastrebov has undergone the same evolution from Orthodoxy to Islam.

[274]   Thus, the skinheads, who are usually materialistic teenagers, bid farewell to their fallen comrades by saying "See you in Valhalla". [Valhalla is the Hall of the Slain in Norse mythology where Odin received the souls of slain heroes. Editor]

[275]   For example, when E. Limonov, who proclaimed his atheism many times, created an image of the leader, he tells about his own clairvoyance, etc., up to his walks with the Devil. (See Limonov E. *Anatomiya geroya* ..., pp. 176-178).

[276]   See: Barker A. *Novye religioznye dvizheniya*. St. Petersburg: Izdatel'stvo Russkogo Khristianskogo gumanitarnogo instituta, pp. 166-170, 1997. The author does not provide a definition of that term, but he lists a number of typical and distinguishing

For instance, the "Commandments of the National Bolshevik"[277] say: "1. Russia is thy God; the Party is thy Church. The Party shall not be questioned; Thou shall believe in the Party". The style plays a big role there, of course, but let us go on: "6. The leader of the St. Petersburg NBP Andrey Grebnev has said: I have broken up with anyone outside the Party. Right on, Andrey! Do as Andrey does. People outside the Party, narrow-minded people who care only about their personal lives and emotions shall be despised. An NBP member shall call them 'veggies'. The word *cadre*, as borrowed by A. Dugin from the vocabulary of the Old Believers, should apply to the people of the System". One can find many similar quotations in NBP publications and in other ultra-right-wing materials.

As A. Shatrov writes, "the internal structure of the NBP and the code of behavior of its members demonstrate the sectarian character of the party and that is true for most radical organizations"[278]. While there may be more reason to draw the same conclusion with respect to other right-wing radical parties, we chose the NBP as an example exactly because it positions itself as a non-religious organization. Others, including both Orthodox and neo-Pagan groups, may be more easily associated with sects, i. e. new religious movements.

Therefore, the right-wing groups are religious groups as much as they are political ones. They occupy the least "political" and the most "religious" part of the political spectrum. The adjective "religious" may be interpreted both in a narrow sense (i. e. the religion plays a more important role for right-wing radicals than it does for other ideological movements) and in a wider sense (the right-wing radical groups and the new religious movements have a substantial number of common characteristics – value systems, their view of the world, etc, even to common phraseology).

---

characteristics. Here are some: the relative youth of the membership, a strong desire to change themselves and / or the world, an authoritarian style of control, alienation from the non-members, expectation of the end of the world, etc.

[277]   Zapovedi natsbola. *Limonka*, No. 83, January, 1998. The document is signed as "NBP ".

[278]   Shatrov A. *Natsboly: ot staroobryadchestva...*

Conclusion

Anti-Semitism, xenophobia, ultra-nationalism, right-wing radicalism and religious intolerance are undoubtedly important problems in contemporary Russia. This study, which does not claim to be comprehensive, discussed the role of anti-Semitism in the mass consciousness of our compatriots, in the ideologies of political parties and in the teachings of the main religious denominations.

We intentionally avoided bold generalizations and farfetched conclusions. The nature of this study is descriptive, rather than theoretical. The reader is free to draw his or her own conclusions, while our task was to provide the necessary information to the reader.

We attempted to avoid making the book polemical; at least, we tried to conceal our emotions and attitudes towards characters mentioned in the book. Perhaps, we did not always succeed – well, totally unbiased social sciences do not exist.

The intended audience for this book consists of civil servants, political consultants, journalists, historians, professors and students of history, sociology and political science, as well as everyone interested in the political life of contemporary Russia.

Vyacheslav Likhachev
Moscow – Jerusalem – Kiev
2002 – 2003

Selected Bibliography

Агурский М. Идеология национал-большевизма – Paris: YMCA-PRESS, 1980.

Антифашистское движение в регионах России: проблемы и перспективы – М.: АМД, 1998.

Арендт Х. Истоки тоталитаризма – М.: ЦентрКом, 1996.

Бабинцев В., Бердников А. Национальный вопрос в программах и документах политических партий и общественных движений современной России – М., 1994.

Барыгин И. Основные тенденции эволюции современных крайне правых// Политико-правовое устройство реформируемой России. Вып. 3. СПб., 1995.

Беленкин Б. Российские периодические издания о национал-экстремизме. 1992-1996. Библиографический указатель – М., 1997.

Беликов С. Скинхеды. Все о бритоголовых – М.: Издательский центр РГГУ, 2002.

Бурцев В. В погоне за провокаторами. "Протоколы сионских мудрецов" – доказанный подлог – М., 1991.

Верховский А. Государство против радикального национализма. Что делать и чего не делать? – М.: РОО "Панорама", 2002.

Верховский А., Папп А., Прибыловский В. Политический экстремизм в России – М.: Институт экспериментальной социологии, 1996.

Верховский А., Прибыловский В. Национал-патриотические организации в России. История, идеология, экстремистские тенденции – М.: Институт экспериментальной социологии, 1996.

Верховский А., Прибыловский В. Национал-патриотические организации. Краткие справки. Документы и тексты – М.: ИЭГ "Панорама", 1997.

Верховский А., Прибыловский В., Михайловская Е. Национализм и ксенофобия в российском обществе – М.: ООО "Панорама", 1998.

Верховский А., Прибыловский В., Михайловская Е. Политическая ксенофобия. Радикальные группы. Представления лидеров. Роль Церкви – М.: ООО "Панорама", 1999.

Верховский А., Михайловская Е., Прибыловский В. Национал-патриоты, Церковь и Путин – М.: ООО "Панорама", 2000.

Галкин А. Российский фашизм// Социологический журнал, № 2, 1994. С. 17-27.

Ганелин Р., Bune О. и др. Национальная правая прежде и теперь. В 3 т. – СПб., 1992.

Губогло М. Три линии национальной политики в посткоммунистической России// Этнографической обозрение. № 5,1995, С. 110-124; № 6,1995, С. 137-144.

Гудков Л., Левинсон А. Отношение населения СССР к евреям и проблема антисемитизма// Вестник Еврейского университета в Москве, № 1, 1992.

Гудков Л., Левинсон А. Изменение в отношении к евреям населения республик на территории бывшего СССР// Вестник Еврейского университета в Москве. № 4, 1993.

Дадиани Л. Фашизм в России: мифы и реальность// Социологические исследования. № 3, 2002. С. 103-111.

Дадиани Л. Размышления о современном русском фашизме – Социальное согласие и толерантность в современом мире. Т. 3. М.: Центр общечеловеческих ценностей, 2002. С. 172-191.

Дадиани Л., Червяков В. Политологическое заключение Института социологии РАН от 28 апреля 1999 по назначению Южно-Сахалинского городского суда (по политической идентификации РНЕ) – Дела 7, 8, 9. "Русское национальное единство" против журналистов. Судебные дела о защите чести, достоинства и деловой репутации. Ред. Симонов А. Фонд защиты гласности. М.: Магеллан ОЕ, 2000. С. 327-366.

Дейч М., Журавлев Л. "Память" как она есть – М., 1991.

Дело № 6. "Русское Национальное Единство" против журналиста Галины Туз. Материалы судебного процесса. Ред. Граев В. Фонд защиты гласности. – М.: Барс, 2000.

Дела № 7, 8, 9. "Русское национальное единство" против журналистов.

Судебные процессы по защите чести, достоинства и деловой репутации. Ред. Симонов А. – М.: Магеллан ОЕ, 2000.

Дрейлинг А. Движение "Русское национальное единство"// Политический монитор, № 2 (37), Ч.2, 1995.

Дугин А. Консервативная революция – М.: Арктогея, 1994.

Дудаков С. История одного мифа: Очерки русской литературы XIX – XX веков – М.: Наука, 1993.

Евгеньев М. [Е.Мороз]. Языческий сталинизм. Учение "Внутреннего Предиктора СССР"// Барьер. Антифашистский журнал, № 1(5). 2000. С. 54-66.

Ерунов И., Соловей В. Русское дело сегодня. "Память" – М., 1991.

Золотаревич В. "Кремль кошерен так же, как и Белый Дом". Русские национал-патриоты отстали от немецких// Независимая газета, № 71, 16 апреля 1993. С. 5.

Золотаревич В. Каганович – тайный начальник Сталина и своего кузена Берия. Антисемитские бредни// Независимая газета, № 174, 14 сентября 1993. С.5.

Золотаревич В. Терминологический ликбез. О значении слов "антисемитизм", "юдофобство", "жид"// Международная еврейская газета, № 46, декабрь 1998. С. 1, 3.

Золотаревич В. Станет ли знак беды символом грядущней России?// Диагноз – антифашистское обозрение, № 3, июнь 1998. С.10-11.

Илюшенко В. Русский фашизм и религия// Диа-Логос. 1998-1999. Вып. II. С. 160-172.

Кандидаты-99. Федеральные списки – Сост. Белонучкин Г., Михайловская Е. М.: ООО "Панорама", 1999.

Карта ненависти. Национализм, авторитаризм и ксенофобия в регионах России – М., 1999.

Касьянова К. Религиозный фундаментализм – Она же. О русском национальном характере. М.: 1994.

Козлов Н. Проблемы экстремизма в молодежной среде – Система воспитания в высшей школе, вып. 4. М., 1994.

Кон Н. Благословение на геноцид. Миф о всемирном заговоре евреев и "Протоколы сионских мудрецов" – М.: Прогресс, 1990.

Костюк К. Православный фундаментализм// Полис (политические исследования), № 5, 2000.

Коргунюк Ю. Современная российская многопартийность – М.: Региональный фонд ИНДЕМ, 1999.

Лакер У. Черная сотня: происхождение фашизм в России – М.: Текст, 1994.

Лимонов Э. Анатомия героя – Смоленск: Русич, 1998.

Лимонов Э. Моя политическая автобиография – СПб.: Амфора, 2002.

Лихачев В. Современная русская правая и антисемитизм: эскалация конфликта или примирение? – Тирош. Труды второй молодежной конференции СНГ по иудаике. Вып. II. М., 1998. С. 146-153.

Лихачев В. Антисемитизм как часть идеологии праворадикальных политических течений современной России (национал-социализма, неоязычества и "традиционной правой") – М.: ООО "Панорама", 1999.

Лихачев В. История антисемитизма: ненависть сквозь века – М.: Еврейский мир, 2000.

Лихачев В. Холокост в идеологии и пропаганде современных российских праворадикальных движений (от апологетики до отрицания) – Материалы Седьмой Ежегодной Международной Междисциплинарной конференции по иудаике. М.: Пробел, 2000. Т. 1. С. 247-254.

Лихачев В. Антисемитизм в современной Российской Федерации: религиозный аспект – Материалы Восьмой Ежегодной Международной Междисциплинарной конференции по иудаике. Тезисы. М., 2000. С. 286-289.

Лихачев В. Мифологема о "двух еврействах" в рамках праворадикальных политических идеологий современной России – Тирош. Труды по иудаике. Выпуск IV. М., 2000. С. 279-287.

Лихачев В. Антисемитизм в современной России// Еврейское слово, № 6 (28), 7-13 февраля 2001.

Лихачев В. Религиозный фактор в идеологии и деятельности современных российских праворадикальных политических партий и движений – Российская государственность XX века. Материалы межвузовской конференции, посвященной 80-летию со дня рождения профессора Н.П.Ерошкина 16 декабря 2000 г. М.: Издательский центр РГГУ, 2001. С. 105-110.

Лихачев В. Русские правые радикалы: кто они?// Еврейское слово, № 17 (39), 2-4 мая 2001.

Лихачев В. Роль религии в идеологии и деятельности современных российских праворадикалов// Диа-Логос. Религия и общество. Альманах. Выпуск III. 2000-2001. М.: Духовная библиотека, 2001. С. 139-156.

Лихачев В. Антисемитизм и православная церковь в постсоветской России – Тирош. Труды по иудаике. Вып. V. М., 2001. С. 292-314.

Лихачев В. Ревизионизм Холокоста – М.: Еврейский мир, 2001.

Лихачев В. Реалии и тенденции российского национал-радикализма// Международная еврейская газета, № 26 (352), июль 2001.

Лихачев В. Антисемитизм в современной Российской Федерации – Десять років єврейського національного відродження в пострадянських країнах: досвід, проблеми, перспективи. Збірник наукових праць. Матеріали конференції 28-30 серпня 2000 р. Київ: Інститут юдаїки, 2001. С. 169-179.

Лихачев В. Скины. Бритоголовые в России (в трех частях)// Международная еврейская газета, №№ 38-40 (364-366), октябрь 2001.

Лихачев В. Нацизм в России – М.: РОО "Панорама", 2002.

Лихачев В. Национал-радикалы в современной России: идеология, деятельность и отношения с властью – Национализм, ксенофобия и нетерпимость в современной России. М.: Московская Хельсинская группа, 2002. С. 253-281.

Лихачев В. Антисемитизм, православная Церковь и государство в современной России – Терроризм и политический экстремизм: вызовы и поиски адекватных ответов. М.: Институт политического и военного анализа, 2002. С. 196-225.

Лихачев В. Российские правые радикалы и Холокост: варианты интерпретации – Проблемы Холокоста. Научный журнал ВБФ "НПЦ "Ткума", № 1, 2002. С. 146-153.

Лихачев В. Антисемитизм, ксенофобия и религиозное преследование: болевые точки (по предварительным итогам 2002 г.) – Антисемитизм, ксенофобия и религиозное преследование в российских регионах/ Сост. Буткевич Н. С. 256-272. М.: НП "Бюро по правам человека", 2002.

Лихачев В., Прибыловский В. Расистский террор на улицах Москвы// Русская мысль, № 4222, 14-20 мая 1998.

Лихачев В., Прибыловский В. Национал-радикалы как криминальная угроза обществу – Политическая ксенофобия. М.: ООО "Панорама", 1999. С. 50-59.

Лихачев В., Прибыловский В. Бандитствующие "патриоты" и патриотствующие бандиты – Между прошлым и будущим/ Сост. Оскоцкий В. М.: Независимое издательство "Пик", 1999. С. 359-375.

Лихачев В., Прибыловский В. Русское Национальное Единство. История, идеология, регионы России – М.: ООО "Панорама", 2001; издание 2-е, дополненное и переработанное.

Менделевич Э. Свастика над городом первого салюта. Процесс баркашовцев в Орле – Воронеж: Центр поддержки малой прессы, 1998.

Митрохин Н. Этнонационалистическая мифология в советском партийно-государственном аппарате// Отечественные записки, № 3, март 2002.

Митрохин Н. Русская партия. Движение русских националистов в СССР. 1953-1985 гг. – М.: Новое литературное обозрение, 2003.

Мороз Е. "Ведизм". Языческая версия русской идеи. Спб, 1992, машинопись.

Мороз Е.В. Борцы за "Святую Русь" и защитники "Советской Родины" – Национальная правая прежде и теперь. Историко-социологические очерки. Часть II, вып. 1. Спб., 1992. С. 68-96.

Мороз Е. Ведизм и фашизм// Барьер. Антифашистский журнал. № 3, 1993. С. 4-8.

Нацистские игры – М.: Независимое издательство "Пик", 2000.

Неоязычество на просторах Евразии – Сост. Шнирельман В. Приложение к журналу "Страницы". М.: Библейско-богословский институт св. Апостола Андрея, 2001.

Нетерпимость в России. Старые и новые фобии – Ред. Витковская Г. и Малашенко А. М.: Московский центр Карнеги. 1999.

Нужен ли Гитлер России? – Сост. Илюшенко В. М.: Независимое издательство "Пик", 1996.

Общероссийские избирательные объединения. Справочник – Ред. Застрожная О. М.: Весь Мир, 1999.

Основные тенденции проявлений антисемитизма в государствах СНГ – Ред. Лихачев В. Киев: Евроазиатский еврейский конгресс, 2003.

Политические партии, движения и организации современной России на рубеже веков. Аналитический справочник – Ред. Барыгин И. СПб.: Изд-во Михайлова В.А., 1999.

Полосин В. Национал-патриоты и Русская Православная Церковь: Всемирный Русский Собор// Диа-Логос. Религия и общество. Альманах. Вып. I. М.: Истина и жизнь, 1997. С. 114-122.

Прибыловский В. "Память". Документы и тексты – М.: ИЭГ "Панорама", 1990.

Прибыловский В. Словарь оппозиции. Новые политические партии и организации России// Состояние страны. Аналитический вестник информационного агентства POSTFACTUM. № 4/5, 1991.

Прибыловский В. Русские национал-патриотические организации. Часть I: Память. Документы и тексты – М.: ИЭГ "Панорама", 1991.

Прибыловский В. "Память" – Национальная правая прежде и теперь. Историко-социологические очерки. Ч. II, вып. II. СПб.: Институт социологии РАН, Санкт-Петербургский филиал, 1992. С. 151-170.

Прибыловский В. Русские национал-патриотические (этнократические) и право-радикальные организации. Краткий словарь – справочник – М.: ООО "Панорама", 1994.

Прибыловский В. Вожди. Сборник биографий российских политических деятелей националистической и имперско-патриотической ориентации – М.: ООО "Панорама", октябрь 1995.

Прибыловский В. Русские национал-патриотические организации. Часть 2: Русские националистические и праворадикальные партии. Документы и тексты, в 2-х частях – М.: ООО "Панорама", 1995.

Прибыловский В. Русское неоязычество – квазирелигия национализма и ксенофобии// Диа-Логос. 1998-1999. Вып. II. С. 137-160.

Прибыловский В. Неоязыческое крыло в русском национализме// http://www.religare.ru/article.php?num=490#1.

Рахшмир П. Фашизм: вчера, сегодня, завтра// Мировая экономика и международные отношения, № 10, 1996.

Резник С. Красное и коричневое. Книга о советском нацизме – Washington, 1991.

Ротарь И. Пылающие обломки империй. Заметки военного корреспондента – М.: Новое литературное обозрение, 2001.

Ротарь И. Под зеленым знаменем ислама. Исламские радикалы в России и СНГ – Научные доклады и дискуссии. Темы для двадцать первого века. Вып. 12. М.: АЙРО-ХХ, 2001.

Русская идея и евреи. Роковой спор. Христианство. Антисемитизм. Национализм / Сост. Крахмальникова З. – М.: Наука, Восточная литература. 1994.

Сендеров В. Русская Православная Церковь и ее отношение к антисемитизму// Диа-Логос. 1997. Выпуск I. С. 123-137.

Скуратовский В. Проблема авторства "Протоколов сионских мудрецов" – Киев: Дух i Лiтера, 2001.

Соловей В. Современный русский национализм: идейно-политическая классификация// Общественные науки и современность, № 2, 1992.

Соловей В. Эволюция современного русского национализма (1985 – 1993)// Русский народ: историческая судьба в ХХ веке. М., 1993.

Соловей В. Русское национальное движение 60—80-х годов ХХ века в освещении зарубежной историографии// Отечественная история, № 3, 1993.

Соловей В. Реальна ли угроза "русского фашизма" в новой России? – Взаимодействие политических и национально-этнических конфликтов. Материалы международного симпозиума 18-20 апреля 1994 г. Ч. 1. М., 1994.

Соловей В. Фашизм в России: концептуальные подходы – Демократия и фашизм. М., 1995. С. 45-54.

Старые церкви, новые верующие: Религия в массовом сознании постсоветской России – Ред. Каариайнен К и Фурман Д. М.: Летний сад, 2000.

Стефан Д. Русские фашисты. Трагедия и фарс в эмиграции, 1925-1945 – М.: Слово, 1992.

Табак Ю. Отношение Русской Православной Церкви к евреям// Диа-Логос. 1998-1999. Вып. II. С. 485-504.

Тарасов А. Skinheads ou naturel. Интервью с комментариями Неприкосновенный запас, № 5 (7), 1999.

Тарасов А. Порождение реформ: бритоголовые, они же скинхеды// Свободная мысль – XXI, № 5, 2000.

Тарасов А., Черкасов Г., Шавшукова Т. Левые в России: от умеренных до экстремистов – М.: Институт экспериментальной социологии, 1997.

Туз Г. Провинциальный фашизм – М.: Независимое издательство "Пик", 1997.

Умланд А. Старый вопрос, поставленный заново: что такое "фашизм"? (теория фашизм Роджера Гриффина)// Политические исследования, № 1 (31), 1996.

Умланд А. Правый экстремизм в постсоветской России// Общественные науки и современность, № 4, 2001. С. 71-84.

Филатов С. Новое рождение старой идеи: православие как национальный символ// Политические исследования, № 3, 1999.

Филатов С., Щипков А. Язычество: Рождение или вырождение?// Дружба народов, 1994, № 11-12.

Фундаментализм – Ред. Левин З. М.: Институт востоковедения РАН, Издательство "Крафт+", 2003.

Христианско-иудейский диалог. Хрестоматия. М.: Библейско-богословский институт св. апостола Андрея, 1998.

Шнирельман В. Евразийцы и евреи// Вестник Еврейского университета в Москве, № 12 (11), 1996. С. 4-45.

Шнирельман В. Русское неоязычество и антисемитизм – Еврейска історія та культура в Україні. Київ, 1997. С. 122-125.

Шнирельман В. Неоязычество и национализм. Восточноевропейский ареал – Исследования по прикладной и неотложной этнологи, № 114, Институт этнологии и антропологии Российской академии наук, М., 1998.

Шнирельман В. Второе пришествие арийского мифа// Восток, № 1, 1998. С. 89-107.

Шнирельман В. Неоязычество на просторах Евразии// Диа-Логос. 1998-1999. Вып. II. С. 201-215.

Шнирельман В. Русское неоязычество: поиски идентичности или неонацизм?// Страницы Библейско-богословского института св. апостола Андрея, том 4, вып. 1, 1999. С. 124-135.

Язык мой... Проблема этнической и религиозной нетерпимости в российских СМИ – Под ред. Верховского А. М.: РОО "Панорама", 2002.

Янов А. Веймарская Россия// Нева, №№ 3–6, 1994.

Янов А. После Ельцина. Веймарская Россия – М., 1995.

Agursky M. The Third Rome: National Bolshevism in the USSR – Boulder, 1987.

Allensworth W. The Russian Question: Nationalism, Modernization, and Post-Communist Russia – Lanham, MD, 1998.

Anti-Semitism, Xenophobia and Religious Persecution in Russia's Regions – Washington, 1999.

Brudny Y. Reinventing Russia. Russian Nationalism and the Soviet State, 1953-1991 – Cambridge, Mass., London, 1998.

Caplan L. Studies in Religious Fundamentalism – Albany, 1987

Carter St. Russian Nationalism: Yesterday, Today, Tomorrow – London, 1990.

Cohen N. The Fundamentalist Phenomenon – Grand Rapids, MI, 1990.

Conradi P. Schirinowski und der neue russische Nationalismus – Duesseldorf, 1995.

Die schwarze Front: Der neue Antisemitismus in der Sowjetunion – Reinberk bei Hamburg, 1991.

Dunlop J. New Russian Revolutionaries – Nordland, Belmont, Mass., 1976.

Dunlop J. The Faces of Contemporary Russian Nationalism – Princeton, NJ, 1983.

Dunlop J. The "Sad Case" of Igor Shafarevich. In: Soviet Jewish Affairs. Vol. 24, 1994.

Dunlop J. Alexander Barkashov and the Rise of National Socialism in Russia. In: Demokratizatsiya: The Journal of Post-Soviet Democratization, 1996, Vol. 4, No. 4.

Dunlop J. Barkashov and the Russian Ministries, 1994-2000 – Paper presented at the Sixth ICCEES World Congress. Tampere, Finland, 29

July – 3 August 2000.

Griffin R. The Nature of Fascism – London, 1993.

Griffin R., ed. Fascism – Oxford, 1995.

Hahn G. Opposition Politics in Russia. In: Europe-Asia Studies, Vol. 46, No. 2, 1994.

Highlights from a September 1999 Anti-Defamation League Survey on Anti-Semitism and Societal Attitudes in Russia. Issued by the Anti-Defamation League.

Kaznacheev P. Report to the Union of Councils for Soviet Jews, August 1999.

Korey W. Russian Anti-Semitism, Pamyat, and the Demonology of Zionism – Jerusalem, 1995.

Laquer W. Black Hundred: The Rise of the Extreme Right in Russia – New York, 1993.

Latin D. Political Sience. In: Encyclopedia of Nationalism: Fundamental Themes. – San Diego, 2001. Vol. 1.

Lewis B. Semites and Anti-Semites. An Inquiry into Conflict and Prejudice – New York, London, 1999.

Likhachev V. Nationalist Radicals in Contemporary Russia: Ideology, Activities, and Relationship to the Authorities. In: Nationalism, Xenophobia and Intolerance in Contemporary Russia. Moscow, 2002. P. 259-282.

Likhachev V. Russian Muslims and Anti-Semitism. In: Jews of Euro-Asia, No. 1(2), January – March 2003 (Shvat – Adar 5763).

Marty M., Appleby S., eds. Fundamentalists and the State (Vol.1), Fundamentalisms and Society (Vol. 2) – Chicago and London, Chicago, 1993.

Messmer M. Anti-Semitism in Post-Communist Russia – Cape Town, 1998.

Nettler R. A Muslim Fundamentalist's View of the Jews – Jerusalem, 1994.

Otto R. Contemporary Russian Nationalism. In: Problems of Communism. Vol. 39, No. 6, 1990.

Parland T. The Rejection of Totalitarian Socialism and Liberal Democracy: A Study of the Russian New Right (=Commentationes Scenarium Socialium. Vol. 46). Helsinki, 1993.

Pribylovskii V. Dictionary of political parties and organizations in Russia – Washington DC, the Center for Strategic and International Studies,

1992.

Pribylovski V. A Political Map of Russia. In: Russian Political Review, No. 1, March-April 1992.

Pribylovsky V. A Survey of Radical Right-Wing Groups in Russia. In: RFE/RL Research Report, No. 16, 1994.

Pribylovsky V. What Awaits Russia: Fascism or a Latin American-style Dictatorship?. In: Transition, Vol. 1, No. 23. 23 June 1995.

Pribylovski V. Le foisonnement des partis russes. In: La nouvelle Alternative, No. 41, mars 1996.

Pribilovski V. Russie. In: Les extremistes, de l'Atlantique a l'Oural, dirige par Jean-Yves Camus. Editions de l'Aube/CERA – Centre europeen de recherche et d'action sur le racisme et l'antisemitisme, 1996.

Reznik S. The Nazification of Russia: Anti-Semitism in the Post-Soviet Era – Washington, DC, 1996.

Rossman V. Russian Intellectual Anti-Semitism in the Post-Communist Era – Lincoln, NE, London, 2002.

Russian Nationalism: Past and Present. Ed. Hasting G., Service R. – New York, 1998.

Shenfield S. Russian Fascism: Traditions, Tendencies, Movements – Armonk, NY, 2000.

Shnirelman V. Russian Neo-pagan Myths and Anti-Semitism (=Analysis of Current Trends in Anti-Semitism, No. 13). Jerusalem, 1998.

Shnirelman V. The Myth of the Khazars and Intellectual Anti-Semitism in Russia, 1970s-1990s – Jerusalem, 2002.

Simonsen S. Alexander Barkashov and Russian National Unity: Blackshirt Friends of the Nation. In: Nationalities Papers, Vol. 24, No. 4.

Slater W. Russia. In: RFE/RL Research Report, Vol. 3, No. 16, 1994.

Spechler D. Russian Nationalism and Political Stability in the USSR – Cambridge, MA, 1983.

Szporluk R. Dilemmas of Russian Nationalism. In: Problems of Communism, Vol. 38, No. 4, 1989.

The Basic Tendencies of th Anti-Semitism in the CIS States. Ed. by Likhachev V. – Kiev, 2003.

Tobarkov I. The "Statists" and the Ideology of Russian Imperialism. In: RFE/RL Research Report, Vol. 1, No. 49, 1992.

Tuminez A. Russian Nationalism since 1956. Ideology and the Making of Foreign Policy – Lanham, MD, 2000.

Jackson W. Fascism, Vigilantism, and the State: The Russian National Unity Movement. In: Problems of Post-Communism, January/February 1999, pp. 34-42.

Williams Ch., Hanson S. National-Socialism, Left Patriotism, or Superimperialism? The "Radical Right" in Russia. In: The Radical Right in Central and Eastern Europe since 1989. Ed. by Ramet S. – University Park, PE, 1999.

Williams R. Culture in Exile. Russian Émigrés in Germany, 1881-1941. – Ithaca and London, 1972.

Yanov A. The Russian New Right: Right-Wing Ideologies in the Contemporary USSR – Berkeley, 1978.

Yanov A. The Russian Challenge and the Year 2000 – Oxford, New York, 1987.

Yanov A. Weimar Russia and What We Can Do About It – New York, 1995.

Zherebyatev M. Russian National Unity: A Political Challenge for Provincial Russia. In: Prism: Jamestown Foundation, 26 March 1999.

Dr. Andreas Umland (Ed.)

SOVIET AND POST-SOVIET POLITICS AND SOCIETY

ISSN 1614-3515

This book series makes available, to the academic community and general public, affordable English-, German- and Russian-language scholarly studies of various *empirical* aspects of the recent history and current affairs of the former Soviet bloc. The series features narrowly focused research on a variety of phenomena in Central and Eastern Europe as well as Central Asia and the Caucasus. It highlights, in particular, so far understudied aspects of late Tsarist, Soviet, and post-Soviet political, social, economic and cultural history from 1905 until today. Topics covered within this focus are, among others, political extremism, the history of ideas, religious affairs, higher education, and human rights protection. In addition, the series covers selected aspects of post-Soviet transitions such as economic crisis, civil society formation, and constitutional reform.

SOVIET AND POST-SOVIET POLITICS AND SOCIETY

Edited by Dr. Andreas Umland

ISSN 1614-3515

1   *Андреас Умланд (ред.)*
    Воплощение Европейской конвенции по правам человека в России
    Философские, юридические и эмпирические исследования
    ISBN 3-89821-387-0

2   *Christian Wipperfürth*
    Russland – ein vertrauenswürdiger Partner?
    Grundlagen, Hintergründe und Praxis gegenwärtiger russischer Außenpolitik
    Mit einem Vorwort von Heinz Timmermann
    ISBN 3-89821-401-X

3   *Manja Hussner*
    Die Übernahme internationalen Rechts in die russische und deutsche Rechtsordnung
    Eine vergleichende Analyse zur Völkerrechtsfreundlichkeit der Verfassungen der Russländischen Föderation
    und der Bundesrepublik Deutschland
    Mit einem Vorwort von Rainer Arnold
    ISBN 3-89821-438-9

4   *Matthew Tejada*
    Bulgaria's Democratic Consolidation and the Kozloduy Nuclear Power Plant (KNPP)
    The Unattainability of Closure
    With a foreword by Richard J. Crampton
    ISBN 3-89821-439-7

5   *Марк Григорьевич Меерович*
    Квадратные метры, определяющие сознание
    Государственная жилищная политика в СССР. 1921 – 1941 гг
    ISBN 3-89821-474-5

6   *Andrei P. Tsygankov, Pavel A.Tsygankov (Eds.)*
    New Directions in Russian International Studies
    ISBN 3-89821-422-2

7   *Марк Григорьевич Меерович*
    Как власть народ к труду приучала
    Жилище в СССР – средство управления людьми. 1917 – 1941 гг.
    С предисловием Елены Осокиной
    ISBN 3-89821-495-8

8   *David J. Galbreath*
    Nation-Building and Minority Politics in Post-Socialist States
    Interests, Influence and Identities in Estonia and Latvia
    With a foreword by David J. Smith
    ISBN 3-89821-467-2

9   *Алексей Юрьевич Безугольный*
    Народы Кавказа в Вооруженных силах СССР в годы Великой Отечественной войны
    1941-1945 гг.
    С предисловием Николая Бугая
    ISBN 3-89821-475-3

10 *Вячеслав Лихачев и Владимир Прибыловский (ред.)*
    Русское Национальное Единство, 1990-2000. В 2-х томах
    ISBN 3-89821-523-7

11 *Николай Бугай (ред.)*
    Народы стран Балтии в условиях сталинизма (1940-е – 1950-е годы)
    Документированная история
    ISBN 3-89821-525-3

12 *Ingmar Bredies (Hrsg.)*
    Zur Anatomie der Orange Revolution in der Ukraine
    Wechsel des Elitenregimes oder Triumph des Parlamentarismus?
    ISBN 3-89821-524-5

13 *Anastasia V. Mitrofanova*
    The Politicization of Russian Orthodoxy
    Actors and Ideas
    With a foreword by William C. Gay
    ISBN 3-89821-481-8

14 *Nathan D. Larson*
    Alexander Solzhenitsyn and the Russo-Jewish Question
    ISBN 3-89821-483-4

15 *Guido Houben*
    Kulturpolitik und Ethnizität
    Staatliche Kunstförderung im Russland der neunziger Jahre
    Mit einem Vorwort von Gert Weisskirchen
    ISBN 3-89821-542-3

16 *Leonid Luks*
    Der russische „Sonderweg"?
    Aufsätze zur neuesten Geschichte Russlands im europäischen Kontext
    ISBN 3-89821-496-6

17 *Евгений Мороз*
    История «Мёртвой воды» – от страшной сказки к большой политике
    Политическое неоязычество в постсоветской России
    ISBN 3-89821-551-2

18 *Александр Верховский и Галина Кожевникова (ред.)*
    Этническая и религиозная интолерантность в российских СМИ
    Результаты мониторинга 2001-2004 гг.
    ISBN 3-89821-569-5

19 *Christian Ganzer*
    Sowjetisches Erbe und ukrainische Nation
    Das Museum der Geschichte des Zaporoger Kosakentums auf der Insel Chortycja
    Mit einem Vorwort von Frank Golczewski
    ISBN 3-89821-504-0

20   *Эльза-Баир Гучинова*
     Помнить нельзя забыть
     Антропология депортационной травмы калмыков
     С предисловием Кэролайн Хамфри
     ISBN 3-89821-506-7

21   *Юлия Лидерман*
     Мотивы «проверки» и «испытания» в постсоветской культуре
     Советское прошлое в российском кинематографе 1990-х годов
     С предисловием Евгения Марголита
     ISBN 3-89821-511-3

22   *Tanya Lokshina, Ray Thomas, Mary Mayer (Eds.)*
     The Imposition of a Fake Political Settlement in the Northern Caucasus
     The 2003 Chechen Presidential Election
     ISBN 3-89821-436-2

23   *Timothy McCajor Hall, Rosie Read (Eds.)*
     Changes in the Heart of Europe
     Recent Ethnographies of Czechs, Slovaks, Roma, and Sorbs
     With an afterword by Zdeněk Salzmann
     ISBN 3-89821-606-3

24   *Christian Autengruber*
     Die politischen Parteien in Bulgarien und Rumänien
     Eine vergleichende Analyse seit Beginn der 90er Jahre
     Mit einem Vorwort von Dorothée de Nève
     ISBN 3-89821-476-1

25   *Annette Freyberg-Inan with Radu Cristescu*
     The Ghosts in Our Classrooms, or: John Dewey Meets Ceauşescu
     The Promise and the Failures of Civic Education in Romania
     ISBN 3-89821-416-8

26   *John B. Dunlop*
     The 2002 Dubrovka and 2004 Beslan Hostage Crises
     A Critique of Russian Counter-Terrorism
     With a foreword by Donald N. Jensen
     ISBN 3-89821-608-X

27   *Peter Koller*
     Das touristische Potenzial von Kam''janec'–Podil's'kyj
     Eine fremdenverkehrsgeographische Untersuchung der Zukunftsperspektiven und Maßnahmenplanung zur
     Destinationsentwicklung des „ukrainischen Rothenburg"
     Mit einem Vorwort von Kristiane Klemm
     ISBN 3-89821-640-3

28   *Françoise Daucé, Elisabeth Sieca-Kozlowski (Eds.)*
     Dedovshchina in the Post-Soviet Military
     Hazing of Russian Army Conscripts in a Comparative Perspective
     With a foreword by Dale Herspring
     ISBN 3-89821-616-0

29   *Florian Strasser*
      Zivilgesellschaftliche Einflüsse auf die Orange Revolution
      Die gewaltlose Massenbewegung und die ukrainische Wahlkrise 2004
      Mit einem Vorwort von Egbert Jahn
      ISBN 3-89821-648-9

30   *Rebecca S. Katz*
      The Georgian Regime Crisis of 2003-2004
      A Case Study in Post-Soviet Media Representation of Politics, Crime and Corruption
      ISBN 3-89821-413-3

31   *Vladimir Kantor*
      Willkür oder Freiheit
      Beiträge zur russischen Geschichtsphilosophie
      Ediert von Dagmar Herrmann sowie mit einem Vorwort versehen von Leonid Luks
      ISBN 3-89821-589-X

32   *Laura A. Victoir*
      The Russian Land Estate Today
      A Case Study of Cultural Politics in Post-Soviet Russia
      With a foreword by Priscilla Roosevelt
      ISBN 3-89821-426-5

33   *Ivan Katchanovski*
      Cleft Countries
      Regional Political Divisions and Cultures in Post-Soviet Ukraine and Moldova
      With a foreword by Francis Fukuyama
      ISBN 3-89821-558-X

34   *Florian Mühlfried*
      Postsowjetische Feiern
      Das Georgische Bankett im Wandel
      Mit einem Vorwort von Kevin Tuite
      ISBN 3-89821-601-2

35   *Roger Griffin, Werner Loh, Andreas Umland (Eds.)*
      Fascism Past and Present, West and East
      An International Debate on Concepts and Cases in the Comparative Study of the Extreme Right
      With an afterword by Walter Laqueur
      ISBN 3-89821-674-8

36   *Sebastian Schlegel*
      Der „Weiße Archipel"
      Sowjetische Atomstädte 1945-1991
      Mit einem Geleitwort von Thomas Bohn
      ISBN 3-89821-679-9

37   *Vyacheslav Likhachev*
      Political Anti-Semitism in Post-Soviet Russia
      Actors and Ideas in 1991-2003
      Edited and translated from Russian by Eugene Veklerov
      ISBN 3-89821-529-6

FORTHCOMING (MANUSCRIPT WORKING TITLES)

Nicola Melloni
The Russian 1998 Financial Crisis and Its Aftermath
An Etherodox Perspective
ISBN 3-89821-407-9

Stephanie Solowyda
Biography of Semen Frank
ISBN 3-89821-457-5

Margaret Dikovitskaya
Arguing with the Photographs
Russian Imperial Colonial Attitudes in Visual Culture
ISBN 3-89821-462-1

Stefan Ihrig
Welche Nation in welcher Geschichte?
Eigen- und Fremdbilder der nationalen Diskurse in der Historiographie und den Geschichtsbüchern in der Republik Moldova, 1991-2003
ISBN 3-89821-466-4

Sergei M. Plekhanov
Russian Nationalism in the Age of Globalization
ISBN 3-89821-484-2

Михаил Лукянов
Российский консерватизм и реформа, 1905-1917
ISBN 3-89821-503-2

Robert Pyrah
Cultural Memory and Identity
Literature, Criticism and the Theatre in Lviv - Lwow - Lemberg, 1918-1939 and in post-Soviet Ukraine
ISBN 3-89821-505-9

Dmitrij Chmelnizki
Die Architektur Stalins
Ideologie und Stil 1929-1960
ISBN 3-89821-515-6

Andrei Rogatchevski
The National-Bolshevik Party
ISBN 3-89821-532-6

Zenon Victor Wasyliw
Soviet Culture in the Ukrainian Village
The Transformation of Everyday Life and Values, 1921-1928
ISBN 3-89821-536-9

Nele Sass
Das gegenkulturelle Milieu im postsowjetischen Russland
ISBN 3-89821-543-1

Series Subscription

Please enter my subscription to the series *Soviet and Post-Soviet Politics and Society*, ISSN 1614-3515, as follows:

❏ complete series   OR   ❏ English-language titles
                                       ❏ German-language titles
                                       ❏ Russian-language titles

starting with
❏ volume # 1
❏ volume # ___
     ❏ please also include the following volumes: #___, ___, ___, ___, ___, ___, ___
❏ the next volume being published
     ❏ please also include the following volumes: #___, ___, ___, ___, ___, ___, ___

❏ 1 copy per volume   OR   ❏ ___ copies per volume

Subscription within Germany:
You will receive every volume at 1st publication at the regular bookseller's price – incl. s & h and VAT.
Payment:
❏ Please bill me for every volume.
❏ Lastschriftverfahren: Ich/wir ermächtige(n) Sie hiermit widerruflich, den Rechnungsbetrag je Band von meinem/unserem folgendem Konto einzuziehen.

Kontoinhaber: _____Kreditinstitut: _____
Kontonummer: _____Bankleitzahl:_____

International Subscription:
Payment (incl. s & h and VAT) in advance for
❏ 10 volumes/copies (€ 319.80)   ❏ 20 volumes/copies (€ 599.80)
❏ 40 volumes/copies (€ 1,099.80)
Please send my books to:

NAME_____DEPARTMENT_____
ADDRESS _____
POST/ZIP CODE_____COUNTRY _____
TELEPHONE _____EMAIL_____

date/signature_____

A hint for librarians in the former Soviet Union: Your academic library might be eligible to receive free-of-cost scholarly literature from Germany via the German Research Foundation. For Russian-language information on this program, see
     http://www.dfg.de/forschungsfoerderung/formulare/download/12_54.pdf.

Please fax to: **0511 / 262 2201 (+49 511 262 2201)**
or mail to: *ibidem*-Verlag, Julius-Leber-Weg 11, D-30457 Hannover,Germany
or send an e-mail: ibidem@ibidem-verlag.de

ibidem-Verlag
Melchiorstr. 15
D-70439 Stuttgart

info@ibidem-verlag.de

www.ibidem-verlag.de
www.edition-noema.de
www.autorenbetreuung.de